REDESIGN

the

MEDICAL

STAFF

MODEL

JON BURROUGHS

REDESIGN

the

MEDICAL STAFF MODEL

A Guide to
Collaborative Change

ACHE Management Series

19   18   17   5   4   3

Library of Congress Cataloging-in-Publication Data

Burroughs, Jonathan H., author.
  Redesign the medical staff model : a guide to collaborative change / Jon Burroughs.
     p. ; cm.
  Includes bibliographical references.
  ISBN 978-1-56793-681-0 (alk. paper)
  I. Title.
  [DNLM: 1. Medical Staff, Hospital—organization & administration. 2. Health Care Reform. 3. Models, Organizational. 4. Organizational Innovation. 5. Personnel Administration, Hospital. WX 203]
  RA972
  362.11068'3—dc23
                          2014024940

The paper used in this publication meets the minimum requirements of American National Standard for Information Sciences—Permanence of Paper for Printed Library Materials, ANSI Z39.48-1984. ∞™

Acquisitions editor: Tulie O'Connor; Project manager: Joyce Dunne; Cover designer: Marisa Jackson; Layout: PerfecType

Found an error or a typo? We want to know! Please e-mail it to hapbooks@ache.org and put "Book Error" in the subject line.

For photocopying and copyright information, please contact Copyright Clearance Center at www.copyright.com or (978) 750-8400.

Health Administration Press
A division of the Foundation of the American
    College of Healthcare Executives
One North Franklin Street, Suite 1700
Chicago, IL 60606-3529
(312) 424-2800

To my extraordinary wife, Anita—animal lover and advocate,
community activist, gourmet chef, fellow skier and hiker,
and best friend—with gratitude for a lifetime of love and laughter.

Contents

Foreword

Some of you who are physician executives will likely remember these old but time-less gags: The "tie vote" of 25-3 at the medical executive committee (MEC) meeting meant that three loud, negative voices scuttled a year's worth of work by hospital leadership. The fact that you missed the last three MEC meetings meant that you were next year's president.

Now, these gags take on a more serious tone: The medical staff leadership reaffirms that a once-a-month, two-hour meeting after office hours will provide sufficient time to deal with all of the impending quality and safety initiatives coming our way under the Affordable Care Act. In fact, these circumstances are no longer mere gags that draw nervous laughter at medical meetings; they need to be seen through fresh eyes in this era of accountability. Enter Jon Burroughs and his contributors, who successfully translate this serious tone to a pragmatic set of approaches that can help even the most reluctant healthcare leaders grapple with the inevitable changes that we face in our industry. With the impressive group of contributors from across the United States whom Burroughs invited to weigh in, he has fashioned a how-to guide that tackles many of the myths of the medical staff structure with the aim of achieving collaborative change.

When one examines the history of the organized medical staff, it is clear that among its traditional priorities were preservation of established referral patterns, maintenance of professional autonomy, and vigilance in its control over nonclinician CEOs to ensure that they protected the physicians' territory. In short, the traditional medical staff's structure, spanning nearly 50 years in the post–World War II era, was about preserving the status quo. Now, with the status quo in our industry largely untenable as a model for the future, Burroughs gives us hope that we can reconcile the situation and emerge with effective strategies for the future.

This book is not for everyone. Surely there remain members of the medical profession who yearn for an idealized, 1965-style era of unfettered professional autonomy and the perceived ability to do everything and anything for every patient and to reap economic reward, even if that reward comes with a poor clinical outcome. Yet others recall the era of "See one, do one, teach one" without analyzing the appropriateness or effectiveness of the *one*. At the other end of the spectrum, some in the healthcare leadership profession believe that the only model for the future is of the employed doctor who works in a tightly managed, hierarchical structure driven by economic incentives to minimize testing.

In my view, Burroughs presents a middle ground that recognizes that social change cannot occur overnight, even in the face of an economic crisis, like the one we face in healthcare delivery. Without hyperbole and with an outstanding supporting cast, Burroughs calmly outlines new structures, tools, and processes that can preserve some of the more laudable aspects of medical staff interaction, such as collegial support, peer review, and a sense of professional community, in a multidisciplinary team–based model. Therefore, this book should be read by all healthcare leaders and stakeholders who aspire to bring physicians and management together to achieve the necessary goal of world-class quality at the lowest possible cost.

Kudos to Burroughs and his contributors. I recommend this book for healthcare leaders at all organizations where physicians are called on to make an important contribution for the future of the organizations in which they work.

David B. Nash, MD
Dean, Jefferson School of Population Health
Thomas Jefferson University

Acknowledgments

I do not recommend that everyone write a book. It is a solitary activity that takes long hours to complete, leads to endless discussion and debate with oneself, and results in many false starts. Fortunately, books cannot be written without a great deal of help and support from others, and it is to these individuals whom I express my appreciation and gratitude.

To the editorial and publishing team at Health Administration Press: Thank you for believing in this book and for encouraging and supporting its design and evolution over a two-year period. Without your expertise and editorial resources, the book could never have been written.

To my acquisitions editor at Health Administration Press, Tulie O'Connor: Thank you for your help and editorial support every step of the way, from the inception of the book through the write, rewrite, and re-rewrite of every chapter, every table, and every reference. Your guidance, expertise, and suggestions have made this a better book and a better read.

To my distinguished group of colleagues and guest contributors, David Nash; Joe Bujak; Michael Callahan; Mary Baker; Stephen Beeson; Alan Zuckerman, FACHE; John Nance; Quint Studer; Maria Greco Danaher; Richard Blakely; Shawn P. Griffin; Chip Caldwell, FACHE; Peter Stille; Ken Cohn; Jim Hogan; Todd Sagin; Kathleen Bartholomew; Ken Mack, LFACHE; Paul Convery; and Carl Couch: Thank you for your contributions to this book; it is better because of your imprint. Thank you also for your expertise, friendship, and passion to improve our healthcare system in such meaningful ways. Your impact is incalculable.

To my colleagues at the American College of Healthcare Executives and the American Association for Physician Leadership: Thank you for providing the network, resources, and support for your ever-blossoming and maturing profession, one that combines art, science, and psychology to create healthcare leaders equal to the task of transforming our healthcare system into one we can be proud of.

To my colleagues, clients, and fellow travelers throughout the United States and beyond: Thank you for teaching me my craft and for granting me the opportunity to continually learn, innovate, and work with such dedicated professionals, leaders, and individuals who care about making the world a little better than they found it and for leaving a meaningful and lasting legacy.

Finally, to you, the reader: Thank you for taking the time to read and reflect on the material here and to help transform your medical staff both as a means to achieve the goals of better quality, service, and cost-effectiveness and as a metaphor for the extraordinary changes that are required in every facet of our healthcare system to achieve those goals. Your comments, feedback, dedication, and impact are what make writing this book ultimately worthwhile.

Jon Burroughs, MD, FACHE, FACPE
President and CEO, The Burroughs Healthcare Consulting Network, Inc.
Glen, New Hampshire
jburroughs@burroughshealthcare.com

Introduction

To achieve high-quality, low-cost, safe care delivery amid healthcare reform requires nothing short of overhauling the entire US healthcare delivery system in the next five years. Not only will we have to offer world-class healthcare under an operating cost structure that is 30 to 50 percent lower than it is currently, but we also will need to make that care seamless and integrated. Furthermore, as healthcare processes become increasingly standardized and commoditized, high reliability will be assumed, and the quality of service will become the key market differentiator.

This magnitude of change does not represent an evolution of our healthcare system but rather a healthcare revolution, in much the same way that the discovery of antibiotics, vaccines, and safe and reliable surgery techniques revolutionized the healthcare system over the past century. Such change, then, cannot be effected by healthcare leaders alone. Organizations must consolidate to gain access to the low-cost capital needed to acquire health information and business intelligence management tools to in turn support more efficient and lower-cost structures. More importantly, organizations need to partner with physicians and obtain the full support of the governing board to accomplish such significant and far-reaching change.

Most physicians, however, are part of an almost century-old institution—the organized medical staff—which is rooted in tradition, advocacy, protectionism, autonomy, and individualistic judgment. The charge for physician leaders is to change that institution into a culture that is responsive; agile; willing to standardize to best practices; service oriented; able to work in multidisciplinary teams; and able to maintain the strong sense of professional dignity, respect, and self-accountability that forms the foundation for a robust professional identity.

The medical staff is not going away; it is rooted in federal and state law and in regulatory and accreditation standards. Physicians control (directly or indirectly) 100 percent of operating revenues and up to 80 percent of direct variable costs by ordering additional or non-value-added hospital days, ancillary services, or elective procedures. I wrote this book to describe what adjustments are needed to the organized medical staff and how they can be carried out in a way that sustains the best of what physicians have to offer in the context of twenty-first-century reform.

Chapter 1 discusses the evolution of physicians' culture from autonomy to collaboration and accountability that must take place for US providers to remain competitive in an increasingly global healthcare economy.

Chapters 2, 3, and 4 look at the selective strategic planning and credentialing/privileging approaches needed to ensure physician–organization alignment and all practitioners' commitment to the same high organizational goals of quality, safety, service, and cost-effectiveness.

Chapters 5 through 10 analyze the components of an effective and rigorous performance management system that enables leaders to negotiate with physicians to reach a partnership characterized by transparent, accountable, and sustainable performance outcomes. Instituting and sustaining such a system requires a collaborative, rather than a top-down, approach so that physicians fully commit to enterprise goals and objectives.

Chapter 11 considers a number of successful models of physician integration and alignment that enable physicians and executive leaders to partner toward achieving continued improvement on all performance initiatives. All integration and alignment models require a cultural transformation based on partnership and mutual trust so that traditional organizational silos are dismantled and physicians work successfully with all members of the organization in a respectful and interdependent way.

Chapter 12 celebrates healthcare organizations large and small, academic and nonacademic that have successfully innovated with their medical staffs to achieve unprecedented cost-effective, high-quality, highly reliable, and customer service–oriented outcomes. As it turns out, healthcare reform will not be accomplished by political parties, federal or state governments, or the US judicial system. It will happen when innovative healthcare professionals of all disciplines come together to innovate, collaborate, and create a better system that focuses on individual patients in both sickness and health.

The good news is that everything in this book can be done—and *has* been done—by many leading organizations of all kinds. The challenge for healthcare leaders is to dismantle the historic infrastructure that served the system well for almost a century but that now must be redesigned and rebuilt for a new healthcare system that requires a different kind of clinical and economic responsiveness. This shift is not optional for US healthcare; it must be carried through for the United States to regain the international credibility and stature of a world-class, comprehensive healthcare system that serves all of its constituents with balance and integrity in an increasingly shrinking and interdependent world.

ADDITIONAL RESOURCES

Centers for Medicare & Medicaid Services (CMS). 2012. *National Health Expenditure Projections 2012–2022: Forecast Summary.* Accessed May 19, 2014. www.cms.gov/Research-Statistics-Data-and-Systems/Statistics-Trends -and-Reports/NationalHealthExpendData/Downloads/Proj2012.pdf.

Government Accountability Office (GAO). 2012. "The Federal Government's Long-Term Fiscal Outlook: Fall 2012 Update." Accessed May 15, 2014. www.gao.gov/assets/660/650466.pdf.

World Health Organization. 2006. *The World Health Report 2006: Working Together for Health*. Accessed May 19, 2014. www.who.int/whr/2006/en/.

The Organized Medical Staff—Moving from Autonomy to Accountability

Change before you have to. If the external environment changes before you do, you will be out of business.
—*Jack Welch, former CEO of General Electric*

During times of stability, organizational structures can remain stable and serve their constituents well. But in times of rapid transformation, traditional structures lose their relevance. They must evolve or be replaced with new models that can adapt quickly to arising complexities and uncertainties.

The organized medical staff is one of those traditional structures: It has a proud and rich legacy but now must change or become obsolete.

THE TRADITIONAL MEDICAL STAFF MODEL

The organized medical staff has been at the center of professional life for physicians and surgeons for decades. It provides a professional, political, and social forum for physicians to discuss clinical issues, define professional perspectives, address professional concerns, and form a network for communicating with each other and with external parties.

Medical staffs and other professional organizations offer many potential benefits to their members. Inevitably, however, they can also pose some problems and challenges.

Beginnings of the Organized Medical Staff

The organized medical staff originated with a set of principles developed by the American College of Surgeons (ACS) in 1919 known as the "Minimum Standard Document." It was the result of six years of work by Ernest Amory Codman, MD, and the ACS's Committee on Standardization. The effort represented an early attempt to address the lax record keeping and significant systemic variation that led to poor clinical outcomes.

The original standard defined the medical staff as a "group of doctors who practice in the hospital inclusive of all groups." Its membership was to "be restricted to physicians and surgeons appropriately trained and licensed" who are "competent in their respective fields and worthy in character and professional ethics." The standard required that the medical staff "initiate and with the approval of the governing board of the hospital, adopt rules, regulations, and policies governing the professional work at the hospital," including the following (ACS 2006):

- Regular monthly meetings
- A regular analysis of the clinical care provided
- Accurate and complete records for all patients
- The availability of competently supervised diagnostic and therapeutic facilities

The ACS's organized medical staff model was so successful that when the organization helped found the Joint Commission on Accreditation of Hospitals (now The Joint Commission) in 1951, the document became an integral part of The Joint Commission's original hospital standards.

The federal government later confirmed the importance of the organized medical staff in 1965, when the US Department of Health and Human Services' Health Care Financing Administration (HCFA; now the Centers for Medicare & Medicaid Services) became significantly involved in the financing of healthcare through the creation of Medicare and Medicaid. HCFA mandated that the original concept of the organized medical staff be fulfilled for the healthcare entity to receive payment from the federal government for healthcare services rendered. That list has evolved to become the CMS Conditions of Participation (CMS 2009).

Benefits of Professional Organizations

A college of peers promotes a sense of professional identity, belonging, and security through its actions to advocate for members and protect the future viability of the profession. It confirms the unique beliefs that form the basis of any highly developed professional culture.

The traditional medical staff has the expertise to govern itself and conduct peer review, credentialing and privileging, and quality oversight functions. The typical structure of a hospital-based organized medical staff—which usually consists of a rotating body of voluntary leaders; a democratic, town-hall approach to meetings and communications; and a cadre of informal leaders with political influence and clout—has provided physicians with a professional guild–like culture that, among other attributes, allows them to share information with each other in a safe, confidential, and protected environment.

Problems Related to Professional Organizations

Any group characterized by a strong professional and cultural identity is vulnerable to issues of professional isolation—even within specialties and subspecialties—and various ingrained tendencies that limit its members' ability or willingness to change and adapt, even when their livelihoods depend on it.

Seeing Issues Through a Predetermined Lens

An important part of any professional social contract is the "give" and the "get" of individuals entering a profession (Kornacki and Silversin 2013). To become physicians, students must agree to make personal sacrifices, including restrictions to personal freedom and time, family support, and potential income for an extended period of time. In exchange, society has promised them an above-average social standing and income and the right to make autonomous decisions that have potentially life-altering consequences.

This social contract is not unlike those of other elite professions that require years of preparation, training, and professional development, such as military command or judicial, religious, and corporate authority. The challenge with social contracts is that external economic, scientific, and political forces and changes often render the original culture unimportant or even irrelevant over time.

The military and other high-risk professions have transformed their cultures from revering autonomy to embracing crew resource management, structured communication protocols, and interdependence. On the other hand, the organized medical staff in general struggles to accept evidence-based practices while its members are individually and uniquely accountable to themselves, their patients, and their state licensing boards.

Perpetuating a Culture of Protectionism

The purpose of any professional organization is to advocate for its members' interests. This goal can be positive when its members hold unique perspectives that need to be understood by the outside world. But it can be limiting when the same perspectives thwart an understanding of and appreciation for other points of view. Executives and managers, board members, patients, community leaders, vendors, regulators, and payers—in addition to physicians—all have a unique stake in healthcare outcomes.

The challenge associated with this tendency is that physicians as a whole continue to hold a protectionist stance and still consider the hospital to be the "physician's workshop." Although physicians are beginning to accept the shift to a balanced care delivery approach, some defend the physician's assumed right to apply his skills independent of the needs and demands of others. Medical staffs today are often split between those who understand the need for interdependence and those who do not, creating a difficult and acrimonious environment in which to adapt to seismic external change.

Resisting Changes Seen as Undermining the Profession

Physicians generally have difficulty supporting change that is clearly necessary but that, to them, represents a threat to their professional identity. For example, a physician might understand that a significant portion of her work (e.g., normal deliveries, routine primary care, low-risk surgery and procedures) can be performed safely and competently by qualified nonphysicians, such as advanced practice professionals (APPs). Yet she continues to block initiatives that support APPs in these roles, fearing a loss of control.

A balance is needed between supporting physician interests and transforming care delivery to provide the highest quality at the lowest cost. Achieving this balance requires physicians to assume leadership roles and organizations to adopt techniques such as Crucial Conversations (VitalSmarts 2014; discussed in detail in Chapter 8) to effectively and safely navigate the future healthcare landscape.

Joseph S. Bujak, MD, FACP, principal of Bujak and Associates, paints an explicit picture of how the traditional medical staff does not meet today's challenges in a meaningful or responsive way.

The Future of the Organized Medical Staff

As more and more physicians move into employment relationships with healthcare organizations, and as essential healthcare services move away from the hospital, the traditional organized medical staff structure becomes increasingly irrelevant. If we agree that the sole purpose of the organized medical staff is to assess and improve the quality of care provided through peer review, credentialing, and privileging—activities that are intended to support continuous quality improvement—the organized medical staff is losing its ability to manage the hospital–physician relationship. A new perspective is required that is not based solely on economics and that transcends the traditional hospitalized patient in addressing the mandate to provide continuity of care.

Specifically, with the trend toward outpatient care delivery, many physicians will no longer work in the hospital, resulting in a lack of access to recredentialing and privileging by the organized medical staff. In turn, those physicians who oversee their peers will no longer be able to directly observe the competencies of those peers being evaluated and must defer to indirect evidence to support what becomes an unmanageable responsibility. Furthermore, because medical staffs are often composed of competing practices, peer review may be outsourced in deference to the internal politics and potential conflicts of interest that can dominate physician relationships.

Governance of employed physicians is provided by the employing organization, so as the percentage of physicians engaged as employees grows, independent physicians fear becoming isolated from their peers and denied access to patients. For this reason, the organized medical staff structure now tends to speak primarily for the independent physicians.

Older physicians tend to be more traditional, autonomous, digitally impaired, and intrinsically motivated to work long hours than are younger physicians. Because most younger physicians are employed and credentialing and privileging are managed by the employing entity, younger physicians often do not attend medical staff meetings and functions because those events are usually scheduled before or after working hours—on their

(continued)

own time. Given these factors, solving clinical problems is a significant challenge, especially when the only vehicle with which to drive integration is the traditional medical staff framework.

The need to orchestrate care in the new world of value-based reimbursement demands sacrificing self-interest for the collective interest. Under the healthcare reform mandate for the provision of coordinated care, the provider community is now responsible for the quality, cost, service satisfaction, and appropriateness of the care offered. One movement toward achieving these goals is to reduce variation and consistently apply evidence-based interventions. Problematic to this trend, however, is the traditional medical staff organization's primary commitment to preserving individual physician autonomy. Coordinating care across professions and specialties conflicts with the departmentalization of the organized medical staff structure, which excludes nonphysicians from participating in that care. As a result, the economically integrated provider community—not the traditional medical staff—will manage quality and cost.

Balanced accountability in the value-based reimbursement model requires a degree of integration not possible in the traditional medical staff organization, making that practice structure an inadequate one for managing relationships in the evolving provider community.

A NEW MEDICAL STAFF MODEL

In the new paradigm of value-based health services delivery, neither board trustees nor senior executives can be considered veterans of the system; thus, neither group can effectively lead the medical staff. The edicts that often emanate from hospital administrators serve only to create conflict, which can undermine trust and lead to organizational divisiveness.

Value-based reimbursement requires a redesigned medical staff, including its leadership model, organizational structure, and operational processes as well as the medical staff–management relationship. In this section, we outline what this redesigned medical staff should look like.

Redesigned Leadership

Physicians need to lead physicians, just as administrative leaders need to lead managers. Not even the chief medical officer (CMO) or vice president of medical affairs (VPMA)—as members of the C-suite—can lead staff physicians where they do not wish to go.

Succession Planning

Rotating voluntary leadership, as democratic as it seems, is no longer a relevant approach to preparing, supporting, and retaining qualified physician leaders. A stable, accountable physician leadership group is required, which is best developed through leadership succession planning. Think of succession planning as being just as essential for medical staffs as it is for any other group of professionals.

Some forward-thinking medical staffs have replaced the traditional nominating committee—the body of physicians on a hospital medical staff that is charged with vetting and recommending medical staff leaders to the organization's governing board and medical executive committee (MEC)—with a leadership succession planning committee. This committee develops criteria for leadership positions, helps identify potential leaders, prepares them for leadership roles, supports them during their term of office or role, and retains them in some leadership capacity following their term. The executive management team may participate as advisers, especially in cases where an individual with senior management potential wishes to grow into a medical director, VPMA, or CMO role.

A Deeper Dive

The medical executive committee (MEC) was developed by the The Joint Commission in the 1980s as organized medical staffs grew larger and more complex. Traditionally, the medical staff was self-governing and held itself accountable through a town hall approach with monthly general staff meetings where initiatives were generated and approved by super-majority consensus. This proved unwieldy in the modern era, and so the MEC, a smaller body made up of medical staff officers and department chairs, was a logical compromise and transitioned the medical staff culture from a democracy to a representative republic.

The leadership criteria that the succession planning committee creates may include the following:

- A specified number of years of qualifying service as a practicing clinician
- The ability to work harmoniously with clinicians, staff, and management
- A willingness to support medical staff–recommended quality, safety, and service initiatives
- Service on medical staff or hospital committees
- Service as a medical staff or hospital committee chair
- Service as a department or clinical service chair or as a medical director (for medical staff officers)
- Formal leadership training

Leadership Training

High-performing organizations often require physician leadership training prior to or concurrent with leadership service. For example, Baylor Scott & White Health in Dallas, Texas, offers a one-day, boot camp–style training seminar hosted by system CEO Joel T. Allison, FACHE, and system senior vice president and CMO Irving Prengler, MD. All physicians who wish to serve in leadership roles are required to complete the training. Other organizations, such as Allina Healthcare in Minneapolis, Minnesota, offer a five-day, 35-hour leadership program for every physician leader in their system. See the sidebar starting on this page for examples of a one-day and five-day program curriculum.

Sample Curricula for Physician Leadership Programs

One-Day Program
1. Orientation to leadership, and how to run a meeting (1.5 hours)
2. Roles and responsibilities, and orientation to the system (1.5 hours)
3. Introduction to performance management (1 hour)
4. Introduction to credentialing and privileging (2 hours)
5. Introduction to peer review (1 hour)
6. How to deal with performance management challenges and behavioral issues (1 hour)

Five-Day Program
Day 1: Medical Staff Structure and Purpose
1. Introduction to the system and program overview (1 hour)
2. Current healthcare challenges (1 hour)
3. Roles and responsibilities (3 hours)
4. Conflict resolution and negotiation (2 hours)

Day 2: Credentialing and Culture
1. Performance management and accountability (2.5 hours)
2. Credentialing and privileging (3 hours)
3. Privileging case study (1.5 hours)

Day 3: Peer Review and Performance
1. Ensuring an effective peer review process (3.5 hours)
2. How to manage poor performance and behavioral issues (1.5 hours)
3. Case studies in ongoing professional practice evaluation and focused professional practice evaluation (2 hours)

Day 4: Legal and Financial Obligations
1. Healthcare law for physician leaders (1.5 hours)
2. Common legal mistakes that healthcare leaders make (1.5 hours)
3. How to manage an investigation, a fair hearing, and an appellate review (2 hours)
4. Healthcare finance and case study (2 hours)

Day 5: Performance Improvement, Patient Safety, and Leadership Skills
1. Medical staff's role in performance improvement and patient safety (2.5 hours)
2. Transitioning from an effective clinician to an effective leader (3 hours)
3. Advanced leadership skills and conclusion (1.5 hours)

Note: In addition to this broad-based education, many organizations offer more focused training to new physician leaders or committee members assuming first-time roles. Topics may include orientation for new MEC members, credentials committee members, peer review committee members, and department chairs and medical directors.

Unfortunately, many physicians assume titled positions with little, if any, orientation, training, or foreknowledge of what the role expects of them, with undesirable results. Instead, job descriptions (many of which are seldom read and only partially described in the medical staff bylaws) should be included as an integral part of this training, to be discussed with each prospective committee member or leader prior to the assumption of her term of office.

Once physicians are trained, it is important to provide ongoing coaching as they make the transition from solving analytical problems for individuals in a rapid and decisive manner to managing people and systems in interdisciplinary team-based settings. Every good manager understands the length of time it takes to master enterprise oversight skills; without real-time mentoring and support, many physicians do not become effective partners with management, despite their best intentions.

Many managers consider leadership training to be just another cost to contend with. A better way to think of it is as an investment with a calculable return on investment (ROI). Exhibit 1.1 shows how the benefits of leadership training can be calculated.

Exhibit 1.1: Hospital Metrics of Leadership Effectiveness

Average length of stay (ALOS): Some chief financial officers in large organizations have quoted a figure as high as $4 million in cash flow differential for ALOS that can be reduced by 0.1 day.

Case-mix index (CMI): Like ALOS, a tenth of a point increase in CMI can have a profound impact on Medicare reimbursement and operating revenue.

Cost per adjusted discharge: Organizations that have installed effective cost accounting software demonstrate up to a 1,000 percent, or tenfold, variation in the way different physicians manage the same patient condition over time. Physician leadership that does not address resource outliers may inadvertently cost patients their lives and certainly costs the organization millions of dollars annually.

Core Measures: By 2016, value-based purchasing (VBP) will have a 2 percent impact on Medicare reimbursement. Even greater will be the impact of third-party payers that monitor the US Department of Health and Human Services' Hospital Compare website (medicare. gov/hospitalcompare/search.html) and create tiered and narrow networks—through both private and public insurance exchanges—to direct patients by offering significant financial inducements (e.g., low or no deductibles, copayments, and coinsurances) to those organizations that achieve high-quality, low-cost care delivery.

Patient safety: Many unsafe behaviors have become deeply imbedded in physicians' psyches during their medical training; these behaviors need to be eliminated and replaced with effective approaches that require continual reinforcement by physician leaders and champions. Standardizing safety behaviors and communication protocols can save tens of thousands of lives per year, whereas inadvertent adverse outcomes from safety breaches may cost human lives and cost an organization its reimbursement, quality measures, community reputation, and market share.

Hospital Consumer Assessment of Healthcare Providers and Systems (HCAHPS): Customer satisfaction and loyalty has a three-pronged impact on healthcare organizations because it not only represents a 30 percent share of VBP but also is a significant indicator of medical liability costs and is the single greatest driver of market share in any industry.

Opportunity cost of lost referrals: It is surprising that many executive leaders never ask individual physicians about the out-migration of referrals; if they did, they would have the opportunity to learn directly how to mitigate the problem. This factor can have a significant impact on operating revenues. Good leaders have ongoing relationships with key physicians and engage in dialogue about the perceived sources of both in- and out-migration.

Elimination of waste in operating systems: A good physician leader works tirelessly to reduce waste and inefficiency, as these conditions are both the bane of physician colleagues who struggle with declining efficiencies and the source of potentially significant reductions in operating costs that can enable a healthier margin.

Standardization to evidence-based practices: Good physician leaders work with physicians to continually optimize quality outcomes by standardizing high-risk, problem-prone clinical situations, such as general intensive care; ventilator management; postsurgical deep venous thrombosis prophylaxis; and the care of patients with congestive heart failure, community-acquired pneumonia, and acute myocardial infarction. Adopting evidence-based medicine not only reduces the cost per adjusted discharge but also, with appropriate horizontal and vertical integration, decreases the rate of avoidable readmissions, which will be subject to a Medicare penalty of 3 percent by 2016.

Elimination of disruptive behavior: A small number of physicians in each organization cost the institution millions of dollars annually in legal fees, lost referrals, staff turnover, medical liability, and community perception. Ineffective physician leadership may promote appeasement and enablement, which undermine morale, compromise quality and financial performance, and may even cost patients their lives.

Diagnosis of and intervention on impairments: In 2003, the American Medical Association estimated that more than 45,000 impaired physicians were practicing in the United States (Ross 2003). Their often preventable and treatable conditions may cause these physicians to commit unanticipated medical errors or cause adverse events because of their failures to communicate or their inability to process complex information quickly or efficaciously.

Physician Leader Compensation

Until recently, physician leaders were volunteers and did not receive compensation for performing their leadership roles. Physician leadership is now shifting to compensated, titled positions, and with that shift comes a set of new realities:

+ Leadership now requires more preparation and commitment than in the traditional medical staff structure. Providing this service for the organization can take a physician out of a busy medical practice at significant opportunity cost.
+ Leaders are increasingly being held to performance expectations and may be accountable for achieving measurable strategic goals and objectives.
+ Many strategic goals and objectives have a calculable ROI. Meeting, and often exceeding, standard ROI metrics (see Exhibit 1.1) is now deemed essential to organizational success.

- Fewer qualified individuals are interested in pursuing leadership roles with real accountability than in the past, when these roles were often symbolic and ceremonial.

Effective compensation models base rates on benchmarking data, such as those provided by the Medical Group Management Association through its annual compensation survey. The floor can be set at the 10th percentile, with incentives that can bring compensation up to the 90th percentile. Categories of incentives include productivity measures, compliance with quality and safety initiatives, patient satisfaction and loyalty measures, cost-effectiveness measures, and corporate citizenship activities (e.g., attendance at meetings, completion of medical records, willingness to serve on committees).

Recruiting Physician Leaders

The level of accountability for physician leaders is clearly increasing, leading to fewer candidates for these roles. To offset this decrease, the medical staff can limit the number of leadership positions and enhance the effectiveness of those that remain.

Taking such a course might require a number of changes in the leadership structure:

- *More flexible terms of office.* Increased flexibility enables (qualified and supported) leaders to serve longer, staggered terms. Key committee chair positions (e.g., credentials, peer review) do not turn over at the same time as the MEC, thus ensuring greater leadership continuity.
- *Aggregate leadership roles.* Combining roles decreases the number of leaders significantly. For example, a medical director could replace the traditional medical department chairs of multiple specialties and subspecialties.
- *No nominations for leadership positions accepted from the floor.* All potential nominees must undergo a vetting process by the leadership succession planning committee to ensure that (1) only qualified nominees reach the floor of medical staff meetings for a vote and (2) individuals seeking office have a clear understanding of the leadership roles, responsibilities, and performance expectations.
- *Dual accountability.* Leaders such as medical directors and service line directors are generally accountable to both the MEC and senior management.
- *Dual clinical/operational focus.* Leadership roles can focus on both the clinical quality of care and the operational and financial performance of clinical services. This approach is often part of a dyad/triad model, in which each service

is overseen by a physician, an administrative or nursing leader, and an executive leader (e.g., COO, CMO) who manage the service together. Dyad/triad structures are discussed in more depth later in the book.

As reimbursement shifts from pay-for-volume to pay-for-value, effective physician leaders are essential for creating a sense of urgency for change among the medical staff. In addition to being necessary for survival in a value-based environment, this new model of leadership is a contemporary and professional approach that ensures a solid partnership with management. Together, physicians and executive leaders can implement important improvements to clinical and operational processes in a responsive and timely way.

Redesigned Structures

Once the organization has effective physician leaders in place, the next step is to reorganize the medical staff structure so that it is dynamic, responsive, agile, and able to partner with management to effect rapid change. Here we introduce the various types of committees; they are discussed in greater depth later in the book.

Medical Executive Committee

Originally, the MEC was made up of medical staff officers (president, vice president, secretary-treasurer, past president); department chairs; and ex-officio members of senior management, including the CEO, CMO or VPMA, and chief nursing officer (CNO), to manage large and unwieldy credentialing, privileging, peer review, and governance bodies. The same individuals who led their departments and served on the credentials and peer review committees oversaw the medical staff as a whole. Department chairs often sought seats on the MEC to protect departmental interests (or their own), and myriad conflicts of interest arose that threatened to damage the integrity of leadership decisions. Some MECs were managed and controlled not by the physician leadership at all but by the CEO, who used medical staff meetings to share management initiatives—without having gained physicians' input or support.

A contemporary approach is to create a small MEC made up of key physician leaders and physicians from both the hospital- and ambulatory-based segments. These individuals should have a desire to serve in a statesperson role representing the best interests of *all* members of the medical staff. This structure appropriately reflects the fact that the majority of physicians no longer practice in the hospital.

Many MECs now also include podiatrists; optometrists; chiropractors; allied health practitioners; and APPs, such as nurse practitioners, physician assistants, certified registered nurse anesthetists, and certified nurse midwives. These professionals represent the views and perspectives of the growing number of nonphysician clinicians on the medical staff. The shift in MEC membership is in line with a proposed change to the CMS Conditions of Participation that expands the definition

---

A Deeper Dive

Structure of the Traditional Organized Medical Staff

The traditional medical staff structure was founded on the ideals of autonomy, independence, and self-accountability. It was designed to protect the relationship between a single physician and his patient—not to adapt to rapid change in complex systems.

The following attributes of the medical staff organizational structure were built into the original model so that the organized medical staff could maintain control of its profession and professional identity and ensure that change was difficult to effect:

- Informal leaders were afforded the ability to drive the medical staff agenda and control formal, titled leaders.
- General medical staff meetings were organized as town-hall gatherings. The expectation was that consensus would be achieved through super-majority voting, thus essentially protecting the status quo.
- Leadership was voluntary and rotated frequently to ensure that no individual gained leadership tenure or skills that would potentially undermine the influence of the majority.
- The leadership of departments, committees, and the MEC overlapped to ensure that one structure did not hold another accountable or modify the other's recommendations.
- A complex set of economic and political relationships was forged through referral channels that were protected at all costs.
- A strong value of professional identity was instilled to promote protectionism.

The paradox in this structure is that when professionals are motivated by fear and resist accountability and transparency, they lose the opportunity to grow and the ability to reach their potential, undermining—albeit inadvertently—themselves and their organizations.

of *physician* to include podiatrists and, for rural health clinics and federally qualified health centers, optometrists and chiropractors (*Federal Register* 2013).

Some large systems have developed a super-MEC structure to focus on systemwide medical staff issues, such as

- strategic planning of and communicating about systemwide medical staff goals and objectives,
- strategic medical staff development, with recommendations made to the system board,
- arbitration of politically or economically charged issues that cannot be fairly or adequately resolved at a member organization, and
- preventive management or arbitration of potential corrective or legal action.

Credentials Committee

Ensuring that every privileged member of the medical staff is qualified to exercise every requested privilege and conducts herself at a high professional level requires a rigorous approach to governance. Physician leaders on the credentials committee must be trained in the technical, legal, regulatory, and accreditation aspects of credentialing and privileging and be accountable to the MEC for the quality and integrity of their recommendations. Some healthcare systems have created system-level credentialing committees—or *super-committees,* as HCA's HealthONE in Denver, Colorado, calls them—made up of the member hospitals' credentials committee chairs and their CMOs or VPMAs. The super-committee helps the hospital credentials committees fulfill their responsibilities by

- creating appropriate policies and procedures for the development of credentialing and privileging structures and processes to address contemporary credentialing and privileging challenges;
- developing and approving credentialing and privileging eligibility criteria;
- overseeing member hospital credentials committees to ensure that they are performing peer review in a transparent, fair, and judicious way;
- serving as a resource for difficult credentialing, privileging, and evaluation issues; and
- auditing or arbitrating complex or divisive credentialing and privileging activities, including those that lead to potential corrective action or civil litigation.

The credentialing and privileging functions are discussed in detail in chapters 3 and 4.

Peer Review Committee

Until recently, most peer review was conducted by a department chair, a departmental committee, or an aggregate committee of medicine or surgery. This approach resulted in numerous conflicts of interest; failures to address quality issues in a substantive or meaningful way, as in the use of the peer review process as a means of rewarding or punishing colleagues because of their political and economic relationships; and other untoward practices. Some peer review committees performed their function well; however, the widespread variation in approaches and intentions among peer review committees often clouded the transparency and marred the integrity of the entire process.

Medical staffs are moving toward a centralized, multidisciplinary model of peer review. Physicians who are motivated by the desire to improve quality are trained and compensated to conduct peer review using a transparent approach with a standardized scoring format and methodology. Improvement opportunities for individual physicians that arise from this process not only support the individual physician being reviewed but also bring to light nursing and systemic issues that can be addressed in tandem.

As with credentials committees, some larger systems are creating a super–peer review committee made up of the peer review committee chairs and the VPMA or CMO of member organizations. An extensive discussion of medical staff peer review is provided in Chapter 7.

Clinical Departments

A service line approach to departmentalization is emerging in medical staffs in response to the problems that come with isolated clinical departments, entrenched interests, and resistance to change. A service line may consist of one or more clinical specialties, and its purpose is to oversee and improve clinical care, operations, and the financial performance of that unit.

Well-conceived service lines offer the following benefits and should be considered part of the organization's overall strategy and portfolio:

- Targeted clinical services provided by interdisciplinary teams
- Branding and marketing that are responsive to the external environment and demand
- A focus on service to both internal and external customers
- Coordination with other service lines and other internal and external organizations
- Strong alignment between quality and safety goals and operational efficiency and financial performance

Service line leadership usually follows the dyad or triad model, with a physician leader, an administrative nursing manager, and an executive leader who work together in all phases of leadership and oversight.

A major cultural difference between the traditional clinical department and a service line is accountability. Many service line–oriented medical staffs have developed a balanced scorecard or dashboard reporting system for the MEC and management. As discussed in Chapter 5, the metrics or targets displayed on the dashboard should be negotiated with full participation of the medical staff and flow naturally from the organizational and medical staff strategic plan.

In a service line, reporting relationships may not be linear, as multiple services and departments may be involved in any given service line. For instance, a vascular surgery service line might include vascular surgery, general surgery, radiology, cardiology, podiatry, primary care, home health care, endocrinology, and a patient-centered medical home. Some physicians may not be psychologically or professionally prepared to transition from autonomous to collaborative decision making, which is essential to achieving a functional service line culture. Both managers and physicians must be realistic when creating service lines. Including individuals who are not compatible with a culture of collaboration may ultimately squander the time and resources spent to build them.

The Integrated Medical Staff Structure

The most successful medical staffs in the United States are fully integrated and aligned with the organizational structure to fulfill a shared mission, vision, and strategy. Integration does not require that the physicians be employed by the hospital, but it does require each member of the medical staff to be aligned with the organization's strategic goals and objectives. Agreements are a key component to building an aligned medical staff. (See Chapter 11 for a detailed description of the integration and alignment process.)

Each physician should have an individual agreement with the organization. A professional agreement can be structured in one of several forms, including employment, co-management, professional services, joint venture, enterprise partnership, and exclusive arrangement. It outlines both the medical staff bylaws and contractual performance expectations, metrics, and targets for the physician and the healthcare organization on the basis of a compensation plan with incentives that is mutually beneficial.

The emergence of these agreements has altered the culture of the traditional medical staff and the relationship between physicians and managers because both are now legally, economically, and clinically interdependent: They rely on each other for achieving goals for mutual benefit. In a conjoined relationship with the organization, the MEC becomes a strategic body, spending little time on areas of self-interest and a great deal of time on organizational strategy; medical staff–wide goals and objectives; physicians' impact on quality, safety, loyalty, operations, and financial performance; and the relationships among the medical staff, management, and board.

Redesigned Processes

Transformed structures need to function in transformed ways. Thus, the work processes used by the medical staff need to transform as well.

Conflicts, and Conflicts of Interest

One key element of transformation is addressing potential conflicts and conflicts of interest to reduce the impact of self-interest on decision making.

Every physician has economic and political relationships with other physicians and managers. A good first step in transforming medical staff processes is to acknowledge that conflicts and conflicts of interest can arise in almost every interaction of a medical staff.

Some medical staffs have created a conflict resolution process that calls on an ad hoc committee to review potential conflicts as they emerge. This approach brings to light the sources of conflict and permits an even-handed method for reaching resolutions. Numerous medical staffs have adopted processes that encourage physicians to voluntarily disclose potential conflicts to the MEC or another decision-making body that can appropriately manage them. Others have developed system-level approaches to deal with commonly occurring conflict situations.

Meetings

The opportunity cost of taking busy physicians out of their practices to attend meetings is significant. According to Merritt Hawkins (2010), physicians generate, on average, $1.5 million in revenues for a healthcare organization per year; some specialties generate almost $1.5 million more. Assuming the average physician works 40 hours per week for 52 weeks per year, for a total of 2,080 hours per year, his work yields approximately $721.15 per hour in revenue ($1,500,000 ÷ 2,080 = $721.15). It follows that a single one-hour meeting with 15 physicians could cost an organization more than $10,000 in lost revenues.

The following guidelines are helpful in reducing the impact of meetings with physicians:

1. Only meet when face-to-face discussion or debate is necessary. Most routine medical staff work can be accomplished online, off-site, or in some expedited manner.

2. Eliminate redundant discussion by diversifying the membership of various committees.
3. Eliminate routine discussions and reports that do not drive change and that no one is interested in. Create a consent agenda, which reflects material that everyone agrees requires no formal discussion or debate.
4. Have a clear vision of what you would like the medical staff or individual departments or service lines to accomplish, and focus their work on essential strategic goals and objectives. Strategy should drive execution, not vice versa.
5. Support off-site participation in meetings by offering GoToMeeting, Skype, or other means of teleconferencing.
6. Do not keep participants in a one-hour meeting—or do not hold the meeting at all—if you have nothing relevant to discuss.
7. Team building is an important exercise; do not relegate it to business meetings.
8. Not everything is equally important; focus on the vital few actions that will drive change and results.
9. Leverage administrative staff to support physician meeting functions, and only tap physicians' input when it is required.
10. Communication is the life blood of any organization, but it does not have to occur in time-consuming meetings.
11. Spend more time developing relationships and less time conducting meetings. (This essential guideline is addressed more fully in Chapter 11.)

Value for the Work Done

Because the medical staff is an organization's most expensive resource, driving physician value is crucial to fulfilling the Patient Protection and Affordable Care Act (PPACA) mandates. Fortunately, in a pay-for-value world, where Value = Outcome ÷ Cost, high quality, high reliability, and service excellence can be quantified by measuring loyalty, market share, and net revenue per adjusted discharge—the most accurate predictor of financial performance (Kaufman 2013). For example, one organization resisted addressing a physician's behavioral issues because he generated $3 million in gross revenues per year. Finally, the leadership assessed his net value to the organization by calculating his opportunity cost and was startled to find that the organization was losing more than $5 million in seepage (out-referrals) annually as a result of the physician's poor behavior and low clinical quality.

Obviously, financial metrics should not be the sole driver of leadership. But placing all of the assets and liabilities of a defined challenge in perspective is a worthwhile exercise to prioritize and support organizational changes and initiatives. The following table illustrates this approach.

Projected revenues	Projected costs
Gross/net revenues per adjusted discharge	Direct variable costs associated with clinical services
Increase in market share/referrals	Cost per adjusted discharge
Increase in ancillary revenue	Leadership time (direct and opportunity costs)
Staff retention savings	Legal costs
Quality/safety/service metrics (positive findings)	Decrease in market share/referrals and related revenues
Quality/safety/service metrics (negative findings)	Turnover costs

Assessing the cost of supporting a peer review program is another example of determining value for the work. As shown in Chapter 7, an effective peer review program that focuses on performance improvement and not merely quality

Example of an Effective Peer Review Program

One medical staff experienced a number of quality events in the intensive care unit (ICU) that resulted in several risk-management and medical liability situations. These events led to a loss of reputation and market share in the community. Medical staff leadership conducted common cause analyses for each event in its peer review process and found that a lack of training and inadequate skill levels were major contributing factors.

The medical staff recommended to the hospital's board of directors that the organization convert the ICU to a step-down unit. It also suggested that the organization require physicians to demonstrate a higher level of training and competence to be eligible to apply for privileges in this unit. The recommendations were accepted and operationalized.

Following implementation, patient turnover was higher, length of stay was lower, and the cost per adjusted discharge decreased while quality, safety, and service metrics improved significantly. These improvements increased the organization's operating revenues and lowered its operating costs.

With the elimination of the ICU, the medical staff agreed to refer all patients requiring critical care services to a regional tertiary care center, which later approached the organization to be included in its network. The move enhanced the local organization's reputation and market share.

This turnaround occurred because an effective peer review program focused on individual, nursing, and systemic improvement and not on placing blame. It demonstrated an ROI that both the medical staff and management could point to with pride.

assurance (the identification of negative outliers) identifies measurable improvements for individual practitioners, clinical services, the entire medical staff, nursing, and the system as a whole. Many of these improvements can be reported on a spreadsheet and quantified easily. See the sidebar on page 20 for an example of how one medical staff improved quality and revived its reputation through the effective use of its peer review program.

Redesigned Medical Staff–Management Relationship

The preceding sections have made clear that physicians, managers, and board members need to work together in new ways to optimize quality, reduce costs, and address conflicts and conflicts of interest in an open and transparent manner. Organizations are beginning to modify their operational structures to support a close and trusting working relationship by placing physicians on the governing board, the senior management team, operating boards, and other hospital-based teams.

Physicians on the Governing Board

Many of today's physicians understand that, like executive and community leaders, they must set aside self-interest if they wish to govern effectively. Good governance includes bringing technical expertise and perspective to the board without the burden of conflicted interests or constituency bias.

Not every physician can play this role, but physicians' unique professional perspectives on quality, safety, and service must be represented directly in the boardroom. The key to selecting physicians for the governing board is that they have a strong character and the ability to insulate themselves from the sometimes intense social and economic pressures of their peers. The expectation is that they represent the organization with undivided loyalty.

Physicians on the Senior Management Team

It has long been common for a VPMA or CMO to be part of the senior management team, but presidents of the medical staff and chiefs of staff have not typically been involved. This exclusion is a missed opportunity to develop a channel of communication to the medical staff, which offers a pipeline for seeking physicians' input and gaining their buy-in on essential management and organizational initiatives.

Physicians on Operating Boards

Operating boards blend governance and operational oversight to approve clinical, safety, service, operational, and financial goals and objectives; convert those goals and objectives to metrics with targets; and hold the operating unit accountable for results. In addition to seating a majority of clinical providers, as mandated by the PPACA (which states that at least 75 percent of an accountable care organization's governing board be controlled by individuals who provide patient care within the structure), operating boards typically include key operational managers; a representative from a strategic corporate sponsor or business partner; legal counsel; a patient advocate; and a few community leaders, who usually lack specific healthcare experience but who offer important community and enterprise perspectives.

Physicians on Committees

The role of the physician serving on a traditional hospital committee is one that many organizations are rethinking. Too often, these committees spend endless hours reviewing subcommittee reports rather than actively discussing, debating, and crafting solutions that produce measurable outcomes. Wise executives redesign these committees to include a committee chair who has excellent project management skills to promote a responsive, adaptive, and focused committee.

One contemporary committee that features robust representation of physicians is the physician–nursing council, an interdisciplinary body made up of physician and nursing leaders that addresses all matters related to the physician–nursing operational relationship in the areas of culture, process, communication, and performance management. Another is the APP interdisciplinary committee.

SUMMARY

The PPACA's mandate that US healthcare providers deliver world-class quality, ensure patient safety, and offer excellent service at a significantly lower cost than in the past requires a medical staff that is far more agile, responsive, and adaptive. Medical staff structures and processes must be transformed, with highly trained and skilled physician leaders at their helm, to develop the kinds of partnerships with management and the board that will enable an organization to respond to demands for continual improvement and change under increasingly tight time constraints.

REFERENCES

American College of Surgeons (ACS). 2006. "The Minimum Standard." Accessed May 19, 2014. www.facs.org/archives/minimumhighlight.html.

Centers for Medicare & Medicaid Services (CMS). 2009. *Conditions of Participation Interpretive Guidelines*. §481.12(a)(5). Baltimore, MD: CMS.

Federal Register Online. 2013. "Medicare and Medicaid Programs; Part II—Regulatory Provisions to Promote Program Efficiency, Transparency, and Burden Reduction; Proposed Rule." FR Doc No. 2013-02421, 78 (26): 9229. Accessed June 20, 2014. www.gpo.gov/fdsys/pkg/FR-2013-02-07/html/2013-02421.htm.

Kaufman, N. 2013. "Net Revenue per Adjusted Discharge Continues to Drive Success." *Journal of Healthcare Management* 58 (1): 8–11.

Kornacki, M. J., and J. Silversin. 2013. *Leading Physicians Through Change: How to Achieve and Sustain Results*. Tampa, FL: American College of Physician Executives.

Merritt Hawkins. 2010. "2010 Physician Inpatient/Outpatient Revenue Survey." Accessed May 27, 2014. www.merritthawkins.com/pdf/2010_revenue survey.pdf.

Ross, S. 2003. "Clinical Pearl: Identifying an Impaired Physician." *Ethics Journal of the American Medical Association* 5 (12): 1–4.

VitalSmarts. 2014. "Crucial Conversations® Training." Accessed June 20. www.vitalsmarts.com/products-solutions/crucial-conversations/.

CHAPTER 2

Strategic Medical Staff Development Planning—Moving from Demographic to Strategic Recruitment and Retention

I only wish the Pareto principle [80/20 rule] applied to our medical staff. In our case, greater than 90 percent of our business comes from less than 10 percent of our staff.

—*Hospital CEO*

High-performing medical staffs do not just happen; they are carefully developed in the context of an organization's overarching strategic plan. What makes medical staff planning strategic? It is based not on demographic analysis but on strategic analysis to determine the specific physicians the organization would like to recruit and retain. These determinations are influenced in part by whether potential physicians possess attributes related to the following carefully defined categories that help drive both physician and organizational success: skill sets, qualifications, organizational fit, personal qualities, economic relationship to the organization, and personal values.

In an era of growing physician shortages, this approach may seem counterintuitive, as many managers feel that the decreasing physician supply will limit and narrow organizations' medical staff recruitment options. However, physicians seek specific types of environments in which to practice. Organizations that exhibit high standards and accountability attract physicians who want to work in that culture. Conversely, organizations that demonstrate little accountability and support poor performance, poor conduct, or loose ethical standards attract poorly performing physicians who feel that they will be protected from discovery through a culture of non-accountability.

Organizations that recruit physicians under a system that relies primarily on demographic analysis—the traditional approach to recruiting—are at risk of suffering the consequences of poor decision making that may have a lasting impact on the competence and culture of the staff.

TRADITIONAL PHYSICIAN RECRUITMENT

The traditional approach to physician recruitment is to compare the number of practitioners in a given specialty per defined population to the current physician roster, which factors in age and anticipated time of retirement for each physician. Such an approach might look like this:

Physician recruitment plan = Specialty-specific demographics
+ physician roster
+ aging analysis
= proposed number of full-time equivalents (FTEs) of each clinical specialty (typically expressed in tenths of an FTE)

Unfortunately, this method is prone to error and has inherent shortcomings, such as those listed in Exhibit 2.1.

The following is an actual case, with identifying characteristics modified, to illustrate how operating under the traditional physician recruitment system can affect an organization.

Case of Dire Need

A rural hospital in a popular ski area has a dire need for an orthopedic surgeon, as it has experienced unexpected turnover, high out-of-state emergency department volume, and growing demand, and the current solo practitioner cannot adequately handle the volume. A highly skilled orthopedist with particular expertise in knee surgery is recruited, and the organization invests considerable funds in bringing the surgeon and her family to the area.

Once she has settled into the area, the orthopedist fails to apply for medical staff membership or privileges but instead sets up an independent surgery center one mile from the hospital, where she performs elective cases on well-insured patients who visit the community. She attends no medical staff meetings, does not volunteer for any kind of leadership role, and takes no on-call coverage. When asked to cover

Exhibit 2.1: Potential Pitfalls of Using Demographic Criteria for Physician Recruitment

- Many physicians are being replaced or supplemented by mid-level practitioners (e.g., advanced practice nurses, physician assistants) to provide routine and low-risk care.
- Many physicians are being replaced or supplemented by hospitalists, laborists, and other contracted full- or part-time practitioners.
- Many specialists provide primary care, and many generalists provide specialty services, thus blurring traditional clinical definitions.
- An increasing number of part-time practitioners or physicians share positions.
- Service areas with very high and very low per capita income tend to create greater-than-average demand for healthcare services.
- Physicians with strong reputations draw above-average panels, whereas physicians with weak reputations attract the opposite.
- Changing technology has a significant impact on demand for services. For instance, an increasing number of older individuals seek screening colonoscopy procedures.
- Geographic variation in demand based on the local medical culture and the supply-to-demand ratio is significant.
- Areas with older populations (e.g., Arizona, Florida) have a greater-than-predicted demand.
- Zip codes may not reflect true service areas or referral patterns (e.g., referral over state lines to regional centers).
- The brand of the organization has enormous power to either expand or contract local, regional, national, and international demand.
- The creation of new models for healthcare delivery, such as multispecialty groups, accountable care organizations, and patient-centered medical homes, significantly modifies local and regional demand.

---

for the existing orthopedist so that he can leave town, she declines, stating, "I never committed to being a part of the medical staff."

The hospital has since lost considerable market share, and because the new orthopedist faces no consequences for her actions or obligations from the recruitment arrangement, it has no recourse but to acknowledge it made a mistake and recruit again.

Comment

Many organizations can cite a case similar to this one, in which the so-called wrong physician is recruited to the wrong organization at the wrong time in the wrong way, all of which undermine, rather than support, the organization's strategic vision. To avoid these costly scenarios, physician recruitment and retention must aim to meet a high level of alignment with the needs of the organization and existing physician groups.

CONTEMPORARY PHYSICIAN RECRUITMENT

The Strategic Medical Staff Development Planning Process

The strategic medical staff development plan is a policy created by the governing board with significant management and physician input. Only the board may open and close the medical staff to membership, and it does so on the basis of objective, economic, non-competency-related criteria, including the following:

- Fulfillment of community need as determined through strategic external market analysis (e.g., focus groups, demographic population analysis, community needs assessment)
- Availability of resources in the organization as determined through an internal analysis of financial and operational capabilities
- The candidate's demonstrated adherence to existing medical executive committee (MEC)–recommended, board-approved credentialing and privileging criteria
- The terms of existing contracts (e.g., exclusive agreements that include carve-outs for specific privileges, such as interventional procedures for radiologists in a community that also supports vascular surgeons)
- Existing organizational and economic structures (e.g., service lines, clinical institutes, joint ventures)
- The candidate's demonstrated adherence to state practice acts and other legal and regulatory requirements
- Input from key, specialty-specific stakeholders, physician leaders, and management

Once the criteria are established, the board may develop specific requirements for medical staff membership that address the number, qualifications, economic relationship, and organizational fit of the physicians required. This activity is performed most often by a strategic medical staff development planning subcommittee of the board, which addresses each clinical specialty and subspecialty. These requirements are placed in the broader strategic medical staff development plan that has been approved by the entire board following comment and input from administrative and/or physician leaders and legal counsel.

Sample language for a strategic medical staff development plan is provided in Exhibit 2.2, reprinted here with permission from Memorial Hospital in North Conway, New Hampshire.

Exhibit 2.2: Sample Strategic Medical Staff Development Plan: Community Hospital

I. OBJECTIVES

Plan and optimally develop the hospital's medical staff into the future. This activity is not designed to close the staff but rather to strengthen the hospital and the medical staff through planned addition of services and providers in a strategic and aligned way.

Generate a quantitative and qualitative basis for discussing the need for more providers with current staff who may otherwise fear increased competition and resultant loss of patients with the addition of more practitioners.

Develop a medical staff that is composed of individuals with the defined background, training, skills, expertise, and alignment needed by the community served by the hospital; limit appointment to the medical staff to providers who satisfy those criteria.

Give the hospital and medical staff greater control over quality of medical care by emphasizing criteria for ranking candidates so that the best qualified can be selected for the open slots in a particular specialty and at particular times.

Provide better or more comprehensive services consistent with the hospital and medical staff's strategic plan.

Enhance the hospital's financial viability as it strives to balance optimum quality with the prudent expenditure of increasingly scarce resources.

Provide the spectrum and depth of quality services necessary to attend to the healthcare needs of the surrounding communities and region.

Prepare for changes in the demographics of communities served in the least disruptive manner possible to members of the medical staff.

COMMITTEE MEMBERSHIP

The Strategic Medical Staff Development Planning Committee is a subcommittee of the Board of Trustees and shall be described in its corporate bylaws.

Membership on this committee shall be determined by the Board Chair with input from the Chief of Staff (COS) and the CEO. Members of this committee shall not represent the interests of any constituency and will serve to support the interests of the hospital and medical staff with undivided loyalty. No individual shall be present on the committee when his/her specialty is being evaluated except to provide information to the committee as requested. Membership shall be divided between representation of the Executive Committee of the Board, the Medical Executive Committee (MEC), senior management, and community leaders as desired. Terms will be six years with staggered rotations, so that one-third of the committee rotates off the committee every two years. The Board Chair, the CEO, and the COS shall be ex-officio members with vote.

II. SERVICE CHANGES

Alternations in service (expansions, additions, reductions, or eliminations) as determined by strategic consideration are used to assist in the selection of the numbers and types of providers for medical staff development based on demographic data of the primary and secondary service areas and the strategic goals of the organization and system.

(continued)

OPEN CATEGORY REQUESTS

Provider categories are opened when a demonstrated need is defined. An individual, a practice, or a leadership group or team may request an opening and present the need to the committee. The committee will hold a meeting with all relevant stakeholders, to include the individual(s) who are requesting the opening; all relevant stakeholders who may be affected by the opening; and representatives from the medical staff, senior management, and governing board leadership groups to consider all demographic, political, economic, and quality factors. If the committee votes to open a category, the MEC is charged with

A. developing position specifications relative to background, training, experience, alignment, and other desired qualifications and
B. seeking relevant provider feedback on the proposed opening and the proposed criteria.

    Requests for all categories of providers—MD, DO, and nonphysician—must undergo this process.

    Once a candidate or candidates has/have been identified, the Recruitment Ground Rules, which define the conditions to be met prior to the Medical Staff application process, must be completed.

All Providers

All providers being recruited under any specialty will be interviewed by the MEC (with committee member feedback to individual or sponsoring group) prior to an offer, an employment agreement, or a contract being made.

Application Process

An application for appointment to the medical staff is only sent upon request to those individuals, according to the medical staff bylaws, who (1) appear to be eligible for appointment to the medical staff, (2) are qualified to provide care and treatment to patients for conditions and diseases for which the hospital has facilities and personnel, and (3) indicate an intention to utilize the hospital as required by the staff category to which they desire appointment.

Those individuals who meet the basic criteria for appointment to the medical staff are given an application for appointment. Individuals who fail to meet the basic criteria are not given an application and are so notified.

Multiple Applicants—Same Specialty

When more than one applicant is to be recommended by the MEC in a specialty that is open, the MEC evaluates the applicants according to the following guidelines:

1. The likelihood that the applicant delivers quality professional services and care to patients
2. The likelihood that the applicant is interested in committing his/her professional services to the community, the medical staff, and the hospital
3. The training, professional background, and experience of the various applicants, including
    a. specialty board certification;
    b. length of prior practice experience in other hospitals;
    c. specific training, background, and expertise commensurate with the criteria recommended by the MEC and established by the Board;

d. alignment and desired association with the medical staff and the hospital in support of the hospital's mission;

e. prior hospital medical staff appointments, offices, and committee appointments; and

f. publications, educational, research, and other honors and professional positions.

4. The likelihood that a particular applicant satisfies the competitive and service needs of the hospital

General factors to be considered include the applicant's commitment to utilize Homestead Hospital, taking into consideration the other hospitals in which the applicant presently exercises privileges and the applicant's probable impact on hospital admissions or clinical procedures. Most importantly, the following specific factors are used to facilitate ranking of applicants:

Priority Rank 1: An applicant *replacing* a productive staff appointee who has had a long history of meritorious service to the hospital, provided that both the new and replaced physicians generally practice at this hospital. This applicant would replace a member of an active group or take over the practice of an existing solo practitioner. Such applicant would have the highest probability of showing an immediate and significant impact on admissions and other ability to serve the hospital.

Priority Rank 2: An applicant who would be joining an individual or a group presently holding medical staff privileges, provided that both the existing member or group and the applicant generally practice at this hospital.

Priority Rank 3: An applicant joining an individual or a group that does not generally practice at this hospital but that has a significant percentage of its practice at this hospital, or an applicant in solo practice recently established in close proximity to the hospital who intends to practice generally at this hospital.

Priority Rank 4: An applicant in solo practice who is appointed to multiple staffs and who has a significant percentage of his practice elsewhere so that such applicant has a low probability of having a significant impact on admissions or procedures.

All applicants are ranked by the MEC to the extent possible in the order that they meet hospital needs. The MEC develops recommendations regarding applicants who best meet the needs of the hospital and forward them to the Board. If all applicants are equal but only some can be accommodated, a first-come, first-served basis is used.

The work of the medical staff does not change as a result of the Medical Staff Development Plan, as the plan does not deal with clinical activities in the hospital. The MEC is still required to review and evaluate applicants and make recommendations to the Board.

Those applicants not selected are deferred until additional openings exist in the appropriate specialty. At that time, they are reconsidered. Deferral does not entitle an applicant to the hearing and appeals process.

(continued)

When the hospital again determines to accept applications in a particular specialty, applicants who have been deferred are notified and asked to inform the CEO if they are still interested in appointment and clinical privileges.

SPECIALTIES IN CLOSED CATEGORIES
For the specialties listed below, there is no demonstrated community need at this time:
Podiatry nephrology
Anesthesiology pediatric cardiology

Categories in which no new providers are needed
When a provider specializing in a category that is closed requests an application, he/she is informed that the hospital is not accepting applications for those specialties at the present time. The provider is also told when the hospital's need in that specialty is expected to be reevaluated and is advised to inquire again at that time if still interested.

When a closed specialty is opened
When the Board adopts a change to the Medical Staff Development Plan that opens a specialty that was formerly closed, the CEO informs physicians in that specialty who had inquired about an application that there are a specific number of openings and asks them to notify him if they are interested in applying.

Specialties exceptions
It is assumed that any specialties not identified in this plan are those in which the hospital is not accepting applications. Specialties not previously addressed in this plan are reviewed upon request by the Strategic Medical Staff Development Committee subcommittee. Recommendations for changes are forwarded to the Board.

CALENDAR FOR PERIODIC REVIEW AND UPDATE
The Strategic Medical Staff Development Committee meets at least every month until the immediate strategic needs of the organization are stabilized, and then at least every six months to review and reassess hospital needs. If necessary, the Board again reviews recommendations and adopts the necessary changes.

ADOPTION
This plan has been adopted by the Board of Trustees as attested by the signature below.

_____   _____

President, Board of Trustees   Date

Source: Adapted with permission from Memorial Hospital, North Conway, New Hampshire.

With the plan in place, the organization should update it monthly to reflect any high-priority specialty or subspecialty recruiting needs that have arisen. Participants in the updating process should include all key stakeholders so that the board gets a balanced perspective of relevant political and economic issues.

TENETS OF STRATEGIC MEDICAL STAFF DEVELOPMENT PLANNING

Tenet 1: Right Number

Analyzing demographics, aging trends, anticipated transitions or departures, and care utilization is a necessary but insufficient part of medical staff planning. Some physicians are much more productive than others, certain clinical services may no longer be needed, and so on. For instance, if an organization closes its intensive care unit (ICU), it may no longer need a board-certified intensivist or critical care specialist on staff.

Community support has a significant impact on demand, as a physician who is trusted and well established can often create higher demand than others on staff can, not only for himself but also for affiliated practitioners.

Determining the right number of staff should also take into consideration several circumstances that are not related to the number of available practitioners:

- Modifications to a physician's practice (e.g., a pulmonologist no longer performs ICU consultations)
- Revenue cycle policy changes by independent physicians (e.g., a solo practitioner no longer accepts certain insurances because of low or nonpayment practices of insurance companies)
- Variations in the practice policies of independent physicians with regard to scheduling, wait times, follow-up evaluations, and treatment of the uninsured who present to the organization's emergency department
- Practices within the medical staff that control referrals into and out of the organization and create an artificially high or low demand
- Modification to physicians' practices with age
- Modification to call coverage arrangements over time
- Political conflicts and conflicts of interest within the medical staff
- Modification to evidence-based practices over time with rising or falling clinical demand

- Modification to reimbursement methodologies over time with increased or decreased utilization
- Environmental factors that may increase or decrease demand (e.g., seasonal tourism levels)

Furthermore, the emergence of service lines, integrated networks, and accountable care organizations (ACOs) has created new physician leadership opportunities, the fulfillment of which may alter the physician demographic landscape.

Tenet 1 Case: Unmet Demand

A local pulmonology group opens a sleep management practice, and its members relinquish their hospital privileges so that they will no longer be obligated to take call or provide inpatient or ICU consultations. One member of the group was a former ICU director and resigned her position, creating a leadership void for the ICU as well. Demographic analysis reveals no need for a pulmonologist despite the fact that every physician questioned and every community focus group convened agrees that significant pent-up demand exists for a pulmonology specialist. As a result, the hospital must recruit and employ pulmonologists who are willing to serve full time in an intensive care setting and provide inpatient consultations.

Comment

Demographics provide partial information that is only relevant if it can be interpreted properly, taking into account external and internal factors that have a significant impact on community need.

Tenet 2: Right Skill Set

Conducting a focused needs assessment of the specific clinical and leadership skills required (e.g., general surgeon who performs breast or endovascular surgery) is an essential part of strategic medical staff development planning. This process calls for comprehensive physician input because the scope of services provided by each clinical specialty and specialist rapidly evolves and is often complex to dissect and analyze. For instance, many family physicians no longer perform obstetrics or critical care; emergency physicians now routinely perform ultrasound evaluations, which were conducted by radiologists in the past; and many interventional radiologists perform complex endovascular procedures, previously performed only by general or vascular surgeons. Recruitment can be made even more complex by the fact that every physician may have a slightly varied scope of practice, potentially increasing the difficulty of completing an inventory of clinical skills within a defined department or section.

Thus, a sufficient number of clinicians may be available within a clinical specialty, but an insufficient number may be qualified to perform specific, high-demand services for the community. For example, a hospital's medical staff may technically have enough nurse anesthetists or anesthesiologists to fulfill general demand but not enough with advanced skills in pain management, which a needs assessment has determined to be necessary for the service area.

Another interesting phenomenon is that recruitment for a specific clinical skill may either drive up or drive down the need for other clinical skill sets. For example, if the organization recruits an interventional radiology team skilled in endovascular procedures, the demand for skilled radiology technologists who can assist in these procedures goes up, and the demand for surgeons performing non-endovascular procedures laparoscopically or through open procedures goes down. If an individual with this skill suddenly leaves the community and cannot be immediately replaced, the demand may reverse for the long term and thus require a strategic response.

Reimbursement has a significant impact on the demand for clinical skills. Organizations that embark on risk contracting, for example, perform fewer procedures and ancillary studies and invest more resources in preventive and ambulatory care. As a result, the demand for procedurists goes down and the demand for primary care providers goes up.

To anticipate these variables, the organization can view the required skill sets in terms of an organizational portfolio of services to be managed rather than privileges to be compartmentalized or isolated. Internal and external environmental factors have a profound impact on the changing nature of service lines and clinical capabilities required, and these must be continually analyzed, balanced, and managed to plan accurately for needed skills.

As with attaining the right number of medical staff members, political and economic forces play a role in recruiting physicians with the desired skill sets, as the recruitment of a needed clinical skill may alter the existing availability of clinical resources. For instance, in rural or inner-city areas, general surgeons may rely on endoscopic procedures to support their surgical practices, whereas the community may express pent-up demand for gastroenterology services. The successful recruitment of gastroenterologists may undermine the general surgical practices and cause out-migration of surgical cases and lack of call coverage availability due to insufficient demand to support the current number of surgeons. To avoid this imbalance, input from physicians is required to anticipate these downstream consequences prior to investment of significant recruitment resources.

Each defined skill set interacts with other skill sets to either elevate or depress demand, and subtle shifts in reimbursement methodology, regulatory and legal requirements, or accreditation standards have significant impact on these interactions.

Tenet 2 Case: Don't Assume

The organization recruits a nationally respected bariatric surgeon to head up its new bariatric surgery program and builds a significant infrastructure to support him, including the purchase of new equipment capable of handling higher-weight patients and the recruitment of nutritionists, home health specialists, and clinical psychologists. Following great fanfare and a hearty welcome, the chair of general surgery quietly says to the new surgeon, "I assume that you will provide call coverage for all bariatric patients?" When the bariatric surgeon replies that he assumed call coverage would be shared equitably among all surgeons, the chair says, "We don't have the clinical skills to handle these kinds of emergencies. You'll have to handle them yourself." The bariatric surgeon then approaches the CEO and demands that either the organization provide additional coverage for bariatric patients or he will be forced to break his recruitment agreement and leave.

Comment

Some managers and board members do not take clinical nuances, such as available expertise for call coverage, into consideration when creating investment strategies for potential clinical growth. Early physician input helps the organization anticipate inevitable conflicts and conflicts of interest that arise when the existing medical staff's homeostasis is disrupted.

Tenet 3: Right Relationship

With the evolution of medical staffs from open to semi-open to closed membership entities, the contractual relationship between the organization and physician recruits is critically important as growing numbers of self-employed physicians leave independent practice to seek employment and new physician graduates seek employment. Also, in an increasingly integrated environment, many organizations want some form of contractual relationship or partnership with independent, self-employed physicians or physician groups. Thus, the recruitment of new physicians involves a discussion of the types of contractual or business relationships that the organization plans to offer.

Contractual options include employment, lease, co-management, joint venture, partnership, directorship, personal services arrangement, exclusive agreement, and management services. A physician contract may hinge on the physician's participation in a specific practice, depending on the service lines, specialty group practices, or other political or economic structures in place at the organization. For instance, all the hospitalists on staff at an organization may be required to be part of an exclusive arrangement with a third-party vendor, which has the authority to dictate who will be recruited based on jointly negotiated qualifications. A surgical group may be involved in a joint venture with the organization that requires the group's members to contribute some form of equity to be considered. Whatever the arrangement, the specific contract requirements should be discussed with all relevant parties well in advance of launching any recruitment efforts.

In addition, different practice or business arrangements may have different professional qualification requirements. For instance, for branding purposes, a center of excellence may require that every physician be board certified or fellowship trained in a specific area, a requirement that is not necessary for the medical staff as a whole. Some emergency departments affiliated with tertiary care centers that support a regional poison control center may require that their physicians complete a toxicology fellowship to be eligible to practice. The approach to recruitment may be different from that of an emergency medicine group that supports a walk-in center in the community or operates a lower-volume and -acuity suburban practice.

Finally, certain clinical nuances should be considered when developing recruitment plans for specific economic and political entities. The following questions are typical of those that organizations should answer when addressing such structures through recruiting:

◆ How will new and existing physician groups share handoffs, call coverage, consultations, referrals, and other clinical and organizational functions?
◆ Who will handle pre- and postoperative care?
◆ Who will handle follow-up visits for the insured? For the uninsured?
◆ Who will perform which specific procedures?
◆ Who will perform proctoring of new appointees; quality oversight; credentialing, privileging, and peer review; and other organizational requirements?
◆ Who will create standardized clinical or functional pathways within defined specialty practices?

Even with employed physicians, contracts should be structured to encourage strategic partnership with the organization, and a range of options should be carefully considered prior to recruitment (see Chapter 11 for a comprehensive discussion of this topic). This level of planning requires collaboration among the governing body, management team, physician staff, and legal department so that the medical staff and physician leadership are aware of the conditions of the relationship between the new physicians and management's oversight of them.

Tenet 3 Case: A Little Too Much Competition

Welcome Memorial has an open medical staff with a small group of employed cardiologists in a thriving practice. Tertiary Care Cardiologists Inc. presents 20 board-certified and fellowship-trained cardiologists for credentialing, stating that it would like to penetrate this important cardiology market. The hospital cannot deny the members of Tertiary Care appointment to the medical staff, as they are all qualified. Even though they have gained membership to the hospital's medical staff, however, the Tertiary Care cardiologists set up a freestanding interventional cardiology center across the street from the hospital and divert most of the cardiology market share from the hospital.

Comment

The governing board has the right to protect the business interests of the hospital and the community it serves. It is legally permissible for the board to control the number and type of clinical specialties as long as its selections are based on an objective needs assessment and criteria that are clearly defined in a strategic medical staff development plan. Recruiting insufficient or excessive numbers of clinicians in any given specialty is in the interests of neither existing clinical resources nor the community as a whole.

Tenet 4: Right Principles

Assessing the right principles and values for medical staff membership is a process that might traditionally have been called *organizational fit,* and it may be the most significant success factor in any recruitment effort. A professional's principles and values reflect her internal motivation and drivers, which can have a profound impact on her compatibility with the organization and ability to work comfortably with management, colleagues, and staff.

The first issue to address is whether the physician's professional goals are consistent with the organization's mission. For instance, a general surgeon who wants to perform advanced procedures may not be satisfied in a community facility whose mission is to provide basic primary care services. Conversely, a physician with broad-based interests may not be content to limit his practice to an academic or tertiary care environment.

The organization's vision reflects its idealized future state, and as with mission, not every physician is prepared to go on the journey. For instance, a self-trained general internist with a strong interest in oncology may have a successful community oncology practice but may not wish to pursue an oncology fellowship and certification when the organization decides to create a center of excellence and raise its privileging criteria. Conversely, an organization may wish to divest itself of unprofitable services, and physicians who are important to the organization may no longer be required. A typical example is the closure of an ICU or its conversion to a step-down unit that no longer requires intensivist coverage.

The third issue is related to values and culture. These characteristics reflect intangible and tangible manifestations of an organization's way of being and doing business. For example, a small hospital emphasizes a commitment to community service and sacrifice. An entrepreneurial surgeon may not be content in this organization; she may feel stifled in an environment where she is expected to perform uncompensated call coverage and provide care to the poor and indigent within the constraints of limited resources. Another surgeon, who has a strong community orientation, may relish this mission to serve.

Other important factors involve medical staff structures, frameworks for decision making, opportunities for growth, performance management, and contracting. Consider the following examples:

◆ Some medical staffs are hierarchical, and some have a flat organizational structure with few opportunities for a young physician to serve in leadership roles.
◆ The interests and tendencies of a physician may determine whether his professional goals are consistent with the culture of the medical staff and the organization.
◆ An organization's center of excellence or service line may make decisions collaboratively using evidence-based clinical and functional pathways. Some physicians are not comfortable working in a collaborative environment and instead prefer to work independently, using their unique way of providing services. Other physicians may not be compatible with key physician leaders or members of a service line group.
◆ One physician with an MD and an MBA may not find suitable leadership and management opportunities to satisfy his career aspirations. Another physician's style or personality may make the CEO feel uncomfortable.
◆ Most medical staffs have performance expectations, metrics, and targets as part of their ongoing professional practice evaluation (OPPE) and focused professional practice evaluation (FPPE). A new physician may have an issue with an organization's performance management approach.

- Some contracts include noncompete or nonsolicitation terms that have been negotiated over time. These terms may not be consistent with a particular physician's professional or personal goals. Other contracts may have unique performance expectations and requirements that differ from the agreements of others on the medical staff, which may create potential conflict.

It is important for an organization to take these and other considerations seriously when recruiting a physician to ensure that the organization's and medical staff's needs are compatible with the individual recruit.

Tenet 4 Case: Oil and Water

A highly qualified academic emergency physician is recruited to a community hospital to lead a well-established emergency group. The group is extremely compatible and has worked well with the medical staff for years. The new medical director has high professional expectations, wants to lead clinical research, and believes that every physician in her group should take on leadership and research projects to enhance the function and prestige of the group. The group rebels because its members are interested in providing good clinical care but not in investing long hours into nonclinical work that disrupts their personal interests and family lives. Shortly following the recruitment of the new director, the tenured members of the group inform management that this recruit is not going to work out.

Comment

Organizational fit is as important as professional qualifications and cannot be overemphasized. It is vitally important that management and the board consider all relevant organizational factors when investing resources and time to bring a physician on staff.

Tenet 5: Right Values

Values transcend feelings, define cultures, and represent the deepest motivators of an individual. An essential part of the recruitment process is to get to know the individual personally through an interview process so that key organizational leaders can probe and assess what makes this physician recruit tick. His deeply embedded and often intangible values may have the greatest impact on organizational fit and tenure among the membership selection factors.

Does the physician value autonomy and the ability to determine a unique practice style, or will he work collaboratively with others in a consensus-driven clinical approach? Is the individual a perfectionist, and will she be satisfied in an organization that is content with good enough? How does the physician feel about a culture of transparency and accountability? Will he feel threatened when asked to discuss performance data with a physician peer? How well does the individual work with others? Does she treat nurses and other nonphysicians in an equitable and nonhierarchical way? Is the physician comfortable with management's style, and does he work well with the management team? Is he interested in transformational change, or would he rather be in a more stable environment?

Answering these questions helps determine an individual's ability—or lack of ability—to work in your organization and to participate on the medical staff in a constructive and meaningful way. Having a realistic sense of what the organization is and is not helps point to which physicians will be an asset and feel comfortable making the necessary transition from a prior environment to the current one.

Tenet 5 Case: Not a Good Fit

A long-standing clinician becomes interested in management when he is selected as the president of the medical staff, becomes certified as a physician executive, and earns an MBA with honors. He finds that neither management nor physician leaders are interested in striving toward excellence but instead are content to be in part of a competent organization that balances professional and community pursuits. He urges the board and management to seek affiliations and partnerships with top-tier organizations and not to settle for average performance. Because of the inevitable culture clash, leaders are relieved when he moves on so that they will not feel encumbered by expectations that they feel are unrealistic.

Comment

Professionals seek environments to work in that are compatible with their internal values and goals. Not every environment can accommodate every individual, and it is important for both the organization and the individual to understand when it is best to work together and when not to. Individuals and organizations change over time. An individual may be initially compatible with an organization's prior values but not with its defined future state. This is particularly true for strongly independent, autonomous professionals who choose not to transition with an organization toward increasing standardization and teamwork or those who find an organization is unwilling to make the same journey that she must make.

ECONOMIC CREDENTIALING

A key part of strategic medical staff development planning is anticipating factors that will be involved in credentialing in the near future. One such factor is economic credentialing.

Credentialing on the basis of economics is the use of non-competency-related criteria for credentialing and privileging in a healthcare organization. Economic credentialing is a misnomer, as it does not usually pertain to economic criteria (e.g., volume of business referred) but rather to privileging criteria that address the specific qualifications, skill set, organizational fit, and contractual obligations of a physician recruit. Professional organizations, such as the American Medical Association (AMA), have come out against policies that allow economic credentialing, yet most healthcare organizations no longer have purely open medical staffs because of the potentially disruptive nature of unmanaged competition and economic relationships that challenge existing contracts and organizational values.

Most legal decisions have upheld the governing board's right to make sound business decisions on behalf of its organization and community needs, and few would contest the fiduciary responsibility of the board to protect the quality and solvency of its organization's healthcare services. One notable case that challenges this authority is *Baptist Health v. Murphy* (2004), in which a healthcare organization challenged a cardiologist and five cardiology colleagues' right to compete as investors in Arkansas Heart Hospital against Baptist Health while maintaining membership and privileges at both. Baptist created a conflict-of-interest policy to disqualify the competing cardiologists from applying, which was found to be tortious interference of the doctor–patient relationship by the Arkansas Circuit Court.

On the other hand, in a more typical case, *Rosenblum v. Tallahassee Memorial Regional Medical Center* (1992), the court sided with the healthcare organization when a cardiothoracic surgeon was denied membership and privileges as a result of his role as the developer of a competing heart surgery program at another hospital. In this case, the Florida Circuit Court upheld the governing board's right to develop what the board called "economic criteria" for membership and privileges if that individual would have an economic impact on the organization's ability to maintain viable clinical services to its community.

Economic credentialing is becoming increasingly prevalent. With the evolution of pay-for-value, bundled payment, and capitated payment methodologies, organizations must not only determine the right number of physicians on staff but also monitor the quality, safety, service, and cost of the care they provide. Fulfilling this responsibility requires a close evaluation of a physician's impact on the organization in all areas, and one way to do so is through economic credentialing.

Attorneys generally recommend that the economic factors be tied directly to quality so that patient safety is the primary concern when establishing economic credentialing criteria. For instance, increases in the cost of care may have an impact on the organization's ability to provide high-quality services to the community in key areas. This shift may in turn affect the provision of other services that are dependent on the high-margin services for their survival. As with other potentially controversial and contentious approaches, economic privileging policies should be developed only after legal counsel has been consulted.

Michael R. Callahan, Esq., *senior partner at Katten, Muchin, and Rosenman LLP and a nationally respected healthcare attorney, summarizes economic credentialing from a legal perspective.*

Economic Credentialing—An Idea Whose Time Has Come?

Overview

The term *economic credentialing* is an old phrase that carries different meanings for different people, especially physicians. Simply stated, it is typically defined as any medical staff credentialing decision that is based solely on economic or financial factors unrelated to a physician's professional qualifications. To engage in economic credentialing has been seen as sacrilegious by most physicians, and such practices have been almost uniformly challenged by medical staff bylaws or any other medical staff rule, regulation, or policy.

Yet medical staff membership decisions based on economic factors vary widely among organizations, and some economic-based decisions have been in common use for many years. For example, exclusive contracts with hospital-based groups such as anesthesiologists, pathologists, and radiologists, which preclude physicians from applying for membership, have been the norm for at least two decades. Although they were challenged as anticompetitive and therefore a violation of state and federal antitrust laws, courts have universally upheld these agreements based on the argument that patient care is improved as a result of better continuity of treatment, 24/7 coverage, greater efficiencies, and other similar factors that are present when exclusive contracts are in place.

But what about some examples of what I call pure economic credentialing practices, in which the connection to improving quality is questionable

(continued)

and the decision is almost exclusively financial? Are such practices still to be considered sacrilege, or rather, in light of rapidly changing healthcare industry dynamics, are the decisions made on the sole basis of financial factors becoming more acceptable?

Appointment Decisions Based on Economic Factors

The extent of merger and acquisition activity and clinical integration at all levels has never been higher, and more is expected. Any stand-alone or unaffiliated hospital, even in a rural area, has been or will be forced to consider whether it can survive in a rapidly changing environment where access to capital is limited and reimbursement is based on the value of services provided rather than the volume. The Affordable Care Act mandates the reduction of Medicare and Medicaid payments, and private payers are following suit. Meanwhile, both the government and private payers expect to see decreased utilization and the achievement of high quality standards based on pay-for-performance measures. Many physicians now eagerly, if not frantically, approach hospitals to purchase their practices or to join a hospital staff as an employee, especially younger physicians coming out of their residency programs. Otherwise, depending on the marketplace in which they practice, physicians often join megagroups in an attempt to remain "independent."

One might therefore ask, How does a hospital make a credentialing or membership decision without taking economics into consideration? For example, what action should a hospital and medical staff take if it receives an application request from a physician who is employed by or whose practice was recently purchased by a competing health system that is aggressively purchasing practices in the hospital's primary service area? The assumed goal of the applicant is to attract business away from the hospital and refer or admit patients to its hospital employer. What if the applicant owns a competing surgicenter or just became a member of a competing ACO?

Under these scenarios, it arguably would be economically imprudent to place these physicians on the medical staff. But is denial of membership illegal or susceptible to a successful legal challenge? A number of courts have addressed such challenges and have supported the hospital's decision to deny a physician's request for an application or the actual application based on the hospital's duty of care and legal right to exercise reasonable business judgment so as to protect the hospital's financial viability and mission to serve its patient community.

But how far can a hospital go in its denials of membership on the basis of economic factors? As a general rule, a hospital and medical staff have the most legal leverage on the front end—before a physician becomes a member of the medical staff. Courts usually do not even exercise jurisdiction in initial application disputes as long as the hospital follows its own bylaws and is not engaged in pure discriminatory, as opposed to financial, activity. Physicians do not have a legal right to obtain membership at a private hospital; even if denied the economic benefits that may accrue from being given privileges and access rights, the denial does not equate to antitrust injury or true injury to competition.

But let's say that a hospital does not want to accept a physician who has a high Medicaid and indigent care patient load and therefore is not likely to generate positive revenue for the hospital. Hospitals that receive Medicare and Medicaid payments are required to staff a sufficient physician population willing to treat Medicaid patients in its community by specialty. Therefore, denial could be challenged on different grounds than denial of a physician's right to make money.

A more likely scenario in which denial would go unchallenged in light of the shift from volume to value is where the physician applying has a record of high or overutilization. Hospitals now commonly distribute periodic reports to physicians that provide the following information: average length of stay, cost per patient visit, number of medication orders and whether they are for generic or brand-name drugs, number of referrals made, consultants used, and other metrics. This information is likely available upon request from other hospitals considering an applicant for privileges. If the applicant indeed demonstrates a pattern of overutilization and has shown no improvement, unless she has some unique skill or practices in a needed specialty, why would the hospital employ this person or place her on the medical staff? Why take the economic risk? I believe a decision to deny an application or a membership to this individual is prudent and defensible.

Reappointment Decisions Based on Economic Factors

Whereas applicants to a medical staff generally have no legal rights, just the opposite is true for current medical staff members. Once a physician is on staff, he is typically entitled to all the rights and privileges afforded to other medical staff members, including rights to a fair or judicial hearing and appellate review. Moreover, decisions that affect a physician's privileges and membership are based on the bylaws, rules, regulations, and policies of

(continued)

the medical staff, which most likely do not recognize or permit termination for failure to be competitive in the marketplace or for employment by a competitor. Unless the hospital's decision to terminate or adversely affect privileges is based on quality of care or disruptive behavior considerations, especially without a hearing, it will likely be challenged and could attract the attention of the AMA and the state medical society.

Such was the case in *Baptist Health v. Murphy*, mentioned earlier in this chapter. Here, the hospital board of directors unilaterally adopted a conflict-of-interest policy whereby all existing medical staff members and their family members had to divest themselves of any financial, economic, or ownership interest in a competing hospital. If current members did not divest, they would not be reappointed; potential new members who held such interests would not be given applications. Five physicians sued, arguing that the policy violated the federal anti-kickback statute, the Arkansas Medicaid Fraud Act, the Arkansas Medicaid False Claims Act, and the Arkansas Deceptive Trade Practices Act and that it illegally interfered with the physician–patient relationship. The case received much attention and ultimately was decided by the Supreme Court of Arkansas, which held in favor of the five physician plaintiffs, who had a direct or indirect investment interest in the competing Arkansas Heart Hospital.

Several unique factors in the Baptist case led to this outcome. One key finding reached by the court hinged on the fact that the policy was unilaterally adopted by the board based on unsubstantiated claims about the dire financial impact that would result if the physicians did not divest or were permitted to remain on the staff when, in fact, the hospital had an extremely strong financial performance. Another finding was that physicians could be terminated without a hearing. One physician testified that she was threatened with termination even though her husband, not she, had an interest in Arkansas Heart Hospital. The husband was threatening her with divorce if she did not accept termination.

While the Baptist case has limited precedential impact in other jurisdictions, it does reinforce the difficulty a hospital will have in trying to adversely affect the membership and privileges of existing physicians without some form of hearing and without support for this action in the hospital bylaws. While the challenge is not insurmountable and some legal arguments support such decisions by a hospital, the political repercussions and legal expenses associated with defending a challenge are substantial.

Common-Sense Economic Credentialing

While I doubt that there is a single approach around which consensus can be reached when considering economic factors in credentialing decisions, the reality is that hospitals and physicians are inextricably bound together as the healthcare industry continues to consolidate and rapidly evolve as a result of reform initiatives. The current model is not sustainable. And while many hospitals are slowly moving toward an employed medical staff or a foundation-type model of employment, others will maintain an independent medical staff for a while to come. In the interim, and perhaps for a very long time, a cooperative and symbiotic—common sense—approach should be considered. Key elements of successful economic credentialing include the following:

Sharing economic, quality, and related information with the medical staff. Physicians are not trained to run hospitals or determine what impact their practices have on the bottom line. Yet when given the right amount of information, most will typically adjust their practices to reduce unnecessary or redundant utilization and alter other behaviors that can adversely affect the hospital's finances and, in turn, its ability to hire nurses, recruit physicians, purchase equipment, and so on. Hospitals need to go over this information with physicians and develop a two-way relationship that takes into account the physician's perspective and any potential adverse impact that adjustments may have on patients. Progress on improvement should be monitored and additional support provided to assist lagging physicians in achieving clearly stated goals.

Coordinating with medical staff leaders. Any effort to inform and educate the medical staff will fail unless these efforts are coordinated with medical staff leaders. Some of the best information to be obtained in terms of cost impact and better, more efficient practices comes from physicians directly. Having informed medical staff leaders who can advise on how to best work with the medical staff greatly facilitates implementation of a plan or policy designed to reduce costs while maintaining—if not improving—quality.

Developing and implementing a performance improvement plan. Just as hospitals have developed OPPE and FPPE plans for physicians to address quality-of-care concerns, so should plans be adopted to help physicians improve practices that are out of line with their peers relating to utilization, average length of stay, cost per patient visit, and other relevant factors. The emphasis of these plans should be on education and not the imposition of disciplinary measures.

(continued)

If performance does not adequately improve to within an acceptable range, progressive remedial measures should be considered that do not trigger traditional hearing rights, as a reduction, suspension, or termination of privileges does. These measures could include taking the practitioner off the physician referral list, limiting and possibly excluding her from a managed care plan, and limiting or excluding her from ACO participation.

Considering disciplinary measures. As is true with quality-of-care concerns, the collective goal of the hospital and medical staff should be to find ways to get the physician back on track so that true disciplinary measures can be avoided. Only the attorneys benefit if you are forced down the hearing and litigation path. While other options, such as proctoring, monitoring, and requiring consultations, are effective and should be used when dealing with repeated quality-of-care concerns, they are not useful if the physician consistently fails or refuses to adjust his practice to adhere to norms and standards embraced by both the hospital and medical staff.

The biggest question is whether, under the right circumstances and when all other remedial efforts have failed, the medical staff is willing to support termination or suspension of a physician's membership and privileges. Such a decision is not reportable to the state medical society if it is made on the basis of financial or economic factors rather than quality-of-care problems; a physician's licensure will not be adversely affected. The physician may have problems linking up with a new medical staff, physician group, or ACO if seen as a recidivist overutilizer, but that outcome is not assured.

Although a hospital should make every effort to work with the medical staff to develop a policy or plan and incorporate it into the medical staff bylaws, if it is not successful in this attempt, the hospital's choices are to (1) impose measures, such as those mentioned here, that fall short of taking away privileges or (2) proceed with suspension or termination with the understanding that some kind of challenge is likely to occur. While I do not necessarily advocate the second path, steps to consider when taking this course of action include the following:

1. *Document, document, document.* Documentation should include the plan or policy adopted, how the metrics were developed, the decision to use a performance improvement plan, and how the physician failed to improve or meet the standards despite efforts to assist him.

2. *Provide a hearing.* Assuming that the medical staff will not support or recommend termination for utilization or economic factors, an administrative hearing should be provided in lieu of a medical staff bylaw hearing. If possible, engage willing physicians to participate and afford the same rights as given under the medical staff bylaws for the administrative hearing. An appeals process is not required by law but can be considered.

3. *Update board bylaws or policy.* The administrative hearing process should be formally developed and adopted by the governing board and referenced in the corporate bylaws or a board policy.

The development of a shared vision between hospitals and physicians that takes into account the financial realities of all parties is fundamental to establishing and implementing a successful strategic plan in this highly competitive and volatile market. Recognizing that all credentialing decisions have some degree of economic impact that can either benefit or undermine the entire enterprise is the first step in creating a balanced approach to membership decisions, whether on a medical staff, in an ACO, or for another clinically integrated entity. The financial resources of all parties are already strained; engaging in continued debates and challenges over whether privileging decisions, such as those based on economic credentialing, are illegal will solve little.

SUMMARY

Demographic analysis is no longer sufficient to effectively recruit and retain a qualified medical staff. Quality, safety, service, and economic factors must be taken into consideration so that new physicians enhance the organization's ability to meet its strategic goals and objectives as consistent with its organizational vision.

REFERENCES

Baptist Health v. Bruce Murphy et al., No. 04-430 (Arkansas Circuit Court, July 1, 2004).

Rosenblum v. Tallahassee Memorial Regional Medical Center, No. 91-589 (Florida Circuit Court, 1992).

CHAPTER 3

Credentialing and Privileging—
Getting More Selective

After dealing with a disruptive physician for more than 15 years, the chief of staff of one hospital performed a retrospective review of her credentialing and privileging processes by calling all of the original references for that physician from 15 years prior. One of the references asked incredulously, "You hired her? She almost ruined my practice due to her disruptive conduct!" The chief of staff replied that the reference had rated the physician as excellent clinically and "fair" for professional conduct. The reference responded, "That was your clue to pick up the phone. There's no way that I could have put my comments in writing."

In the pay-for-volume era, physicians were seen as revenue assets to be recruited, credentialed, and privileged with impunity. Today, healthcare organizations want to recruit and select physicians who commit to quality, safety, service, and cost-effectiveness and desire to work in interdisciplinary teams with both staff and management to achieve organizational goals. Credentialing and privileging lay the foundation for ensuring that the right physicians are recruited and retained and create a framework in which to proactively and effectively deal with any performance issues that emerge.

ACCOUNTABILITY FOR QUALITY

Originally, healthcare organizations were not responsible for physician performance because they were protected under the doctrine of charitable immunity as not-for-profit entities. This status changed in 1965 with the *Darling v. Charleston Community Memorial Hospital* ruling, in which the Illinois Circuit Court determined that the hospital had an independent duty to the community to affirm the competence of any physician granted clinical privileges. This legal standard was raised in 1981 when the Wisconsin Circuit Court, ruling in *Johnson v. Misericordia Community Hospital*, determined that a hospital must use "reasonable care to grant only competent medical doctors the privilege of using facilities" when it found that the organization did not exercise due diligence in evaluating the credentials application of a problematic orthopedic surgeon.

In 1991, the Pennsylvania Circuit Court expanded the hospital's role further yet when it affirmed that hospital authorities must be notified so that appropriate action may be taken if an attending physician fails to reasonably act after noting patient abnormalities (*Thompson v. Nason Hospital,* 1991). Finally, in 2007, the Illinois Circuit Court determined that when a hospital fails to follow its own privileging criteria, it fails to meet reasonable standards of competence (*Frigo v. Silver Cross Hospital,* 2007).

The Department of Justice and the US Department of Health and Human Services Office of Inspector General have recently instructed US attorneys to prosecute those hospitals for Medicare fraud under the False Claims Act that fail to effectively address quality and safety issues because they profit from practitioners of "poor quality" (Honig 2013). Thus, healthcare organizations assume an increasing role in ensuring that only competent physicians and healthcare practitioners are recommended to the governing board for membership and privileges.

Also in past years, healthcare organizations were eager to credential and privilege as many physicians and healthcare practitioners as possible. The screening process was based on a quality assurance approach that sought to eliminate negative outliers from the application pool, assuming that the absence of negative information signaled clinical competence. Professional references were provided as opinions rather than as performance data and were often political and rife with potential conflicts of interest. Privileges were categorized under vague terms (e.g., general surgery), they were often undefined, and little effort was made to distinguish those applicants who performed the privileged procedures often from those who either rarely performed them or were never properly assessed.

CREDENTIALING AND PRIVILEGING DEFINED

To close this gap, organizations have begun to separate membership from privileges, defining credentials as pertaining to eligibility for membership (e.g., political rights) on the medical staff and privileges as authorization to care for specific patients, perform specific procedures, and oversee specific diagnostic categories.

As defined by The Joint Commission (2013), credentialing "involves the collection, verification, and assessment of information regarding three critical parameters: current licensure; education and relevant training; and experience, ability, and current competence to perform the requested privilege(s). Verification is sought to minimize the possibility of granting privilege(s) based upon the review of fraudulent documents." It defines privileging as "the criteria that determine a practitioner's ability to provide patient care, treatment, and services within the scope of privileges requested. Evaluation of all of the following are included in the criteria: current licensure and certification, relevant training, evidence of physical ability to perform the requested privilege, data from professional practice review, and peer/faculty recommendations" (Joint Commission 2007, MS.06.01.05, EP2).

Originally, privileges included everything that a physician was willing to do. By 1951, the American College of Surgeons had introduced the so-called laundry list denoting each privilege. When this list became overly complex due to the number and variety of clinical specialties, core privileges were introduced in the 1990s, which stratified privileges into those clinical activities that any reasonably trained specialist should be competent to perform and those that only some specialists should be competent to perform as the result of additional training, volume of practice in that specialty, or skill set.

Over the past decade, and in response to concerns that attempts to describe every practitioner's competence based on a defined core privilege was inadequate, competency clusters were created that define the specific privileges that a practitioner is competent to perform based on all of the defined criteria listed earlier. The specific cluster of privileges that each practitioner is qualified to exercise requires some degree of customization, as both the Centers for Medicare & Medicaid Services (CMS) and the other deemed status accreditation organizations (The Joint Commission, the Healthcare Facilities Accreditation Program [HFAP], Det Norske Veritas, and the Center for Improvement in Healthcare Quality) require that the medical staff and governing board affirm the clinical competence of all practitioners who are assessed through the medical staff process for *every* clinical privilege that is requested by the physician. Many practitioners within the same clinical specialty have different skills and knowledge gained as the result of their specific training, interests, and abilities; these must now be taken into consideration when defining each practitioner's specific scope of privileges.

It is possible to be credentialed but not privileged, as with emeritus or administrative physicians who participate in medical staff affairs but no longer practice clinically. It is also possible to be fully privileged with incomplete political rights, as with physicians and mid-level or allied health practitioners who are new to the staff, have multiple medical staff appointments, or are not interested in medical staff affairs. (This approach partially solves the low- or no-volume practitioner problem that is discussed more fully in Chapter 4.)

Accountable care requires governing boards and medical staffs to establish specific criteria for membership and privileges that are consistent with nationally recognized standards in multiple dimensions of performance. The Joint Commission had essentially raised that bar in 2007 (MS.06.01.05) when it introduced the concepts of ongoing professional practice evaluation and focused professional practice evaluation. It asserted that current clinical competence had to be defined on the basis of performance data (objective and evidence based) and not solely on professional opinion (references) or the absence of negative information (quality assurance). This step was considered a game changer in clinical performance management. Specifically, The Joint Commission required that "The decision to grant or deny a privilege(s) and/or to renew an existing privilege(s) is an objective evidence based process." This standard is consistent with the CMS (2009) Conditions of Participation, which require that "the criteria for selection are individual character, competence, training, experience, and judgment."

On the basis of the foregoing standards, governing boards and medical staffs must establish criteria within the following dimensions of performance:

- Medical or clinical knowledge
- Practice-based learning and improvement
- Interpersonal and communication skills
- Professionalism
- Systems-based practice

Objective measures of performance should be developed for each dimension and applied consistently. This process, which is more rigorous than what has been applied in the past, enables an organization to define its performance standards in advance, create a performance management system around it, and use the credentialing and privileging process to identify professionals who meet the medical staff–recommended, board-approved criteria.

CREDENTIALING AND PRIVILEGING CASE STUDIES

The healthcare organization is ultimately responsible for the integrity and veracity of its credentialing and privileging process, and the board depends on management and the medical staff to make appropriate recommendations for it to uphold its fiduciary responsibilities to the community (and stockholders in for-profit entities). The following represent actual situations (with identifying characteristics altered to protect individuals and organizations) that illustrate key principles of a high-performing credentialing and privileging process in the new era of accountable care.

Case 1: Workaround

The president of the medical staff asks the CEO to sign off on temporary privileges for a locum tenens physician so that a busy surgeon can take a last-minute holiday. The president states that the surgical chair checked his credentials and that he is "good to go." What should the CEO do?

Comment

The Joint Commission (2013, MS.06.01.13) permits temporary privileges to be granted under only two circumstances:

- To fulfill an important patient care, treatment, and service need
- When an applicant for new privileges with a complete application that raises no concerns is awaiting review and approval by the medical executive committee (MEC) and governing board

Typically, The Joint Commission does not consider a physician's desire to take a holiday as an important service need. Furthermore, in this case, the locum tenens physician's application has not been fully vetted by the clinical department or credentials committee. In addition, The Joint Commission (2013, MS.06.01.11, EP1) requires that the organization "develop criteria for an expedited process for granting privileges," which typically includes a rigorous evaluation for any potential issues that would preclude a candidate from being considered for expedited approval.

Although it is tempting to perform a workaround of a process that is inconvenient to some individuals, the risk to the organization and its patients is greater than anyone's immediate wishes. In this case, the organization should have followed its customary process to determine the standard against which the organization is held accountable in the event of a credentialing or privileging decision that leads to an adverse outcome.

Case 2: "I Cannot Give You Further Information"

The organization has spent a great deal of time and money to recruit a surgeon to its community. On the clinician's professional reference, she is rated "excellent" for technical skills and "satisfactory" for professional conduct. When the medical staff contacts her reference, he claims that he cannot give them any further information. On the basis of this information, what should the MEC do?

Comment
According to The Joint Commission (2007, MS.06.01.05, EP8):

> Peer recommendations include written information regarding the practitioner's current:
> - Medical/clinical knowledge
> - Technical and clinical skills
> - Clinical judgment
> - Interpersonal skills
> - Communication skills
> - Professionalism

Thus, an essential component of a good credentialing policy is a consistently applied definition of when an application is complete. Completion of an application has often been characterized as when all requested materials have been received by the hospital and verified. However, this threshold is insufficient for determining the suitability of an applicant for the medical staff, as problematic issues may arise at any time during the application (or reappointment) process. It is essential to address them in a direct and cost-effective way, which is not necessarily possible if the application has been determined to be complete.

A better approach in this case would have been for the MEC to view this surgeon's application as incomplete until all requested materials were received and verified *and* no issues came to light that required further information or clarification.

The organization might have used the following language in its credentialing and privileging policy to define the completion of an application:

> An application shall be deemed incomplete if any required items are missing or if the need arises for new, additional, or clarifying information in the course of reviewing an application. Any time in the application process that it becomes apparent that an applicant does not meet all of the eligibility criteria for membership or privileges,

the application process shall be terminated, no further action shall be taken, and the applicant shall not be entitled to a fair hearing.

Furthermore, this organization should have put the burden on the surgeon applicant to obtain any requested material from her reference, as healthcare organizations are held accountable to secure a meaningful professional evaluation in each area specified by The Joint Commission, particularly if a patient suffers an adverse outcome. It may even have required the applicant to speak directly to the reference to authorize him to share additional information with the requesting organization.

Case 3: An Odd Request

A respected general surgeon approaches the MEC to request privileges for performing breast augmentation and reduction, stating that he took a rigorous two-week course in these procedures and was deemed qualified to perform them. What should the MEC do?

Comment

As mentioned earlier, CMS requires that privileging decisions be based on medical staff–recommended, board-approved criteria along several dimensions of performance, including character, competence, training, experience, and judgment. The appropriate response to this case (and every case like it) is to ask the medical staff to determine what the current credentialing and privileging criteria are for this request. If no such criteria exist or they are inadequate for the request at hand, the medical staff should stop the application process and thoughtfully deliberate on whether they should recommend new or modified criteria prior to processing this request and others like it.

Many hospital and health system leaders ask whether it is appropriate or even legal to modify a process once it has begun to accommodate an unexpected or unusual request. The challenge is that dealing with issues on an ad hoc basis leaves an organization vulnerable to charges of corporate negligence when an adverse patient care event occurs and the organization is found to base its judgments on inconsistent or poorly documented criteria. The key to avoiding these concerns is to apply the criteria consistently, fairly, and in the best interests of good patient care.

The Joint Commission reinforces this point in the following standards:

All of the [privileging] criteria used are consistently evaluated for all practitioners holding that privilege. (Joint Commission 2007, MS.06.01.05, EP3)

The hospital's privilege granting/denial criteria are consistently applied for each requesting practitioner. (Joint Commission 2007, MS.06.01.07, EP5)

In this case, the MEC could have consulted the Credentialing Resource Center (CRC) White Papers (published by HCPro Inc.) or the American Medical Association's *Graduate Medical Education Directory* (known as the "Green Book"). The CRC White Papers publish sample privileging criteria, and the AMA Green Book documents the required elements of training for residency and fellowship programs for each clinical specialty and subspecialty. In addition, privileging criteria may be freely shared between organizations of similar size and demographics. This organization could have compared criteria to gain a sense of how others deal with similar situations.

If the organization in the case study had consulted these references, it would have found that general surgical residency programs do not provide comprehensive training in cosmetic surgery (most general surgical residents spend no more than two months rotating through a plastic surgical service), and few (if any) healthcare organizations include cosmetic breast surgery in their general surgical privileging criteria or delineation.

Medical staffs that find themselves in a situation such as the case study hospital should inform physicians who are interested in expanding their scope of practice to consult with the credentials committee or MEC *prior to* obtaining additional training or experience. An in-depth discussion of this topic is provided in Chapter 4.

Case 4: "What's a SPARC Procedure?"

The operating room (OR) nurse manager calls the medical staff office to ask if a particular ob-gyn has privileges to perform a "SPARC" procedure that is on the OR schedule for the next day. The nurse manager says that he has never heard of a SPARC procedure and has no idea how to set it up. The director of the medical staff office cannot answer the question based on information in the current core privileging document and consults the chief medical officer (CMO).

The CMO researches SPARC in the literature and finds that it is a suprapubic arc procedure that involves elevating the bladder to correct urinary incontinence (leakage) with a suture that is placed blindly through the pelvic bone. She also discovers that a significant number of inadvertent injuries to the bladder have occurred as a result of this surgery. Upon reviewing the ob-gyn's background, the CMO determines that the physician has neither the privileges nor the training to perform cystoscopic evaluation or repair of the bladder necessary to handle potential bladder injuries and cancels the case, resulting in frustration and anger for the patient and the surgeon.

Comment

This case is a corollary to Case 3 and demonstrates how potentially negative consequences can be avoided by vetting privileging criteria in advance of a procedure. The system worked in this case, and no one was harmed; however, two key issues were raised.

1. When is a clinical privilege an extension of the core privileges that a practitioner is already authorized to exercise? As in Case 3, the CRC White Papers, AMA Green Book, and other privileging resources are helpful. In addition, it is important to know that a privilege may fall outside of the core if it involves different training, skill, judgment, technique, equipment, or ability to manage complications. As in this case, most ob-gyns do not receive significant training in conducting cystoscopic procedures to evaluate the bladder and treat related conditions or any complications arising from the use of the cystoscope. Therefore, most organizations do not include the SPARC procedure as part of an ob-gyn's core privileges.

2. Does the healthcare system have appropriate checks and balances to catch unauthorized privileges before they have the potential to cause injury or harm? Most organizations have a computerized manifest of every practitioner's current clinical privileges, and staff consult this list if any doubt or question arises as to the extent of a physician's privileges, as in this case study. Management's role is to reinforce this important responsibility so that no injury occurs as a result of an unauthorized clinical privilege that places patients, physicians, and the organization at risk.

Case 5: Scope Creep

A nurse practitioner (NP) is asked to write orders for her collaborating physician in the intensive care unit (ICU). The ICU nurse manager asks the ICU medical director if the NP has privileges to write orders in the unit. What should the medical director do?

Comment

Each state's licensing board determines the scope of practice for advanced practice professionals (APPs). Hospitals may grant a scope of practice that is up to but not beyond the state's statutory authorization. The medical director in this case should have checked the NP's scope of privileges to see if she was authorized to write orders in the ICU. If the medical director had found that she was not authorized to do so under her licensure, he should have communicated this finding immediately to the NP and the collaborating physician to stop the NP from writing an order in this and future instances.

Clinical practitioners are authorized by law to provide services assuming an unlimited scope of practice *only* in emergency situations in which a patient requires life- or limb-saving treatment. If the NP in this case had injured a patient following her writing of the elective care order, she, her collaborating physician, and the organization might have been held negligent, which could result in charges of battery or aggravated battery, corporate negligence, and individual liability of all involved parties. Furthermore, neither organizational indemnification nor individual liability coverage or protection would be applicable to protect the entities.

One step this organization could have taken prior to any question of authorization is to develop an MEC-recommended, board-approved policy for APPs that outlines the following:

◆ Scope of services provided (consistent with state law) that determines which APP specialties will be used
◆ Scope of practice defined for each APP specialty
◆ Level of oversight provided for each practitioner (e.g., direct or in person; indirect or immediately available; available often by text, message, or phone; or available per policy or clinical protocol)
◆ Clinical and administrative oversight (e.g., medical staff office and human resources department)

This case demonstrates the challenge of scope creep as practitioners, under increasing pressure to improve efficiency, introduce workarounds that seem innocuous but may have dire consequences.

Case 6: A Matter of Organizational Fit

An orthopedist completes a knee surgery fellowship program and requests privileges to perform knee surgery only. The medical staff is concerned by this limitation, as the organization needs all of its general orthopedists to provide call coverage for routine emergencies after hours. What should the medical staff and management do?

Comment

As mentioned earlier, the hospital has the right to approve facility-specific privileging criteria that determine a practitioner's ability to provide patient care, treatment, and services based on recommendations from the organized medical staff and approval of the governing board. If, as in this case, the board (with medical staff input) feels that the community requires general orthopedists to handle routine orthopedic emergencies after hours, it may define its eligibility criteria accordingly so that an orthopedist who requests knee privileges only would be ineligible to apply. (In terms of case law surrounding economic credentialing, discussed in Chapter 2, this decision would not be a reportable event for documentation in the National Practitioner Data Bank because the orthopedist does not qualify to apply and was not denied as a result of clinical incompetence or issues related to professional conduct.)

Case 7: Convicted Felon, Altered Identity, and Knowing Misrepresentation

A nurse anesthetist applies for medical staff membership. The medical staff conducts a criminal background check and finds that the applicant has been convicted of a felony for selling drugs. On his application, the nurse anesthetist had provided an alias and checked "No" when asked if he had ever been convicted of a felony. What should the medical staff do?

Comment

This case presents three separate but related issues: felony conviction, altered identity, and knowing misrepresentation on the application. The medical staff should have a clear policy to address each of these problematic issues. As described earlier in Case 3, if the medical staff does not already have such policies in place, the application process should cease pending the creation of medical staff–recommended, board-approved policies to be applied in a clear and consistent manner.

Issue 1: Felony Conviction

Many medical staffs do not allow convicted felons, regardless of the circumstances, to apply to their staff. This type of policy is overly simplistic and denies the medical staff the opportunity to work with some fine individuals. Felonies can be either major (e.g., criminal activity) or relatively minor (e.g., possession of marijuana). They may have occurred recently or in the distant past. They may indicate a significant character flaw (e.g., fraud) or a temporary lapse in youthful judgment (e.g., felony violation for driving while intoxicated). Therefore, a more nuanced approach to crafting policy is called for, which may include language similar to the following:

> If convicted of a felony related to misuse of controlled substances, illegal drugs, fraud or abuse, violence, or any act that would reflect adversely on the reputation of the healthcare organization and/or the confidence of the community, the practitioner shall automatically and voluntarily relinquish membership and privileges without right to a fair/judicial hearing or review.

This type of approach affords the MEC and governing board the discretion to make customized decisions based on each applicant's unique presentation and supports decisions that are in the organization's best interest on a case-by-case basis.

Issue 2: Altered Identity

Deception related to an individual's identity is a growing issue with our dependence on information technology and the ability of individuals to use it for deviant motives. As a result, many organizations now require the following items to confirm the identity of each applicant:

- Social Security number
- Photo identification (typically a passport or state-issued driver's license or identification card)
- Criminal background check

Are fingerprints and iris scans to come? It is not an unlikely scenario.

Criminal background checks are relatively new to healthcare and were stimulated by the publication of *Blind Eye*, by James Stewart (1999), which tells the story of Dr. Michael Swango, whose criminal activity went undetected as he murdered untold numbers of patients in multiple states and several countries because the healthcare system failed in its due diligence. As of 2013, 44 states require criminal background checks and fingerprints as a condition of medical licensure, and this number is likely to increase in the near future (FSMB 2013). Regardless of your state's regulations, this is a recommended practice to help avoid serious consequences.

Issue 3: Knowing Misrepresentation on an Application

Any knowing, substantive misrepresentation should terminate the application process without recourse to procedural rights. The following is recommended bylaws language:

The applicant attests to the accuracy and completeness of all of the requested information in the application and agrees that any substantive inaccuracy, omission, or misrepresentation may be grounds for termination of the application process without right to a fair/judicial hearing or an appellate review.

As with policies regarding felonies, this approach gives the medical staff and governing board the discretion to determine whether an inaccuracy, an omission, or a misrepresentation is substantive or not.

Case 8: "Like Riding a Bike"

A cardiothoracic surgeon decides to cut back on her practice and return to operating on hernias, gallbladders, and appendixes. She has not performed any of these procedures in more than 20 years but claims it is "like riding a bike" and she will be up to speed in no time. What should the medical staff do?

Comment
In accordance with The Joint Commission's (2007, MS.06.01.05) statement that "The decision to grant or deny a privilege(s) and/or renew an existing privilege(s) is an objective evidence based process . . . that includes data from professional review by an organization that currently privileges the applicant and review of the practitioner's performance within the hospital," the MEC correctly determined that this cardiothoracic surgeon is ineligible to apply for general surgical privileges because she has no professional review data to evaluate and therefore does not meet the privileging criteria.

Michael R. Callahan, Esq., *senior partner at Katten, Muchin, and Rosenman LLP and nationally respected healthcare attorney, summarizes the legal precedents that inform the medical staff's, management's, and board's legal obligations when evaluating a prospective applicant for medical staff membership or privileges.*

How to Avoid Negligent Credentialing Liability
In the seminal decision *Darling v. Charleston Community Memorial Hospital* (1965), the Supreme Court of Illinois held for the first time in the United States that a hospital is legally responsible for making sure that a physician

(continued)

---

seeking appointment or reappointment to a medical staff is qualified to exercise each and every clinical privilege that is granted to him as determined through the hospital and medical staff's credentialing and privileging procedures. If the hospital fails in its duty and knew, or should have known, that the physician is unqualified and the physician subsequently commits an act of negligence that injures a patient, the court opined, the hospital can be held separately liable for compensatory damages under what is commonly known as the doctrine of corporate negligence.

Since the decision was issued, approximately 40 states have adopted this liability standard. Sometimes referred to as "negligent hiring or selection" or "negligent retention," this duty applies not only to hospitals but also to managed care entities, such as physician–hospital organizations and independent practice associations. Similarly, The Joint Commission, other hospital accrediting bodies, and state licensing boards impose clear and detailed obligations on hospitals and medical staffs to vet physicians' qualifications at the time of appointment and reappointment and to continuously monitor their practices to ensure ongoing compliance with accepted standards of patient care services.

Standards for a Negligent Credentialing Claim

To succeed in a negligent credentialing claim, a plaintiff must establish that the hospital had a duty to the patient, this duty was breached, the breach caused the patient's injury, and the patient suffered resultant damages. These standards, and the defenses that can be asserted by a hospital, are discussed in more detail next.

Duty

Hospitals owe a duty to make sure that physicians appointed and reappointed to the medical staff are qualified to exercise each and every clinical privilege granted to them. Consequently, this is the easiest element of the tort claim of corporate negligence to prove. This duty applies irrespective of whether the physician is employed or is independent. The only difference is that if an employed physician is found to be negligent when he injures a patient, the hospital will be held directly liable under the doctrine of respondeat superior, whereas if the physician is an independent member of the medical staff, the plaintiff must not only prove that the physician is negligent but further that the hospital either negligently appointed or reappointed him or that it knew, or should have known, he was unqualified but still permitted him to exercise clinical privileges.

Breach of Duty

If the plaintiff is able to show that the physician was negligent, the next requirement is to establish that the hospital was negligent in appointing, reappointing, or otherwise allowing the physician to render the patient care services on which the claim is based (*Darling v. Charleston Community Memorial Hospital* 1965).

An illustration of this breach-of-duty standard can be found in *Frigo v. Silver Cross Hospital* (2007). In this case, the plaintiff was a patient of a podiatrist who had been appointed to the medical staff and allowed to perform category 2 surgical privileges, which include bunionectomies. When the physician was first considered for appointment, the standard for granting membership and privileges for these procedures was that he have some postgraduate training or be board certified or deemed board eligible by the American Board of Podiatric Surgery. He was approved as a member of the medical staff even though he did not meet these established qualifications.

By the time he came up for reappointment two years later, the qualifications had been elevated to manage the high influx of applications from other podiatrists seeking surgical privileges. Now, podiatrists had to complete a 12-month surgical residency training program, complete and pass the written portion of the board-certification examination, and prove that they had participated in at least 30 category 2 surgical procedures within the previous 12 months. When it was pointed out that the podiatrist up for reappointment had not satisfied this higher eligibility standard, much less the previous standard, the decision was made to reappoint him anyway because the quality of the care he provided had been acceptable and he had received no patient complaints. No attempt was made to grandfather him or create a documented exception to his remaining on staff with his previously delineated privileges.

Two or three years later, the podiatrist performed a bunionectomy on a diabetic patient for whom he had successfully performed the same procedure on her other foot the previous year. At the time of the surgery, the patient had an infection near the surgical site. Rather than wait until the infection cleared, the podiatrist proceeded with the operation. Because her postoperative care was poorly managed, the patient's foot became infected and had to be amputated. The patient subsequently sued.

The plaintiff's theory against the hospital was simple and straightforward. She argued that the hospital was directly negligent because it granted

(continued)

surgical privileges to a podiatrist even though he had not satisfied the privileging standards established by the hospital. The fact that he had no prior lawsuits or patient complaints was seen as irrelevant.

Stated in legal terms, the hospital's duty to grant privileges only to qualified podiatric surgeons was breached when it failed to follow its own established eligibility standards. Had it done so, this podiatrist would not have been granted the privileges and the patient would not have lost her foot. The jury awarded the plaintiff nearly $8 million, and the verdict was upheld on appeal under the doctrine of corporate negligence.

Frigo and other similar decisions teach us several lessons for preventing hospitals from breaching their duty to patients, which include the following.

Create Robust Appointment and Reappointment Processes

Hospitals and medical staffs must expend reasonable efforts in determining whether a physician is qualified for membership and clinical privileges. Most application and reappointment forms contain detailed questions as a means of detecting any issues or concerns related to a physician's ability to exercise the requested privileges. During the appointment phase, the hospital has all of the leverage. The burden should be on the physician to answer all questions and concerns to the satisfaction of the hospital and medical staff.

Following are some steps to follow and suggested provisions to include in the bylaws:

1. Applications must be complete before they are processed by the hospital.
2. The application process should not go forward until all questions and issues are addressed.
3. A physician's failure to respond completely should result in the withdrawal of the application with no fair hearing or other procedural rights.
4. Bylaws should contain a provision stating that if the physician does not respond truthfully or completely or if the answers are misleading, the application will be terminated without action or access to procedural rights either at the time of initial processing or retrospectively if discovered after membership and privileges have been granted.

5. The hospital should seek to further evaluate and follow up on any and all substantive issues from the original source and not rely solely on the physician's representation of the circumstances.
6. The hospital must establish and comply with eligibility criteria for credentialing and privileging and apply them uniformly. Failure to follow them exposes the hospital to liability claims.
7. Physicians must be subject to continued monitoring. If adverse events or issues are identified, the hospital and medical staff must establish and follow appropriate peer review and quality improvement policies and procedures to address identified problems as soon as possible.
8. All relevant quality, utilization, and other data should be collected from all available sources and thoroughly reviewed at the time of reappointment (although they should also have been monitored throughout the two-year reappointment period).
9. Where necessary, if problems arise, remedial measures should be put into place. These include monitoring and proctoring, which do not trigger hearings under the bylaws or a data bank report, as set forth by the Healthcare Quality Improvement Act of 1986.
10. If remedial measures fail, the hospital should trigger an investigation or request corrective action.
11. To achieve medical staff buy-in to a rigorous privileging process, the hospital should adopt a just-culture environment in which the emphasis is on acknowledging issues without fear of reprisal or loss of membership or privileges.

Align Criteria and Qualifications with Best Practices

Delineation criteria and qualifications should be tied to industry practices and standards of care—and once adopted, they must be followed. If they are not followed, the hospital must document the objective basis for granting an exception.

Have Remedial Measures in Place

Courts and juries are more likely to rule against the hospital if no remedial measure has been imposed despite the existence of a clearly substandard pattern of practice.

Causation

The third prong of a tort claim is to establish that the patient's injury was caused by the breach. As noted in *Frigo*, the patient's need for an amputation

(continued)

was caused by both the physician's negligence and the hospital's act of granting privileges to an unqualified podiatrist based on a self-imposed standard. Most cases are not so straightforward. Hospitals do not guarantee outcomes and do not constantly look over the shoulders of their physicians. The fact that the physician was negligent does not mean that the hospital was negligent in granting him privileges. The outcome in *Frigo* likely would have been different if the podiatrist had met the established privileging standard even though he was found to be negligent. There was nothing in his record that otherwise would have suggested that he was not qualified: no patient complaints, no bad outcomes, and no previous malpractice suits. In fact, he had a reputation as an expert in treating podiatric patients with diabetes.

In addition to the earlier recommendations, some steps to consider when establishing lack of causation include the following:

1. Establish appropriate peer review and quality improvement policies and proof of compliance. Bear in mind that confidentiality statutes do not allow the hospital to introduce into evidence confidential peer review information, and therefore the hospital needs to develop a separate paper trail to establish that it abides by all required licensure and accreditation standards. Hospitals should consult with legal counsel on proper steps to take.
2. Introduce evidence that the physician has had no pattern of lawsuits, patient complaints, or other evidence to suggest he Is unqualified.
3. Where evidence does exist, such as past lawsuits with similar claims, establish that the hospital and medical staff took appropriate remedial measures to improve care and avoid repeat behavior. The hospital is not legally required to terminate or suspend a physician for a single bad outcome.

Injury

The last prong is that the patient must have suffered some compensable injury as a result of the physician's and hospital's negligence. Using the *Frigo* case again as an example, if the patient's bunionectomy had been successful and the patient did not suffer an injury, even though the hospital had negligently granted surgical privileges, she would have no claim. (That being said, if no injury had occurred, it's likely that no lawsuit would have been brought in the first place.)

Case 9: "I Heard It Through the Grapevine"

The hospital expends a great deal of resources to bring a top-name neurosurgeon to the staff to head the organization's new center of excellence. Through the grapevine, members of the medical staff hear that documentation, behavioral, and administrative issues have followed the neurosurgeon from his current organization. His references are all "outstanding" and his record is clean on paper. What should the MEC do?

Comment
The overarching theme of this chapter is to use the credentialing and privileging process proactively to identify potential performance issues and address them early on so that they do not lead to harm. We do not know if any of the rumors about this physician are true; however, ignoring important clues to potential issues is not a good idea, despite the investment costs already expended. Courts will hold an organization liable for information that is available through ordinary channels, and more importantly, our fiduciary obligations demand that we take every precaution to protect patients, the communities we serve, and the reputation of the organization. Thus, the MEC should resolve the unsubstantiated claims by either validating or invalidating them to ensure that potential performance issues are addressed at the door and not after the fact.

SUMMARY

Creating a high-performing medical staff is not an accident. It is the result of clear credentialing and privileging criteria that are thoughtfully developed, consistently applied, and intended to continually raise the bar in providing patients with the best possible care.

REFERENCES

Centers for Medicare & Medicaid Services (CMS). 2009. *Conditions of Participation Interpretive Guidelines*, §482.12(a)(6). Baltimore, MD: CMS.

Darling v. Charleston Community Memorial Hospital, 33 Ill. 2d 326, 211 N.E. 2d 253 (Ill. 1965).

Federation of State Medical Boards (FSMB). 2013. "Criminal Background Checks: Board-by-Board Overview." Retrieved June 4, 2014. www.fsmb.org /pdf/grpol_criminal_background_checks.pdf.

Frigo v. Silver Cross Hospital and Medical Center, 377 Ill. App. 3d 43, 876 N.E. 2d 697 (Ill. App. 1st Dist. 2007).

Honig, D. B. 2013. "The False Claims Act and Quality of Care." Hall Render Blog. Published February 13. http://fcadefense.com/false_claims_act /whistleblower/qui_tam/the-false-claims-act-and-quality-of-care/.

Johnson v. Misericordia Community Hospital, 99 Wis. 2d 708, 301 N.W. 2d 156 (Wis. 1981).

Joint Commission. 2007–2013. "Hospital Accreditation Standards," MS.06.01.03, .05, .07, .11, and .13. Oakbrook Terrace, IL: Joint Commission.

Stewart, J. B. 1999. *Blind Eye: The Terrifying Story of a Doctor Who Got Away with Murder*. New York: Simon and Schuster.

Thompson v. Nason Hospital, 527 Pa. 330, 591 A.2d 703 (1991).

CHAPTER 4

Privileging Challenges

One day, the medical staff credentials committee received several unusual requests: a family physician wanting to do Botox injections, a general surgeon wanting to do endovascular surgery, and an ob-gyn requesting to do a SPARC procedure. A member of the committee suggested that these physicians undergo proctoring to make sure they are competent to perform these procedures. Another committee member raised the question, "What are our criteria for these privileges, and are these physicians eligible to make these requests?"

Clinical and administrative leaders understand how important it is to narrow the range of acceptable performance competencies in an environment that demands world-class quality at a fraction of the prevailing cost. But they may not be well versed in how to go about it. This chapter focuses on the most common and problematic privileging challenges and how to manage them in the current high-stakes climate.

COMPETENCY CLUSTERS

As practitioners began to specialize and subspecialize, the definition of *clinical competence* became increasingly narrow. Accreditors, regulators, and payers required healthcare organizations to assess the clinical competence and professional conduct of all practitioners granted clinical privileges for each and every privilege authorized, even if they were seldom (if ever) exercised. Establishing core privileges seemed like a logical way to manage privileging because it separated low-risk privileges that every reasonably trained practitioner should be able to safely perform from higher-risk privileges that required additional training, experience, expertise, judgment, technique, or special equipment to safely perform.

Today, with more than 130 specialties and subspecialties recognized by the American Board of Medical Specialties, assessing clinical competence continues to evolve as the acceptable scope of practice for each specialty and subspecialty narrows. In response, the healthcare industry has moved to adopt competency clusters, or tightly defined areas of expertise derived from a practitioner's *actual practice and practice patterns*. Privileging through competency clusters avoids inadvertently granting clinical privileges for clinical services that the organization no longer offers or privileging practitioners who are no longer competent to perform specific privileges within a narrowly defined scope of practice.

Typical clusters that exist today include the following:

- Primary care physicians who no longer care for hospitalized patients and exercise ambulatory privileges only
- Primary care physicians who give up certain areas of traditional practice (e.g., obstetrics, critical care, pediatrics) to focus on a more narrow practice (e.g., ambulatory care without obstetrics or critical care privileges)
- Orthopedic, plastic, and general surgeons who restrict their practice to certain types of procedures (e.g., knee, hip, or ankle; cosmetic)
- Surgeons who restrict their practice to certain settings (e.g., ambulatory surgery centers)
- Specialists who restrict their practice to specific freestanding imaging or interventional ambulatory settings (e.g., radiology, cardiology)
- Pulmonologists who restrict their practice to certain types of practices or procedures (e.g., ventilator management, sleep study, ambulatory pulmonology)
- Fellowship-trained subspecialists who focus on a narrowly defined area of that subspecialty (e.g., spine, vascular neuroradiology, neuropathology of the cerebrum, retinal pathology)

To determine the appropriate level of privileging, organizations must define each practitioner's scope of practice according to her specific training and experience. A key question is, What procedures has she performed in sufficient numbers and with sufficient quality to demonstrate current clinical competence? The challenge emerges when granted privileges overlap other areas of competence. A general surgeon who frequently performs abdominal procedures in the bowel will eventually encounter a rare condition that requires an enhanced or modified skill set. The medical staff should anticipate such areas of overlap and identify guidelines for when a practitioner should seek an appropriate consultation or turn the case over to a more qualified colleague.

Any narrowing of clinical privileges leads to political power shifts, new group dynamics, and adjustments to existing procedures. Medical staff organization and structure, specialty affiliation, call coverage, handoffs, and patient flow can all be affected by the introduction of competency clusters that alter the organizational matrix of physicians and how they practice.

Medical Staff Organization and Structure

The introduction of new privileges and specialties may require the reorganization of clinical departments, sections, service lines, and accountable care structures. For instance, the medical staff that recruits physicians who bring a new or specialized expertise (e.g., endovascular surgery) might consider creating a separate organizational structure to support the subspecialty or generate community awareness of the new capability. It may also reorganize related specialties into a service line (e.g., cardiovascular, oncology) with narrow definitions of clinical competence to support a higher standard of quality, safety, and service. New clinical skills naturally introduce new privileging criteria, which change the dynamic of an organization and its clinical portfolio of services.

Call Coverage

This problematic area should be dealt with before taking any action to narrow clinical privileges to avoid safety issues and potential conflict. When one organization in North Carolina introduced bariatric surgery as an incoming service line, the new bariatric surgeons assumed that general surgeons would be "happy" to take call for them. However, the chair of general surgery informed the new head of bariatric surgery that general surgeons were not trained or prepared to properly manage bariatric complications and thus would be unable and unwilling to take call for those specific procedures.

Similar scenarios are often seen in the orthopedic specialties. If a fellowship-trained orthopedist decides to perform only joint surgery at his small hospital, which provides general orthopedic call coverage after hours, the medical staff may or may not be able to accommodate his desire to limit his practice and his call coverage responsibilities to that narrowly defined area. The hospital's medical staff may need all orthopedists to take call coverage and handle routine orthopedic emergencies, which may not be consistent with an individual orthopedic surgeon's practice and

skills. This orthopedist's decision to limit his practice might compromise call coverage, leaving the rest of the staff responsible for situations they may or may not be able to handle and place him in professional jeopardy to perform procedures (complex closed reductions of fractures) that he may no longer be competent to perform safely. In the bariatric surgery service line case, a task force worked out a new call coverage approach acceptable to both surgery departments: General surgeons would cover the new service line's call but have bariatric backup support available to deal with clinical issues beyond their expertise. Contingencies should always be worked out in advance so that patients can receive competent care and members of the medical staff do not feel unreasonably encumbered or placed in clinical situations they are not trained to handle.

Handoffs and Patient Flow

As the amount of inpatient care decreases and the number and variety of ambulatory-based services increase, the ways in which patients are screened, evaluated, stabilized, observed, monitored, and transferred to various levels and settings of care must be redefined, mapped, and measured to ensure that high-quality, cost-effective care is delivered. How an organization defines the clinical privileges it authorizes is but one reflection of evolving medical structures and processes.

This evolution has had an impact on the fundamental processes of care. For example, when hospitalists are introduced to the clinical setting, traditional primary care specialists may no longer care for inpatients or perform perioperative care. With the addition of a palliative care unit, hospitalists may no longer care for patients with end-of-life issues. Thus, all aspects of care, including the formulation of evidence-based clinical and functional pathways, should be revisited to ensure that they are relevant to the evolving matrix of clinical competencies.

LOW- OR NO-VOLUME PRACTITIONERS

The prevalence of low- or no-volume practitioners is significantly increasing as the result of the confluence of several factors, including the following:

- Changes to financial incentives, which are driving most physicians into ambulatory settings
- Increasing evidence-based performance expectations around the care of patients with acute medical and surgical conditions

- New Leapfrog Group recommendations that call for evidence-based referrals of acutely ill and injured patients to high-volume clinical care settings, where they are most likely to receive high-quality, low-cost care
- Increasing payer expectations of high quality and low cost with the creation of narrow and tiered networks of coverage and referral
- Lifestyle preferences of younger physicians to lead a balanced life and to focus on a more narrowly defined and controllable scope of practice

The challenge with this trend is how to incorporate these low- or no-volume practitioners into the medical staff safely. The traditional approach is to give carte blanche clinical privileges whether or not they meet medical staff–recommended, board-approved privilege criteria. This avenue was often taken through the courtesy, consulting, or affiliate categories of membership, in which full privileges were granted with a limited volume of practice at the local facility. But if a patient is injured at the hands of a physician who does not meet the privileging criteria, the organization will be held accountable and negligent for not upholding its own internal standards. The best approaches balance the need to integrate and align physicians who are important to the mission of the organization with the expectation that privileging standards and criteria will be upheld at a high and uncompromised level.

Low- or no-volume practitioners being considered for medical staff membership either have or do not have adequate quality data compiled from their work in other clinical settings to help measure their level of competence. Even those on staff who *can* produce these data may not have the specific clinical data or experience that is relevant to the inpatient privileges requested. Say a surgeon who performs routine, low-risk procedures in an ambulatory setting asks for inpatient surgical privileges for the infrequent complex case. If she meets the minimum inpatient volume criteria or has performed procedures in the ambulatory setting that are equivalent in scope and complexity to the privileges requested, the organization is likely to be safe in granting these privileges. However, this is not often the case, and many hospitals inadvertently put their patients at risk for injury and themselves and their physicians at risk for liability when they grant privileges inappropriately in these situations.

Building a Balanced Approach to Medical Staff Acceptance

Practitioners who lack *relevant* quality data clearly do not meet the minimum criteria for inpatient privileges, but that does not mean they should be excluded from the medical staff. The first step in establishing a process for this type of privilege request is to separate medical staff membership from clinical privileges. *Membership* confers political rights to physicians, such as the right to hold office, form a quorum, chair a department or committee, and vote at an open meeting. *Privileges,* on the other hand, define the clinical activities a physician is authorized to perform. Thus, a physician could have full membership rights without any clinical privileges or be granted clinical privileges without full membership rights. This separation enables the organization to engage and align with strategically important physicians, who are committed to supporting the mission of the medical staff and organization, while ensuring that only those who meet medical executive committee (MEC)–recommended, board-approved privileging criteria are authorized to care for patients.

Once this separation is institutionalized, the categories of membership essentially can be reduced to three:

1. Active staff, with full political rights and varied privileges
2. Associate staff, with partial political rights and varied privileges (e.g., new members, advanced practice providers, locum tenens practitioners, consultants, telehealth providers)
3. Honorary staff, with limited political rights and varied privileges

Partial political rights can be defined in any terms the organization chooses. Typically, they include the right to serve and vote on committees, participate in medical staff and hospital affairs, and provide input when requested and exclude the right to hold office, chair a department or committee, and vote at an open medical staff meeting.

The second step is to create privileging gradations so that physicians and practitioners who meet different levels of criteria may be granted different types of privileges. Gradations may be divided as follows:

1. *Independent privileges:* The traditional privileges authorize a licensed independent practitioner to function without direct supervision and to make independent clinical decisions.
2. *Co-management or collaborative privileges:* These privileges permit a physician or practitioner to work under the supervision of a physician or practitioner who has independent privileges and may permit varied levels of independence as deemed appropriate by the supervising clinician.
3. *Dependent privileges:* This type of privilege denotes the traditional relationship between a physician and an advanced practice provider (APP) or allied health practitioner (AHP) who lacks independent privileges (particularly in those states that do not permit independent practice).

4. *Refer-and-follow, ambulatory, community, or continuity-of-care privileges:* This set of privileges includes the right to refer a patient to the hospital, to access protected health information under the Health Insurance Portability and Accountability Act, and to contact and communicate with any practitioner involved in a patient's care. This privilege type does not include authorization to write orders or notes in the chart or to make clinical decisions.

The third step is to create a systemic approach to privileging practitioners whose strategic value to the organization and conformance to board-approved privileging criteria vary. The following list describes several examples:

- *Clinically active physicians who have accrued sufficient quality data:* These individuals may be eligible for independent privileges. Typically, new members of the medical staff are placed in this associate-level category with limited political rights until they have been on staff for a defined period (typically one to two years) and demonstrated satisfactory performance. APPs are also assigned to the associate staff with independent, co-management, or dependent privileges depending on state statute (maximum allowable scope of privileges) and hospital or medical staff policy.
- *Clinically active physicians who come with sufficient and relevant quality data compiled elsewhere:* These individuals may be eligible for independent privileges as long as the quality data are available and relevant to the data required for the inpatient privileges requested. As with the first category, new members and APPs may be assigned to the associate staff with varied privileges depending on state statute and hospital or medical staff policy.
- *Clinically active physicians with sufficient but irrelevant quality data elsewhere:* These individuals should not be eligible for independent inpatient privileges if their data do not meet the level of care required for high-acuity or high-complexity patients. They may be granted co-management privileges to work toward sufficient volume with appropriate oversight and focused professional practice evaluation (FPPE) to become eligible to apply for independent privileges.
- *Clinically active nonmembers with sufficient quality data:* These individuals typically include APPs; new members of the medical staff; consulting or visiting clinicians; locum tenens practitioners, who provide temporary services for existing practitioners; telemedicine providers, such as radiologists and psychiatrists; proctors from outside organizations; and others. They may be assigned to the associate staff and be granted varied gradations of privileges on the basis of their professional and specialty training consistent with state statute and hospital or medical staff policy.

- *Members or nonmembers who are decreasing their clinical volume or scope of practice:* These individuals typically include older practitioners who are narrowing their scope of practice or moving to the outpatient setting. The medical staff should pay close attention to the volume and scope of these practitioners so that privileges may be adjusted accordingly. For instance, a physician with independent privileges may drop her volume to the point that she no longer accrues enough quality data to perform proctoring duties or be eligible for her current clinical privileges.

- *Clinically inactive members who offer a strategic advantage to the organization:* An increasing number of healthcare providers take time off for personal, family, or professional reasons, but their lower inpatient volume does not necessarily translate to decreased value to the hospital. The organization should have a systematic approach in place for determining these individuals' privileges. They could, for example, remain on active or associate staff—depending on the extent of their strategic benefit to the organization—without privileges or with limited privileges until they request reinstatement or require reentry. This situation is discussed more fully in the section titled "Leave of Absence and Reentry," beginning on page 89.

- *Clinically inactive members who offer no strategic advantage to the organization:* These practitioners might be direct competitors to the organization or demonstrate a lack of support for the organization's mission, vision, strategic plan, or values. They may be excluded from any medical staff with a board-approved strategic medical staff development plan as long as the circumstances are consistent with predetermined, board-approved criteria that are based on an internal and external analysis of community need. Potential exclusion from the medical staff is fully covered in Chapter 2.

NEW TECHNOLOGY AND PRIVILEGES

As technology and innovative care processes proliferate, organizations must have a medical staff–recommended, board-approved process established to vet new technology—and new privileges to use it—so that the hospital can offer up-to-date services to the community while protecting the safety of patients. Whenever a request for a new technology or related privilege is made, a deliberative body designated by the MEC or credentials committee should consider the request using an objective process, such as the approach described in the next subsection. Ideally, this body should be interdisciplinary and made up of physician and management leaders who have an interest in vetting and analyzing medical technology–related requests.

For example, the University of California–San Francisco's Healthcare Technology Assessment Program includes 20 physicians of varied specialties and six managers representing the areas of nursing, nurse education, value analysis, purchasing, human factors research, hospital contracting, operations, health plan strategy, and contracting (UCSF 2014; Gutowski et al. 2011).

Another option is to convene a value analysis committee made up of physician and management leaders who share an interest and expertise in quality, patient safety, strategic planning, contracting, supply chain management, marketing, and finance. Typically, criteria are established that define when a request must be reviewed by this committee and may include technology or privileges that are outside the current scope of service or practice; new technology that requires a predefined dollar investment or a significant programmatic change; technology that involves multiple specialties; new or modified infrastructure; or changes that require further inquiry regarding efficacy, safety, or cost-effectiveness.

Systematic Approach to Privileging for New Technology

A recommended process for setting privileges on the basis of new technology includes the following steps:

1. The request should be forwarded by the new technology committee to the board or a board subcommittee with a recommendation on whether to include this new technology or privilege as a part of the *organization's scope of service*. If the decision is made not to approve this new technology or privilege, the process is complete and the requesting physician is notified. If the new technology or privilege is approved as a part of the organization's scope of services, the issue is sent back to the deliberative body for consideration of privileging criteria and any relevant and related political or economic concerns that must be addressed.

2. As explained in Chapter 3, privileging criteria generally include the privilege-specific training, background, experience, evidence of current clinical competence (minimum threshold of volume and quality measures), and physical capacity to perform the privilege safely. The deliberative body considers privileging of new technology using the same references and resources as with other privileging criteria (see Chapter 3 for a discussion of those sources).

3. The privileging criteria are presented to representatives from relevant clinical departments, sections, and service lines for input and potential

modification. The recommended criteria are then presented to the credentials committee for review and revision.

4. The credentials committee presents its recommended privileging criteria to the MEC for its review and modification.

5. The MEC presents its recommended privileging criteria to the board for review and approval or modification. If modified, the criteria should be remanded to the MEC for final review, modification, and presentation to the board for final approval.

6. The criteria are implemented.

Common challenges that arise during this process include conflicts and conflicts of interest (discussed in Chapter 5); infrastructure challenges (e.g., new investment, training, supplies, or processes); and changes in the interrelationship of and dynamics among care providers—which should not be underestimated—including the introduction of hospitalists; APPs; and potentially disruptive, innovative technology, such as robotics, endovascular stenting, and telemedicine.

AGING AND IMPAIRMENT ISSUES

An essential and often overlooked privileging criterion is the physical capacity of a practitioner to safely exercise a granted clinical privilege. Although CMS and the accreditation agencies require organizations to assess practitioners for potential impairments, a stigma is still attached to this process, and physicians are often reluctant to pursue evaluation in this sensitive area. This stigma inadvertently creates a "conspiracy of silence" that undermines the ability of medical staffs to advocate for their colleagues in the most meaningful way possible—by helping them accept and effectively address the realistic impact of potential impairments.

The best predictor of a potential impairment is a change from a practitioner's baseline performance. It may be subtle at first, and a leader needs personal and clinical acumen to distinguish an emerging impairment from the occasional "bad day."

The success of any process for addressing impairments relies on having a systematic policy in place to guide physician leaders and managers through a sensitive and confidential course that respects the rights and dignity of healthcare practitioners while ensuring patient safety and appropriate adherence to relevant federal and state laws.

A few medical staffs have created a policy and procedure to identify, evaluate, treat, and manage acute and chronic impairments in a way that closely follows The Joint Commission's guidance to promote "assistance and rehabilitation rather than discipline to aid a physician in retaining or regaining optimal functioning consistent with the protection of patients" (Joint Commission 2013).

The medical staff advocacy committee develops a wellness pathway for referring colleagues for a *fitness-for-work evaluation* to determine whether any physical, cognitive, or behavioral issues exist that would preclude that practitioner from safely exercising his clinical privileges. Asking a physician to "get a physical" from his primary care physician is a waste of everyone's time and resources. A fitness-for-work evaluation is a formal vocational assessment performed by physicians with advanced training in vocational medicine who can evaluate the physical, cognitive, and behavioral requirements of specific clinical privileges and correlate them through a comprehensive individual assessment.

An excellent resource when considering fitness-for-work evaluations is your state licensing board, which likely maintains a list of individuals and organizations that it contracts with for its own internal evaluations. The following are a few nationally recognized organizations that offer these evaluations:

◆ Physician Assessment and Clinical Education (PACE) program, University of California San Diego
◆ Center for Personalized Education for Physicians (CPEP), Denver, Colorado
◆ Drexel University, Philadelphia, Pennsylvania
◆ Vanderbilt University, Nashville, Tennessee

The organization should directly pay for this evaluation so that the quality of the evaluation and the integrity of its findings are controlled by the credentials committee or MEC.

Once the medical staff receives the findings of the evaluation, leaders can sit down with the practitioner and work out a plan for managing the impairment that ensures that both the physician and her patients are supported and protected. Terms of the plan may include a medical leave of absence, voluntary modification of clinical privileges, or a combination of these with ongoing assessment and treatment. As long as changes to a physician's clinical privileges are made voluntarily and not accompanied by a threat of an investigation, the organization has no obligation to report the impairment to most state licensing boards or to the National Practitioner Data Bank (NPDB). A few states, such as Oregon and New York, require that all modifications of clinical privileges be reported; however, this action does not necessarily trigger a state licensure investigation, particularly if the organization demonstrates that it supports the physician's voluntary request.

As discussed in the earlier section on managing low- or no-volume practitioners, if the medical staff separates membership from privilege requirements, there is no inherent reason a practitioner with an identified impairment cannot maintain full membership rights with a short- or long-term modification of clinical privileges (e.g., independent, co-management, dependent, refer-and-follow). The variety of options that separation creates allows as smooth a transition as possible back to independent privileges, assuming that is the ultimate goal of the physician and medical staff leadership.

Aging

Each individual ages in both a unique and a predictable way. In 1994, Harvard University psychologist and researcher Douglas H. Powell, with Dean K. Whitla, published his landmark and controversial work in a book titled *Profiles in Cognitive Aging*, in which Powell compared more than 1,000 physicians and 600 nonphysicians from ages 25 to 92 using the Micro-Cog assessment tool. He found that, overall, physicians scored higher in cognitive functioning than nonphysicians from ages 25 to 55 but thereafter experienced a consistent and precipitous decline with increasing age in cognitive function, inductive reasoning, verbal memory, and reasoning, to the point that the overall scores of the two groups began to equalize with increasing age (Burroughs 2012).

Thus, as physicians (like nonphysicians) age through their 60s and 70s, the incidence of impairment due to aging increases. Most physicians have the insight to recognize this decline and self-modulate and narrow the scope of their clinical practice as they near retirement. On rare occasions, a physician is either unable or unwilling to acknowledge a change in performance, posing a dilemma for the medical staff and a risk to his patients. Some medical staffs have created an aging practitioner policy and procedure to address this issue in a thoughtful, balanced, and sensitive manner.

Process for Addressing Aging in Clinical Practice

For physicians who reach a predefined age (typically set at 70, based on research that the likelihood of potential impairments increases significantly by that time), the medical staff should shorten the reappointment cycle from two years to one year and require an annual fitness-for-work evaluation. It may further shorten the reappointment cycle to six months once a clinician reaches the age of 80, when the incidence of potential impairment is high.

It is not necessary to require mandatory retirement in medicine, as the Federal Aviation Administration does at age 65 for pilots, if this process is carried out consistently and provides physicians with mutually acceptable options, such as gradations of privileges or ambulatory-only privileges without call. For example, some organizations offer senior physicians the opportunity to receive a salary and corporate benefits for providing part-time call coverage for their clinical services with or without office or clinic responsibilities. Such options are often welcomed by practitioners who want to keep their hands in clinical practice in a sustainable way while taking more time for personal pursuits.

Legal Considerations Related to Aging

Two laws that should be taken into consideration during deliberations over aging and potential impairments are the Age Discrimination in Employment Act (ADEA) of 1967 and the Americans with Disabilities Act (ADA) of 1990. The main principle of the ADEA is that for employees 40 years of age or older, age cannot be used as a criterion for employment by any business with at least 15 employees. The ADA requires that any business with more than 15 employees consider a reasonable accommodation for an individual with a declared and defined disability. It does not oblige an organization to provide an accommodation if doing so may place an organization at risk. The hospital should consult with legal counsel to appropriately interpret and apply these federal laws.

The most important aspect of addressing potential impairments is doing so before they have an adverse impact on patients or on a physician's professional life and career. Tragically, the medical staff, out of a misplaced sensitivity to a practitioner's privacy, may inadvertently isolate that individual, leaving her to deal with a physical, cognitive, or behavioral issue without help or support.

PROFESSIONAL CONDUCT ISSUES

In 2005, The Joint Commission (2006) studied the root causes of unexpected injury to patients and found that communication failures ranked first among the common causes, with an incidence of 68 percent. As a result of this study, the accrediting body released Sentinel Event Alert #40, which states (Joint Commission 2008):

> Intimidating and disruptive behaviors can foster medical errors, contribute to poor patient satisfaction and to preventable outcomes, increase the cost of care, and cause qualified clinicians, administrators, and managers to seek new positions in more professional environments. Safety and quality of patient care is dependent on teamwork, communication, and a collaborative work environment. To assure quality and promote a culture of safety, healthcare organizations must address the problems of behavior that threaten the performance of the healthcare team.

Physician conduct issues are improving throughout the country; however, a small subset of individuals still subscribes to the traditional social contract, which holds that technical excellence and robust operating revenue excuse occasional, or even a well-established pattern of, unprofessional conduct. These few individuals cost organizations a disproportionate amount of time, energy, frustration, and resources and, on rare occasions, may hold an organization back from achieving a collaborative culture and high levels of care and service.

The Studer Group studied the impact of communication on clinical outcomes and found that patients who give physicians and organizations "top box" Hospital Consumer Assessment of Healthcare Providers and Systems (HCAHPS) scores are the most compliant with evidence-based recommendations, by a factor of four. In addition, organizations with a prevalence of low-box HCAHPS scores have a 24 percent greater length of stay and 28 percent higher mortality than those that consistently receive top-box ratings (Studer Group 2013).

These findings are supported by the American Health Lawyers Association, which has demonstrated the following (Stelfox et al. 2005):

◆ Each 10 percent decrease in patient satisfaction scores leads to a 6 percent increased incidence of complaints and a 5 percent increase in risk management episodes.
◆ Only 3 percent of victims of inadvertent negligence sue the physician or healthcare organization involved; the inciting issue for those who sue is usually poor communication.

Since the 1990s, courts have upheld healthcare organizations' right to protect the quality and safety of its services by assertively managing professional conduct that may affect patients and the patient care environment. Cases in which such rulings have occurred include the following (White and Burroughs 2010):

◆ *Bessman v. Powell* (1998): Defendants awarded attorney fees when sued by a hematologist-oncologist who inappropriately delegated clinical responsibilities to unqualified individuals and attempted to retaliate against hospital employees when sanctioned for violations of medical staff policies.
◆ *Gordon v. Lewistown Hospital* (1998): The hospital suspended an ophthalmologist on the basis of disruptive conduct and successfully defended itself against resultant legal claims of antitrust.
◆ *Freilich v. Upper Chesapeake Health, Inc.* (2002): The court upheld the hospital's decision to not renew a nephrologist's membership and privileges on

LEAVE OF ABSENCE AND REENTRY

As mentioned earlier, growing numbers of healthcare practitioners are taking voluntary leaves of absence for increasing periods of time. Many of these individuals return to the full- or part-time practice of medicine, but organizations typically do not have a systematic way to assess a practitioner's current clinical competence, particularly when he has not taken part in any clinical activity for more than a year. This issue also arises when a practitioner who currently practices in one specialty or subspecialty wants to shift back to a previous specialty after a significant period of nonpractice or clinical inactivity.

Conditions of Reentry

CMS and the deemed status accrediting organizations require a rigorous assessment of competence based on medical staff–recommended, board-approved privileging criteria. As with the low- or no-volume practitioner discussed earlier, a leave-taking practitioner may have no recent or relevant performance data to offer toward meeting the medical staff's eligibility criteria to apply or reapply for clinical appointment and privileges and ensuring compliance with federal, state, accreditation, and bylaws requirements.

Interestingly, each state medical licensing board takes a different approach to reentry following a leave of absence. For example, states vary widely (one to five years or more) in the amount of nonpractice time that requires a mandatory reentry program, based on years of clinical inactivity. Some states prefer to adjudicate such matters on a case-by-case basis and offer no specific guidance.

An approach that satisfies most common reentry regulations is to divide leaves of absence into three time frames: less than one year, one to two years, and more than two years.

Less than One Year

Most healthcare practitioners can safely resume clinical practice within one year of taking leave and clinical inactivity as long as their licensure, Drug Enforcement Administration (DEA) registration, and liability coverage are maintained and their continuing medical education (CME) is up to date. All practitioners should undergo some form of FPPE or proctoring to ensure that they are clinically competent to exercise all of the clinical privileges requested.

One to Two Years

Some states (e.g., Nevada) require a formal reentry program following a year of clinical inactivity; however, most practitioners can safely resume clinical practice with a formal preceptorship, which is more extensive than routine proctoring. A preceptorship includes not only the objective and observational assessment that proctoring provides but also coaching, direct support, and supplemental coursework or didactic training (as in a procedure laboratory or with a simulator). The preceptor decides when the practitioner is ready to resume regular proctoring or FPPE and can safely practice without direct supervision or co-management.

More than Two Years

Many states do not require formal reentry following two years of clinical inactivity; however, many organizations do. The healthcare environment is changing so rapidly that a return to practice after an extended leave comes with a bit of "future shock" from new technology; updated computerized provider order entry and information technology systems; new quality, safety, and service metrics; and the emergence of interdisciplinary teams and accountable care organizations, to name a few recent changes. Thus, a medical staff may require that a physician complete a formal reentry program typically overseen by an academic medical center with accredited residency and fellowship programs. Reentry programs are expensive (usually between $10,000 and $15,000 per month) but provide a comprehensive evaluation and assessment with a focused and concentrated clinical experience over a one- to three-month period.

Organizations that have well-established reentry programs include Drexel University, Vanderbilt University, Cedars-Sinai Medical Center in Los Angeles, CPEP, PACE, Albany (New York) Medical Center, and Texas A&M Health Science Center in Fort Worth (AMA 2014).

Once a practitioner successfully completes a reentry program, she may be assigned a local preceptor who determines when the practitioner may advance to independent privileges and regular proctoring.

Wise MECs and credentials committees take a proactive approach to physician reentry by offering guidance prior to a practitioner taking an extended leave. The committee should, at a minimum, recommend to the leave-taking physician that she maintain her

- licensure,
- board certification,
- CME credits,
- DEA registration,

- membership in professional organizations (e.g., specialty societies),
- membership on the medical staff,
- minimum clinical threshold (volume) through part-time practice in her regular specialty,
- ongoing communications with the medical staff office, and
- ongoing communications with the department chair and MEC.

Taking this preemptive step saves the practitioner and organization a great deal of time and resources and helps ensure a smooth transition back into full- or part-time clinical practice following a desired leave.

ADVANCED PRACTICE PROFESSIONALS

As discussed in Chapter 1, APPs will assume an increasingly important role in healthcare delivery as a result of the need to cut costs and leverage physician skills. Many organizations use APPs to handle routine, high-volume, low-risk care guided by functional and clinical pathways or protocols, freeing physicians to serve in a consultative and oversight role and minimizing cost-to-revenue ratios.

APPs can also function in many organizational roles to support physician and nursing activities, including the following:

- Administrative support for physicians and nurses through the timely completion of histories and physicals, progress notes, and discharge summaries
- Support for clinical documentation improvement projects through documenting and coding in specific clinical specialties, thereby improving the organization's revenue cycle management performance (Wise organizations support training to enable the APP to obtain certification as a coder for a specific clinical specialty.)
- Primary call coverage for all clinical specialties to provide medical screening examinations, in compliance with the Emergency Medical Treatment and Labor Act, enabling physicians to serve in a consultative role for emergent care or surgery, critical care admissions, and emergent after-hours consultations
- Follow-up care and indigent care services to protect self-employed physicians from bearing burdensome opportunity costs
- Liaison activity between the medical staff and nursing staff to foster cohesive and collaborative interdisciplinary teams

To implement an APP strategy efficiently and coherently requires that a medical staff–recommended, board-approved policy and procedure be in place to guide the organization in its overarching goals and objectives. It should address the following questions (see the sidebar starting on this page for additional comments):

1. What is the APPs' scope of care for each clinical specialty or subspecialty?
2. What will be the role of APPs on the medical staff (e.g., member versus nonmember)?
3. For each APP, what scope of service (privileges) will the board authorize?
4. Who will be responsible for the credentialing and privileging process for each APP? (As mentioned in Chapter 3, APPs who offer a medical level of service must be credentialed and privileged by the organized medical staff.)
5. What type of oversight will each APP receive, and by whom?
6. What quality metrics will be used to assess the ongoing and focused professional performance of each APP?
7. How will peer review be performed for APPs, and by whom?
8. Will a new medical staff structure be created to support the medical staff's role in working with and overseeing APPs?

This policy should be a living document, as the legal framework supporting the autonomy of APPs—especially advanced practice nurses—continues to evolve with the growing physician shortage and the need to provide access to care for those in rural and inner-city areas. As of this writing, according to the American Association of Nurse Practitioners (2014), 17 states permit advanced practice nurses to function independently without any physician oversight, and this number is expected to rise over time.

A Deeper Dive

Considerations When Developing an APP Strategy

Scope of Service Authorized by the Board

The extent of board-authorized privileges granted to APPs may be up to or less than the state's statutory limits, but it may not exceed them. It is important to define in protocols or policies the specific privileges that the APP may exercise and when physician involvement is necessary. For example, a certified nurse midwife may perform low-risk deliveries without physician consultation as long as the mother's glucose level is <100, her diastolic blood pressure is <90, she has no proteinuria or hyper-reflexia, the fetus is in the vertex position with good quickening, the mother has no vaginal bleeding, and labor is progressing normally.

Responsibility for Credentialing and Privileging

The medical staff is required to perform the credentialing and privileging function for advanced practice nurses and physician assistants. However, for newer clinical specialties, such as surgical technician and doctoral-degreed physical therapist, this responsibility may be negotiated between the organized medical staff and the human resources department.

Oversight

Many healthcare organizations break down oversight by licensed independent practitioners of nonlicensed independent practitioners into four categories:

1. Direct supervision (on-site and immediately available or physically present)
2. Indirect supervision (on-site and available)
3. Available (may be off-site)
4. By policy (a clinical/functional pathway or policy defines when the collaborative physician must be contacted or involved)

Quality Metrics

The organized medical staff is responsible for the clinical performance of all practitioners credentialed and privileged through that body. However, APPs may also have employment agreements with the healthcare organization that require contractual oversight and management. Thus, performance oversight responsibilities through both the organized medical staff and management should be negotiated to avoid ambiguous leadership responsibilities and accountabilities.

Peer Review

Peer review is a required function for all members of the medical staff. Because physicians provide collaborative oversight, the role of APPs in quality management and peer review is essential and often overlooked.

Political Structure

Many organizations have an interdisciplinary advisory committee made up of representative APP leaders to advise the MEC on APP credentialing, privileging, quality, and performance management issues. Some medical staffs have even taken the step of empowering APPs to become voting members of the medical staff, although per the CMS Conditions of Participation, they may not serve as medical staff president.

SERVICE LINES AND ACCOUNTABLE CARE ORGANIZATIONS

More and more physicians recognize the need to form accountable care organizations and integrated healthcare networks, to standardize care, and to work in interdisciplinary teams. These professionals and their organizations narrow the range of tolerable variation; define excellence with specific quality, safety, service, and cost-effectiveness metrics; and position themselves to assume risk contracting to address population health. By doing so, they elevate the credentialing and privileging standards or criteria so that only those colleagues who meet them may apply to and participate on the medical staff. Mayo Clinic has operated under this premise for years through the Mayo Medical School, which enrolls only 50 students per year and maintains a closed medical staff that permits membership by invitation only. The culture of Mayo Clinic recognizes that excellence is not achieved by everyone and not everyone should be asked to adapt and contribute to its specific and highly evolved professional culture.

Physicians who are credentialed by and obtain privileges from a hospital generally agree to

- practice medicine at the highest level according to evidence-based research and peer recommendations;
- follow evidence-based practices to achieve the highest level of quality, safety, service, and cost-effectiveness;
- work in collaborative interdisciplinary teams to optimize the delivery of healthcare services 24/7 across the continuum of care;
- use information technology to support health exchange networks and share timely and accurate healthcare information;
- work with peer groups to create recommendations for evidence-based practices and techniques;
- contribute to clinical and functional pathways and oversee their implementation;
- mentor and support nonphysicians as key members of the healthcare team; and
- work collaboratively with management to provide high-quality, low-cost services.

Large employers and third-party payers understand this differentiation and have created narrow and tiered networks to preferentially refer employees, beneficiaries, family members, and enrollees to organizations and health plans that offer high-quality, low-cost care. Many third-party payers, such as Aetna in Houston, Texas, for the Memorial Hermann MD Clinical Integration Practice, agree to pay higher rates of reimbursement for outstanding cost-effective care that differentiates itself from its competition.

Legally, management is permitted to set different standards for different parts of the organization (e.g., center of excellence) as long as those standards are applied consistently. As mentioned earlier in the book, through standards MS.06.01.05, EP2, and MS.06.01.07, EP2, The Joint Commission (2007) recognizes that credentialing and privileging criteria should be facility specific on the basis of recommendations by the organized medical staff and approval by the governing body to control for the differences in resource availability and external and internal environmental factors.

Mary Baker, DHA, CPMSM, CPCS, president and principal consultant of Medical Staff Plus Consulting LLC, describes how to evaluate and use credentialing software to make the credentialing and privileging process seamless and efficient.

The Decision to Use Credentialing Software

The need to streamline the credentialing verification process is driven by the increasing demand for better verification documentation and data maintenance as well as the need for quicker turnaround time in processing applications.

Information Management

Today's medical staff services professional (MSSP) serves as a resource to the medical staff and healthcare organization in the development of reports that present provider-specific data. That individual must be able to understand technology analysis, application, implementation, and support. Practitioner credentialing software, when well maintained and properly used, enables the MSSP to automate the collection and management of practitioner data, such as medical licensing information; the distribution and pre-population of reappointment applications, the generation of hospital affiliation and peer reference queries, and the verification of expirables (e.g., license, DEA registration, liability coverage). Credentialing staff supervisors can view the distribution of work among employees in real time and monitor a watch list of outstanding items that need immediate attention.

(continued)

Available Credentialing Software

Many credentialing software programs are available, including Visual Cactus (Cactus), Echo (HealthLine Systems), IntelliCred (IntelliSoft Group), and MSOW (Morrisey Associates). Several offer similar credentialing verification and tracking capabilities and can be used in multiple settings, such as hospitals, managed care organizations, credentialing verification organizations, or physician practices. Most vendors also offer add-on modules for performance improvement, focused and ongoing professional practice evaluation, and privileging. They typically provide an online overview of the program functions.

Organizations considering a purchase or an update of their credentialing software should first consider how it will be used and the desired outcome. Will the end product be a simple database to generate basic reports, letters, or queries? Is the organization working toward paperless credentialing? Certainly, the MSSP and health information management department should be involved in the discussion as to which software best meets the organization's needs. The MSSP should request relevant information from each vendor and perform a detailed cost–benefit analysis. Consulting with peers, other healthcare facilities, and physician leaders who have used various vendor products can also be helpful in the selection process.

Cost–Benefit Analysis

Industry statistics indicate that the cost to process an application for privileges ranges from $200 to $400, depending on the information required, regardless of the size of the organization (Baker 2011). This fee covers staff time; computer costs; fees charged by various agencies, such as the NPDB and the American Medical Association; postage; supplies; and filing. The cost to process reappointment applications can range from $150 to $300, again depending on the information required. In my experience, most organizations report application processing time to exceed 90 days. The cost of credentialing software can range from $25,000 (basic program) to more than $100,000 (sophisticated program). In addition, annual maintenance and upgrade fees may apply.

As an example, assume the following scenario: Hospital A has 950 medical staff and APPs or AHPs and receives 100 new applications per year. The medical staff office has three MSSPs who process appointment and reappointment applications. Over a two-year period, its cost of processing applications is approximately $335,000, as determined by the following calculations:

New applicants	$100 \times \$400 = \$40,000$
Reappointment applicants	$425 \times \$300 = \$127,500$
Total for one year	$\$40,000 + \$127,500 = \$167,500$
Total for two years	$\$167,500 \times 2 = \$335,000$

Although the benefit of this technology varies according to medical staff office operating costs, the financial return can be significant. A reduction in labor costs should also be considered in the cost–benefit calculation, as some organizations with credentialing software recognize significant time decreases in the performance of certain tasks. The table that follows offers some examples.

Task	Estimated Time Reduction (%)	Example
Report preparation/ requests for data	99	◆ Manual report preparation: 2 staff @ $15/hour × 4 hours = $120 ◆ Software report preparation: × 5 minutes = $1.20
New-application processing	80	◆ The ease of finding provider-specific information can save staff several minutes or even hours. Once information from the application is in the program, verification letters and other documentation can be generated in seconds.
Credentials tracking and related form letters	60	◆ The ability to prepare labels and form letters for all or a subset of providers saves not only time but also material and resources.

(continued)

Delineation of privileges	50	◆ Department privileges and privileges assigned to each provider are computerized, allowing multiple search options.
Reappointment process	50	◆ Reports save days of preparation and processing time, allowing more time to gather supplementary materials.
Meeting scheduling, notification, and attendance tracking	40	◆ Preparing and sending meeting notices/invitations, preparing sign-in sheets, tracking attendance, and providing reports, as needed, is a time-saver.

Source: Cactus Software. n.d. "Executive Summary." Overland Park, KS: Cactus Software.

Final Thoughts

The question should not be whether to use credentialing software but rather which software best meets the needs of your organization. Although the medical staff office is not generally thought of as a revenue-generating department, when credentialing and privileging tasks are performed efficiently and effectively, practitioners can begin practicing sooner, thus generating revenue for the organization.

SUMMARY

The establishment of credentialing and privileging criteria is the most important part of any performance management system, as it is through this process that the governing board, medical staff, and management team set the bar for clinical performance. Too often, privileging criteria are open-ended, nebulous, or vague and permit the sort of non-value-added variation that does not support the organization in achieving its strategic goals. A thoughtful and frank discussion regarding performance expectations early on will save the organization resources, time, and unnecessary conflict and will help it reach its strategic vision and potential.

REFERENCES

American Association of Nurse Practitioners. 2014. "State Practice Environment." Accessed August 19. www.aanp.org/legislation-regulation /state-legislation-regulation/state-practice-environment.

American Medical Association (AMA). 2014. "Physician Re-entry." Accessed July 18. www.ama-assn.org/ama/pub/education-careers/finding-position /physician-reentry.page.

Baker, M. 2011. "How to Save (at Least) $100 per Practitioner in Your Credentialing Process." PowerPoint presentation to Texas Society Medical Staff Services, San Antonio, TX, April 13–15.

Burroughs, J. 2012. "Dealing with the Aging Physician: Betrayal or Advocacy?" *Physician Executive* 38 (6): 38–41.

Federation of State Medical Licensing Boards (FSMB). 2011. *Report of the Special Committee on Reentry to Practice.* Accessed July 18, 2014. www.fsmb.org/pdf /pub-sp-cmt-reentry.pdf.

Gutowski, C., J. Maa, K. S. Hoo, and K. J. Bozic. 2011. "Health Technology Assessment at the University of California-San Francisco." *Journal of Healthcare Management* 56 (1): 15–29; discussion 29–30.

Joint Commission. 2013. "Hospital Accreditation Standards, Rationale for MS.11.01.01." Oakbrook Terrace, IL: Joint Commission.

———. 2008. "Behaviors That Undermine a Culture of Safety." Sentinel Event Alert #40. Oakbrook Terrace, IL: Joint Commission.

———. 2007. "Hospital Accreditation Standards." Oakbrook Terrace, IL: Joint Commission.

———. 2006. "Sentinel Event Statistics." Oakbrook Terrace, IL: Joint Commission.

Powell, D. H., with D. K. Whitla. 1994. *Profiles in Cognitive Aging.* Cambridge, MA: Harvard University Press.

Stelfox, H. T., T. K. Gandhi, E. J. Orav, and M. L. Gustafson. 2005. "The Relation of Patient Satisfaction with Complaints Against Physicians and Malpractice Lawsuits." *American Journal of Medicine* 118 (10): 1126–33.

Studer Group. 2013. "HCAHPS: The Next Generation: An Addendum to the HCAHPS Handbook." Published January 31. www.studergroup.com /resources/news-media/articles/hcahps-the-next-generation-an-addendum -to-the-hc/.

University of California–San Francisco (UCSF). 2014. "UCSF Healthcare Technology Assessment." Accessed July 18. http://htap.ucsfmedical center.org/.

White, R. D., and J. Burroughs. 2010. *A Practical Guide to Managing Disruptive and Impaired Physicians*. Danvers, MA: HCPro.

CHAPTER 5

Negotiating Performance Expectations

The opposite of a truth is not a lie, but another deeply held truth.
—*Niels Bohr, research physicist*

Most future physicians enter the long and rigorous educational path to ultimately find a professional home where they can lead, function autonomously, make independent decisions, and assume complete responsibility and accountability for their work. This expectation is at odds with the growing need for physicians to work collaboratively, function interdependently, and share responsibility and accountability with others—including patients. Hospital leaders need to support physicians in making this crucial transition without dismissing the values that brought these practitioners into the profession.

Paradoxically, the more management genuinely respects the physicians' professional values of independence, accountability, and leadership, the more benefits this gesture presents and the greater the likelihood that physicians will make the important changes necessary to achieve the goal of interdisciplinary teamwork and co-management.

One challenge of working in interdisciplinary teams is understanding the stark differences in educational and professional culture between physicians and managers. Both professions bring complementary skills, singular perspectives, and biases that are most useful when displayed in a synergistic and constructive forum. When either or both cultures retreat to their default values, the downside of the cultures are demonstrated, to the detriment of all parties involved.

Imagine that a manager takes what seems to the physicians like an excessive amount of time to gather data and develop a plan. In the time it takes administration to prepare, the physicians regress to a defensive posture of provoke and attack, which leads the manager into her own retreat. Similarly, imagine that physicians decide to embark on a complex and risky project on the basis of insufficient data and information. The hospital's administration becomes increasingly passive; allows the physicians to "fail"; and reveals the weakness of their approach, which only frustrates and angers the physicians more than they already were.

Certainly, not all initiatives play out this way, but these situations are usually rife with tension. Atchison and Bujak (2001) note that physicians are selected into and trained for an *expert culture* that values personal achievement, sacrifice of one's personal life for a greater good, intense focus on rapid analytical problem solving on the basis of incomplete information and pattern recognition, and professional risk taking and personal accountability. Managers and healthcare personnel, on the other hand, are selected into and trained for a *collective culture* that values team and organizational performance, interdependence, trust and loyalty, and a willingness to place organizational interests over self-interests.

When charged to work together, individuals from the expert culture may be confrontational, provocative, excessively self-interested, untrusting and untrustworthy, unwilling or unable to work interdependently, and disruptive to the organization's mission and vision. Members of the collective culture may be passive-aggressive; risk averse; unable to make effective and timely decisions; unwilling to assume responsibility or accountability; and, similar to the expert culture, disruptive to the organization's mission and vision, albeit in a more quiet and subtle manner (Atchison and Bujak 2001).

PHYSICIAN–MANAGER PARTNERSHIPS

In an ideal environment, both cultures bring to their collaborations the best of their attributes and minimize their respective downsides to accomplish mutually beneficial goals. To get the best collaborative performance out of each, physicians and managers should base their relationship on mutual respect, trust, a flattened hierarchy that promotes partnership, and an agreement to defer to the expertise available at all levels of the organization.

Mutual Respect

Physicians and managers tend to respect those in their own profession who take on greater responsibilities, achieve accomplishments, and demonstrate a history of success. It is sometimes a challenge for any professional to acknowledge that other professionals bring experience, skills, and expertise that may complement their own skill set and elevate the group's performance. Nevertheless, physicians need to accept that members of the management team bring operational, business, and financial experience that physicians may not possess, and managers need to accept that physicians bring clinical expertise that managers often lack. Both parties can function at a higher level when they integrate clinical and operational or business perspectives in real time than when they come together as an afterthought. Just as management should not present a business plan to the medical staff after it has been drawn up as a token effort to gain their support, physicians should not create functional and clinical pathways that do not take operational and financial exigencies into account.

A failure of either party to respect the other not only dooms the relationship but also wastes valuable resources and time. One CEO presented a board-approved strategic plan—the result of months of research and effort—to the chief of staff, asking her to roll it out to the medical staff for their support. The chief of staff looked the CEO in the eye and said quietly, "I wish you and the board much success in carrying out your plan. Perhaps next time you may wish to involve the medical staff in the creation of a joint strategic plan that we can work on together." The chief of staff felt disrespected by the CEO and board and gave up any prior sense of loyalty or obligation she might have felt.

Trust

Trust is an intangible feeling of reliance, certainty, and interdependence erected on a foundation of positive encounters over time. It is a form of political and social currency that builds or erodes as one experiences positive or negative encounters. When a critical mass of trust is lost, trust essentially ceases to exist. Thus, trust is not bred of a single action but rather a string of events and interactions that often take time to amass, only to be spent by a single thoughtless act of disregard, disrespect, or perceived betrayal. The best leaders invest heavily in building trust over time, maintaining it through regular positive interactions, and revitalizing it when it erodes. For example, one CEO in Alabama (see case studies in Chapter 12) visits with all the committed physicians of the organization monthly, amassing currency with every meeting. When he needs them to support him in a way that they perceive to be difficult or even sacrificial for the organization, he almost always gets their support as a result of the significant social and political capital he has built and invested over time.

Trust is a manifestation of the relational aspect of leadership and cannot be built or maintained easily, yet it is the single transcendental characteristic of successful collaboration.

Linear Partnership

Both physicians and executives are trained and brought up in a hierarchical culture defined by established accountabilities and respect for the hierarchy. For instance, physicians at an academic medical center are trained from internship through residency and fellowship and then move into the ranks of attending staff. Attending staff move from assistant to associate to full professor to chair of the department to dean. Each level of the hierarchy has clearly defined authority, responsibility, and accountability. Similarly, managers rise from frontline associate to manager to middle manager to executive manager, or through nursing or medical staff to operations manager, to CEO.

The pathways that management professionals follow are carefully defined. The medical staff's hierarchy is more fluid and is made up of "insiders" and "outsiders," determined as such by their experience, years of service, political and social connections, clinical competence, years of formal and informal leadership, and cultural fit. Yet, issues inevitably arise that challenge the hierarchy when professionals do not follow traditional organizational structures or track neatly through silos and instead cut across interdisciplinary boundaries. For example, process improvement requires operational, medical and nursing, revenue cycle, and executive management input. When a process fails, it is both wasteful and unproductive to identify an individual to blame. Instead, a new kind of *systems* accountability is needed that relies on complementary skill sets, experience, and perspectives and the ability of the team to work effectively. To bring disparate individuals together to work in new ways, the traditional hierarchy must be flattened so that it does not obstruct the group's ability to work together and solve complex interdisciplinary system challenges.

Deferral to Available Expertise

Traditionally, hierarchy trumped competence, which created inefficiency and potentially lackluster performance, as in these examples:

- A general surgeon with little or no clinical background in anesthesiology oversees the work of an anesthesia department.
- A general internist who lacks expert knowledge in critical care and ventilator management oversees the respiratory therapy department and relies on the knowledge of respiratory therapists to manage ventilation orders in the intensive care unit (ICU).

- The CEO who delegates financial decision making and has little, if any, financial background modifies a financial plan created by the chief financial officer and controller without consultation.
- The board approves a complex and potentially risky privileging recommendation from the medical executive committee (MEC) with little or no medical staff input.

The ideal balance is for the organization to maintain the legal structure and basic organizational hierarchy but be flexible enough to forgo it when outcomes depend on the input or control of individuals with the greatest expertise at the right moment. A clinical example is the surgeon who has an appropriate level of control over the procedure to be performed but yields to the nurse anesthetist on issues pertaining to the airway and to the scrub nurse regarding the correct position of the patient. A management example is when the CEO, who is ultimately responsible to the board for the quality of the financial plan, seeks an independent financial audit and review to ensure that technical and regulatory compliance issues are appropriately addressed.

PHYSICIAN RELATIONSHIP MANAGEMENT

Functional, group-level medical staff–management partnerships are just one fundamental element of successful economic or clinical integration. Also necessary is a solid relationship between the organization and each physician, which can be achieved through customer relationship management.

The term *customer relationship management* was coined in the 1980s by Granroos, Gummesson, and Levitt. Their theory helped convince corporate organizations to move from transactional (or mass) marketing to a relationship-oriented approach that customizes offerings according to individual consumer preferences and needs (Levitt 1983). As a result, they do not waste valuable resources attempting to engage an individual whose needs are not compatible with the goods or services offered.

Similarly, physician relationship management (PRM) recognizes that not all physicians should partner with all organizations. By focusing on a professional relationship based on shared values and goals, both the organization and the physician ultimately save a great deal of time and effort. (It is important for the organization to work with its legal counsel to establish a medical staff–recommended, board-approved governance policy for applying PRM through a strategic medical staff development plan as described in Chapter 2.)

When a physician first pursues entry to an organization, leadership should ask the following questions:

- What are your personal and professional goals and objectives?
- What are your personal and professional values?
- Are your goals, objectives, and values consistent and compatible with those of our organization?
- If so, what type of economic relationship or partnership would you like to pursue with us?
- Can we agree on specific strategic goals and objectives that we will accomplish together?

If an organization is committed to a culture of reliability and collaboration, an independent, entrepreneurial physician who is accustomed to pursuing her own approach may not be compatible with the evolving cultural values of the organization, and this mismatch is best recognized at the outset.

Once a physician is on staff, PRM is operationalized by management to a degree dictated by the physician's potential strategic importance to the organization. The organization uses quantitative and qualitative data to arrive at this factor. Quantitative criteria may include the number of admissions or referrals, revenue and cost per case, gross revenue generated through referrals for admissions, elective procedures, or ancillary testing. Qualitative criteria may include physician leadership skill, the willingness and ability to support or lead change, alignment with the organization's mission and strategic vision, and the ability to work collaboratively with others.

If a physician rates high enough as a result of this calculation to warrant investment of resources, an executive leader is assigned responsibility for managing the relationship. They meet regularly to discuss ways in which the organization can:

- better understand and support the physician's personal and professional needs and aspirations;
- create contractual processes by which the organization can best partner with the physician to accomplish shared organizational and professional goals and objectives;
- address potential or perceived obstacles to delivering high-quality, cost-effective services;
- support the physician in providing effective input at all levels of the organization; and
- support an effective partnership between the physician and the organization.

For self-employed physicians in private or independent practice, many organizations create a management services organization (MSO) through which it can help the physician optimize revenues and lower costs. MSOs allow physicians access to third-party contracts, offer them assistance in the implementation of an electronic health record (EHR), provide them access to the organization's group purchasing organization for supplies, support or provide services to their revenue cycle management, train their office staff and personnel, allow them access to patient management portals, and provide software to automate their office functions. (Legal counsel guides organizations regarding the contractual relationship [e.g., employment, exclusive arrangement] that is necessary in their state to permit such arrangements under Stark and anti-kickback legislation.)

For employed physicians, the opportunity to partner with their employer to drive high quality, safety, and excellent service in the most cost-effective way is rewarding. Successful employment arrangements create risk and opportunity for both the employer and employee so that their mutual success depends on an effective partnership and working relationship. Economic integration strategies are discussed in greater depth in Chapter 11.

Because a PRM program requires significant resources to maintain, its return on investment should be calculated in terms of incremental revenue per market share; physician loyalty; Hospital Consumer Assessment of Healthcare Providers and Systems (HCAHPS) scores; operating efficiency; compliance with quality, safety, and service metrics; adjusted cost per case; and other key financial and operational metrics.

PRM works because it enables organizations to focus their scarce resources on individuals who share common values and whose personal and professional goals are compatible with those of the organizational partner. It establishes a foundation of trust, mutual knowledge, and shared aspirations for an effective economic and clinical partnership that can help an organization meet its ultimate goal of providing world-class quality, ensuring patient and staff safety, and offering exemplary service at a low cost (Burroughs 2013).

The quid pro quo for this level of management investment is that physicians who pursue a partnership arrangement with the organization must commit to the principles of evidence-based quality, safety, and service and to working with management to optimize cost-effectiveness. This commitment involves the willingness to work in interdisciplinary teams to standardize care, service, and supplies and continually improve all key processes throughout the organization.

Example of a Successful Physician Relationship Management Program

The positive results from successful PRM programs are significant. Mount Carmel St. Ann's hospital in Westerville, Ohio, implemented such a program in 2007, and the organization made gains within three years. Net income increased from $14 million to $24 million, case mix–adjusted length of stay decreased from 3.6 days to 3.3, HCAHPS ratings for the "would recommend" measure rose from 50 percent to 80 percent, and adjusted discharges increased by 3,000.

Another organization to adopt a PRM program is HCA Presbyterian Hospital (now Oklahoma University Medical Center) in Oklahoma City. It, too, derived benefits within a three-year period in the following measures: Volume increased by 12 percent; monthly inpatient revenue increased by 15 percent; HCAHPS ratings improved by 23 percent; and, most startling, the cardiology market share saw a positive shift of 40 percent.

For both organizations, implementation of a PRM program resulted in a return on investment of between 400 percent and 500 percent (Mack 2012).

MANAGING PHYSICIANS' PERFORMANCE

Cultural integration, as facilitated by PRM, entails the exploration of a compatible professional and business relationship. It must be in place and successfully maintained before economic integration—the defined contractual relationship—can be pursued. Once the organization is ready to move to this next step, it develops economic integration options through a physician performance management system.

What Is Not Physician Performance Management?

Following years of research and political debate, the Centers for Medicare & Medicaid Services (CMS) now requires organizations to report the following value-based metrics as 1 percent (as of 2013) to 2 percent (by 2016) of their calculated reimbursement:

◆ Twelve process-of-care measures related to congestive heart failure (CHF), acute myocardial infarction (AMI), and community-acquired pneumonia (CAP)—the top three inpatient diagnosis-related groups, as part of the CMS Core Measures

- HCAHPS survey results that pertain to patients' perceptions of care
- Healthcare mortality outcome measures for CHF, AMI, and CAP

These and other reimbursement measures, such as those mandated by the Affordable Care Act, represent the *minimum* expectations of payers as to what is acceptable healthcare quality. But strategic quality does not represent minimum standards. It reflects the organization's vision of what it would like to become and how it would like to differentiate itself from its competitors in the marketplace. Thus, strategic quality represents shared aspirations and commitments among stakeholders in an organization and has little, if anything, to do with standardized processes to achieve minimum expectations. The performance management system is the framework for creating and implementing the strategic goals and objectives that comprise that vision.

Stephen Beeson, MD, *founder and CEO of PracticingExcellence.com, reflects on the challenges of recruiting physician input for quality initiatives.*

Enrolling Physicians in Quality

If such a clear need exists for the pursuit of quality in healthcare, why would any organization hesitate to adopt quality initiatives? Why does healthcare management have such difficulty rallying support around a shared mission of continuous improvement? Despite their straightforward nature, these are complex questions with complex answers. What we do know is that our clinical and behavioral actions have a profound influence on healthcare quality, cost, and the patient experience. So how do we enroll physicians in the call to action to make healthcare better?

Over the past decade, Sharp HealthCare and the Sharp Rees-Stealy Medical Centers in San Diego improved physician satisfaction to the highest level in Sharp's history. The patient experience (as measured by HCAHPS) also improved dramatically, from the bottom decile to the top decile, and the subsequent quality improvement moved Sharp to rank as one of the top-performing healthcare systems in California. In the process, Sharp has won multiple Acclaim Awards and the coveted Malcolm Baldrige National Quality Award for healthcare in 2007. How did the organization achieve such success?

Sharp could not have implemented any strategic plan without the support, enrollment, buy-in, visibility, and leadership of physicians at the local

(continued)

---

level. Physicians' behavior and attitudes are highly contagious; when a few physicians sabotage—either directly or indirectly—an operational effort, the rest of the medical staff align themselves with the resistance. If those same physicians embrace and champion an effort and adopt it themselves, the others follow. Management telling the medical staff what to do is the least effective approach to enrolling them in any initiative. Conversely, when the administration reaches consensus with physicians prior to deploying a strategy, the speed of implementation is radically faster than without consensus and the influence of engaged physicians is the most powerful change driver in any clinical environment.

How do we enroll physicians in the improvement initiatives we must pursue? There is no simple answer, but the solution resides in crafting clear, concise organizational mission and vision statements—with physicians at the table—that are widely known, visible, and vibrant. Physicians rarely reject a plan they help to create.

Physicians must be selected, oriented, and mentored in accordance with the organizational culture, mission, and strategy. When the right physicians are in the organization, the objective is much easier to obtain. Gaining physicians' buy-in also requires physician-selected and -embraced performance metrics and rich feedback loops measuring physicians' success in meeting quality goals. Finally, it relies on a physician leadership team that includes, responds to, rounds on, and provides for physicians who say, "I love this place, what it stands for, the leaders leading it, and the results we can create together. I will do what I can do help." Physicians do for you what you do for them.

As regulatory and pay-for-performance pressures come to bear on organizations, leaders may resort to mandating behavioral change in a panic to improve. Physicians will not respond to this tactic. They respond when they are given a mission to pursue that they believe in, are a key part of the decision-making process, receive the resources necessary to provide good clinical quality to patients, are aware of where they stand in important performance metrics, and receive recognition by leaders when they perform well individually and move together as respected members of the team.

Physicians can help rescue US healthcare and make it great for their patients, their organizations, their communities, and themselves. It is time for physicians to begin leading and partnering with the entire healthcare team to execute care for the patients we serve.

Foundation of Physician Performance Management

Numerous organizations base their performance management system on the aforementioned regulatory quality and minimum requirements, using a series of arbitrary measures that are neither relevant to nor supportive of the organization's strategic plan. Some have no management system at all save the traditional quality assurance efforts to identify negative outliers when they emerge.

Many physicians are still compensated according to volume as measured by work relative value units (wRVUs). In other words, quality equals volume. Because these physicians have little, if any, incentive to provide a high level of service, ensure that care conforms to evidence-based quality and safety practices, and do so in a cost-effective way, the organizations they are affiliated with tend to perform poorly in their quality and safety metrics, receive low HCAHPS scores, and experience high operating costs, none of which helps them achieve their overarching organizational goals and objectives.

If a physician does not feel that improving performance will have a direct impact on patient care or make his professional life easier (e.g., by removing obstacles), he is not likely to embrace or even consider the specific performance metric in his clinical practice. Physicians are so used to being bombarded with regulatory, legal, and accreditation requirements that they have a finely honed filter that enables them to ignore what they consider to be external distractions so they can get about doing their work. Many physicians devise ingenious workarounds to avoid adhering to a requirement that has little or no professional meaning to them, some of which may place patients or the organization at risk.

Thus, it is important that physician leaders communicate to colleagues why a specific metric is valuable and important. A classic example is patient perception and service, which until recently was not considered relevant to quality outcomes and good technique. Recent research demonstrates that a high level of service improves patient outcomes, reduces or eliminates litigation, reduces turnover, decreases medical errors, lowers cost, and enhances loyalty (Zolnierek and Dimatteo 2009).

Alan M. Zuckerman, FACHE, president of Health Strategies and Solutions, Inc., explains the medical staff's role in the organization's strategic planning process.

What Is the Medical Staff's Role in Strategic Planning?

Strategic planning is increasingly a critical function in healthcare organizations. It allows a hospital or healthcare system to lead and direct its future, rather than simply react to external and internal events. In a volatile industry such as healthcare, it will be organizations with clarity of direction and strategy that have the greatest chance of thriving, and not merely surviving.

Strategic planning in healthcare organizations is frequently carried out around physicians rather than with them. That is, physicians are involved in a disjointed and peripheral way in the process. Good strategic planning today is a collaboration of all leaders and stakeholders. Great strategic planning is a team sport and synergistic endeavor, and its result is significantly improved performance and market positioning.

A typical strategic planning process is illustrated in the exhibit below. Physicians, board members (some of whom may be physicians), and senior management (some of whom also may be physicians) provide oversight, direction, and insight to this process through a strategic planning steering committee. With the aid of staff support, the committee carries out the following activities.

© 2014 by Health Strategies & Solutions, Inc.

- *Environmental assessment.* Physicians provide input about organizational strengths, weaknesses, opportunities, and threats through interviews, surveys, or focus groups. Physicians who serve on multiple staffs can provide valuable insights about the competition and external market conditions.
- *Organizational direction.* Physicians provide input about key clinical and quality attributes and strategies that may assist in differentiating the organization in the future. Physicians are important guardians of organizational values and may be catalysts in enhancing those values as well as supporting crucial changes in organizational behaviors in the future. Input mechanisms are similar to the environmental assessment.
- *Strategy formulation.* This key strategic planning activity benefits from physicians' insights about critical organizational goals and how to achieve them. Typical approaches for obtaining these perspectives are interviews, focus groups, and sometimes reactor panels that may be asked to provide feedback regarding a proposed strategic initiative.
- *Implementation planning.* Usually, this stage continues the process started in the formulation of strategy to develop detailed one-year action plans for high-priority goals and initiatives.
- *Execution.* Increasingly, execution is carried out through dyads that pair a physician leader with an administrative leader to direct implementation of strategic plan goals and initiatives. Physicians may also be involved as advisers, consultants, and sources of information to implementation leaders.

The challenge of involving physicians constructively and productively in the process of strategic planning has increased in the past few years. Due to reimbursement and income pressures, most physicians have curtailed their voluntary activities and are unavailable to participate in strategic planning and other health system endeavors that may not affect them directly. Many primary care physicians and even some specialists operate almost exclusively in outpatient settings, often away from and outside the mainstream of health system locations and activities. Some physicians may be involved in ventures that compete with the hospital or health system. Other demands and needs mitigate against strong physician involvement in strategic planning as well.

Nonetheless, these factors do not decrease the need for maximizing physician participation in strategic planning. And other factors, such as the increasing alignment of healthcare organizations and physicians and the trend toward bundled and capitated payment, make it more important than ever for coordinated—or better yet, synergistic—planning.

(continued)

The following guidelines should assist in optimizing constructive and productive physician participation:

- Remember that a physician's time is an extremely precious commodity—don't waste it. Be sure to overprepare for physician interactions and expect to address operational concerns that physicians raise, even if they have limited strategic impact.
- Schedule meetings and other in-person interactions early or late in the day to avoid conflicts with clinical practice.
- Make extensive use of intranet surveys, teleconferencing, web conferencing, videoconferencing, and other approaches that minimize travel or allow participation in strategic planning activities when time permits.

This brief overview of strategic planning and the role of physicians in it sets forth a process for developing highly engaged and supportive physician stakeholders. The process also should lead to better strategic thinking and outcomes, which provide benefits to physicians, their patients, and the entire organization. It is clear as well from examples both within and outside healthcare that more engaged stakeholders lead to higher rates of implemented recommendations and increased adaptability in a rapidly changing environment.

Steps in Developing a Physician Performance Management Program

Create a Medical Staff Strategic Plan

The traditional medical staff model inherently disconnects the activities of senior management and the governing board from those of the medical staff. Physicians were expected to generate revenue, and performance management was little more than reporting on regulatory quality measures and professional compliance or conduct issues. Today's need for rapid transformation calls for complete integration of management, governance, and medical staff activities so that they are a seamless whole, united in their pursuit of organizational goals and objectives.

The medical staff strategic plan should determine what specific performance objectives the medical staff will commit to in support of these organizational objectives, what goals or objectives it will create for itself in support of management's efforts, and how willing it is to hold itself accountable for achieving them. A medical staff strategic plan should cover both short- and long-term periods, consistent with the organization's, and inform all of the activities of the medical staff over the course of the upcoming year.

Create a Medical Staff Operations Plan

Once a strategic plan is created, it makes sense to operationalize that plan. Questions to consider in developing an operational plan include the following:

- *Are the current medical staff organizational structures, such as committees, relevant to the specific goals and objectives established?* Obviously, certain medical staff functions (e.g., credentialing, privileging, peer review) are ongoing; however, if the medical staff commits to working with management to reduce operating costs or building an infrastructure for population health, are interdisciplinary committees in place to accomplish these goals?
- *Does the medical staff include leaders trained to manage the initiatives established?* Using the example in the first bullet point, do physician leaders have training in Lean, Six Sigma, population health, or other change management processes that enable them to lead cost-reduction efforts and build the necessary infrastructure to support them?
- *Has adequate time been budgeted for physicians and physician leaders to come together with management to address the key priorities established?* Traditional MEC, medical staff, or quality meetings are not good venues to address specific strategic issues in a focused way.
- *Are sufficient resources available to support the medical staff's efforts to work with management?* An opportunity cost is involved in taking physicians out of busy practices to solve problems. On the other hand, the opportunity cost for not solving key operational issues may be even greater.

Like the medical staff's strategic plan, its operating plan should be consistent with and supportive of the organization's operating plan so that physicians and management are working in a coordinated and aligned way.

Negotiate Specific and Balanced Performance Expectations

The next step is for physicians to articulate performance expectations that support the medical staff's efforts to accomplish the defined goals and objectives. Recalling the example of reducing operating costs, the medical staff might articulate the following expectations:

- Follow evidence-based approaches as determined by peer group research and recommendations to optimize the use of resources toward achieving high-quality outcomes.
- Determine the most cost-effective approaches for achieving quality outcomes and minimizing the cost of care.

Not every physician will support these initiatives. The "why" must be explained by physician leaders as a commitment to supporting the performance expectations in terms of the relationship between quality and the cost to optimally provide those clinical services.

Every practitioner on staff needs to agree in principle to these expectations; those who do not will undermine the medical staff's efforts to achieve them and further demoralize and frustrate their colleagues. It is the duty of physician leaders to ensure that every physician not only is given a good opportunity to get on board but also commits to the medical staff strategic plan as a fundamental obligation of membership and privileges. On rare occasions, it may be necessary to ask a physician to leave the organization voluntarily because she demonstrates an inability to support the professional goals required. If the practitioner declines to depart voluntarily, the medical staff can recommend to the board that it increase eligibility criteria for its medical staff so she is not eligible to apply or reapply.

Negotiate Specific Performance Metrics with Targets

Once expectations are understood and accepted, the next step is to create performance metrics with specific targets so that members of the medical staff have a means to hold themselves and each other accountable. Numerous organizations provide resources on performance metrics, including the following:

- National Quality Forum
- Agency for Healthcare Research and Quality
- National Committee for Quality Assurance
- CMS
- The professional societies of all medical and surgical specialties (e.g., American Association for Physician Leadership, American College of Surgeons)
- Accreditation organizations (e.g., The Joint Commission, the Healthcare Facilities Accreditation Program, Det Norske Veritas, the Center for Improvement in Healthcare Quality)
- Peer organizations and training programs relevant to a clinical specialty, as applicable

Specific performance measures should be recommended by physicians in the clinical department or service line, modified as necessary, forwarded to the medical staff quality committee and MEC, and approved by the board of trustees on the basis of their relevance to the specific strategic goal they serve.

A good rule of thumb when choosing performance metrics is for two sets of professionals to determine the targets' importance to the organization: The physicians assign the metric on a scale of 1 to 3, as a high priority, a medium priority, or not a priority, respectively. The quality or information technology personnel rate the metric from 1 to 3, where a rating of 1 denotes that data for the measure are easy to collect accurately with little, if any, investment of resources, a rating of 2 means data may be challenging to collect accurately with an investment of new resources, and a rating of 3 represents that the data are impossible to collect accurately or that resources must be invested to do so. If both physicians and managers agree that the measure is a high priority, is highly reliable, and requires few new resources, that measure should be prioritized and chosen.

Choosing the targets within those metrics is part art and part science. Only those targets should be chosen that can be assigned to one of three levels of performance: excellent, satisfactory, and needs follow-up. This framework of three performance levels permits

- formal recognition for outstanding performers (e.g., reappointment with commendation) and hardwiring processes to reproduce and emulate this level of performance throughout the organization;
- stimulation of the large middle group to continually elevate their performance so that they may be recognized; and
- the opportunity to follow up with individuals who do not meet expectations to validate the performance result, work through an improvement process (if necessary), and eliminate performance that does not meet expectations (if possible).

Where to set the performance excellence bar is challenging—too high, and many clinicians become demoralized; too low, and the performance metrics accomplish nothing. Ideally, the targets should be a stretch that individuals can accomplish with effort and diligence.

Another challenge is related to professional branding. A center of excellence, service line, or clinical institute may not want to be viewed as average or competent but rather as a leader in quality performance throughout an international market. Its targets will naturally be higher than regular healthcare environments.

Culture poses a third challenge. Some organizations are not content with good performance, and physicians who seek to "merely" meet expectations may not be welcome. For instance, increasing numbers of high-performing organizations have closed medical staffs that function by invitation only and limit membership to high performers.

Two important caveats in developing targets are worth noting:

1. Do not pay for a set of metrics or targets that is not relevant to your organization's or medical staff's strategic goals and objectives; not chosen or developed by physicians on staff (who thus have no ownership or personal commitment to them); or not relevant to organizational brand, culture, and strategic plan. The sources of performance metrics listed earlier represent external benchmark targets based on regulatory, accreditation, or reimbursement methodology. It is up to each medical staff and organization to determine which metrics will best align medical staff performance with organizational objectives that will drive improvement in the most effective and strategic way.

2. "You are what you measure" is an important aphorism. Lack of time and consideration spent selecting performance metrics and targets lead to poor results and low morale. Good performance management systems drive good performance.

Create Work Plans to Support Performance

Individual and systemwide performance cannot be separated. Nowhere is that more apparent than in healthcare. For example, a medical staff finds that individuals have performance issues in the ICU, only to further discover that the volume of cases for each individual is so low that there is no way performance can be sustained at an acceptable level. Or an organization becomes concerned that professional conduct issues are on the rise without taking into account chronic sleep deprivation, overwork, and unrealistic schedules, which place both physicians and patients at risk. Thus, while physicians and managers monitor and track individual performance, they must also explore systemic issues that have a significant impact on individual performance.

Conducting an assessment of systemwide issues and devising a performance work plan typically require dedicated activity over a limited period by a relevant ad hoc committee. One organization in Montana experienced both quality and cost issues over inefficient call coverage schedules. It created an ad hoc committee, called the Reduce the Burden of Call Committee, which was jointly staffed by physicians, managers, and board members. This body acknowledged the damaging impact on quality, financial performance, and customer service that a traditional call coverage system created. It redesigned and redeployed call coverage to mid-level practitioners and hospitalists and created observation units to stabilize patients experiencing medical emergencies who could likely be discharged home rather than admitted. The output of this committee was a win for everyone: fewer peer review cases, better individual performance profiles, high levels of service for the community, lower cost for both management and physicians, and a more cost-effective approach for regional referrals and self-referrals. The work plan also led to reduced complaints from patients and nurses, fewer conduct issues, higher quality, and more timely care. In other words, it supported the medical staff's and hospital's efforts to improve the level of quality and service at a lower cost.

This example demonstrates the importance of a targeted and narrowly defined approach to improvement that explores a specific systemwide issue in depth. It is rewarding work for both physicians and management because it leverages aggregate performance in a positive and meaningful way with the least expenditure of resources and makes far more sense than going over endless peer review cases that share the same root cause and failure mode over and over again.

Measure Performance in a Credible Way

Management is charged with overseeing the operationalization of tracking, collecting, formulating, posting, reporting, transferring, and storing the data that measure performance. Common questions to address when deciding how to operationalize the metrics and targets include the following:

- Are the data produced reliable, valid, and consistent?
- Does the method used to collect these data make our work easier or harder?
- Does this method allow us to do the work in less time, or does it require more effort over a longer time?
- Can each practitioner's performance be tracked to specific orders, procedures, and decisions?
- Can sentinel events (e.g., near misses) and other key safety occurrences be abstracted automatically?
- Can key performance indicators and targets for each individual, department, and service line be abstracted automatically?
- Can performance data be seamlessly transferred to ongoing professional practice evaluation (OPPE) and focused professional practice evaluation (FPPE) feedback reports?
- Can direct variable costs be tracked for each practitioner?
- Can relevant performance data be seamlessly transferred to credentialing and privileging bodies for review?
- Can customized reports be generated for specific medical staff officers, the MEC, the vice president of medical affairs, the chief medical officer, the CEO, and the board?
- Can customized reports be generated to document the impact of systemic initiatives on individual performance?

Large organizations may convene a data trends council made up of physicians, the chief information officer, the management team, quality department staff, and information technology experts to monitor the accuracy, reliability, validity, and consistency of data. The council can serve as an extra monitor for the governing board, medical staff, and management to ensure that the performance management system is working well.

Organizations with successful performance tracking systems spend years working with vendors, staff, and users to refine and perfect them; the ideal system cannot be implemented off the shelf. Organizations that take the time to do this well (see the Sarasota Memorial Hospital case study in Chapter 12) reap enormous benefits from a highly efficient and effective performance tracking system.

To reiterate, it is better to have fewer data that are credible than more data that are not. Non-credible data damage morale, negatively influence physicians' willingness to participate in performance improvement initiatives, and undermine confidence in the performance management system and leadership at large.

Embed the Performance Management Process in All Contracts

Nationally, physician contracts are beginning to reflect a comprehensive approach to performance management. In the past, there has been a disconnect between the hospital's strategic goals and performance metrics (or OPPE and FPPE) and its expectations as stated in contracts. Even today, contracts typically cover only the dates of employment or engagement for services, generic issues of professionalism and attendance, and pay per hours worked or wRVUs generated. As discussed in Chapter 11, clinical alignment cannot be achieved without cultural and economic alignment, and vague or loose contract terms such as these lower expectations that a physician will work with an organization to achieve its key strategic goals and objectives.

If the medical staff and management spend the time to craft a strategic plan, develop performance expectations, and select performance metrics and targets, these performance management elements should be specified in the contract; otherwise, it lacks relevance and undermines alignment efforts. Imagine, for example, that the medical staff and management strive to foster a culture of service based on "standardizing to excellence" all aspects of care and services provided, but the standard physician contract in place mentions nothing of these activities. Those contracted physicians who ignore medical staff initiatives and focus on churning volume may come out far ahead of their colleagues, leaving their peers and the organization at large feeling defeated. Contracts should be made in service of organizational strategy and not vice versa.

Provide Timely and Supportive Feedback

Providing timely feedback has a profound impact on performance, independent of its content, as it indicates to participants that time and resources are consistently allocated to focus on high-quality care. As found in the famous study that produced the Hawthorne effect theory (*Economist* 2008), when individuals are aware of being measured on a task, they pay more attention to their performance of that task.

A classic example is the ob-gyn who performs a high number of primary cesarean sections on Friday afternoons to avoid coming to the hospital for deliveries during the weekends that she is on duty. The organization implements performance measurement targets related to the inappropriate use of Pitocin to induce labor and tells the physician that data on her performance will be collected, analyzed, and reported—first blinded, and later unblinded. Despite the physician's stated objection that leadership has no right to measure her performance on this metric (she contends that the procedure is performed as a "patient–physician preference"), the ob-gyn's primary C-section rate drops significantly by the time the first target measures data are collected. The reason is simple: The physician does not wish to appear as an outlier before her peers. Such shifts in practice do not always occur, but they are seen frequently enough that being informed about the observation of one's work is seen as a powerful motivator.

Offering supportive feedback signals that a physician leader's intention is to help practitioners improve and be successful. As the leader reviews the data with the physician, the leader should expect and be open to questions of data validity and attribution (ascribing relevant performance data to the correct practitioner), consider systemic factors that might contribute to outcomes, develop strategies for improvement, and create practitioner and leader accountabilities for performance. Any action that results from the feedback must be discussed, negotiated, and agreed on so that both parties have a personal stake in the outcome. Failure to come to a constructive conclusion should be seen as a joint medical staff–leadership issue.

Although performance measurement can provide information about a physician's quality of care, the data offer limited insight. Leaders should enter this interaction with humility and the strength of character to acknowledge those limitations, understanding what can be gleaned from patterns that emerge and what the data do and do not signify. Statistical significance is rarely achieved; a more realistic approach to outcome metrics is to recognize what patterns of measurement signify and how they can be used in a beneficial and constructive way.

Create Improvement Plans for Marginal Performers

Individuals with performance issues require an improvement plan so that they will not continue to perform below the medical staff's self-imposed standard and can reach their personal and professional potential. To ignore low performance is to sanction and support a level of care that is inconsistent with the medical staff's and board's values and betrays the community's trust in the organization. It also undermines the practitioner, as it communicates the message that the medical staff is prepared to allow an individual to fail through a lack of action or intervention.

Consider the general surgeon who failed in his practice because his untreated depression caused him to be nonresponsive to nursing requests for care in the middle of the night. Eventually, his inaction led to the death of two otherwise healthy patients from normal postoperative complications. The physician took a medical leave of absence, got his depression treated, and returned to start anew. At an MEC meeting, he asked the chief of staff why he did not help when the physician was clearly suffering from an untreated impairment. The chief of staff said, "I thought we were helping you by looking the other way."

At the least, physician leaders owe every practitioner the opportunity to succeed. (Clinicians who are unwilling or unable to avoid failure present a separate issue.) Every practitioner who does not meet performance expectations deserves an improvement plan, completed jointly with leadership, that outlines the

- specific element of measureable performance that is at issue,
- amount of measurable improvement expected,
- time frame in which the improvement must occur,
- commitment of the leader and the practitioner to support each other through the improvement process, and
- consequences (positive and negative) that ensue if the performance exceeds or does not meet expectations.

This plan forms the basis for a performance contract that should be approved and overseen by the MEC, as it is this deliberative body's role to support both the practitioner in question and the designated leader to move substandard performance into at least the acceptable range. If the improvement plan is carried out successfully, the practitioner should reach reappointment with no red indicators or metrics on her feedback report, and the medical staff can recommend her for reappointment to the board with impunity.

Create Spreadsheet Scorecards to Report Performance

A common way to present the results of performance measurement is to organize an individual's performance in a Microsoft Excel spreadsheet or Access database, organized as a balanced scorecard or dashboard (Kaplan and Norton 1992). The scorecard should show the practitioner's name and specialty on top, followed by the activity (e.g., admissions, consultations, procedures) being measured and the data pertaining to it.

Organizations often display metrics according to the dimensions of performance developed by the Accreditation Council for Graduate Medical Education, the American Board of Medical Specialties, and The Joint Commission, which include the following:

- Patient care
- Medical knowledge
- Practice-based learning
- Interpersonal and communication skills
- Professionalism
- System-based practice

Within each dimension are two to three performance indicators that pertain to department- or service line–specific measures and generic measures. Examples of performance metrics are the following:

- *Patient care:* Risk- and severity-adjusted mortality and morbidity indexes (e.g., actual performance versus expected performance), number of peer review cases deemed care inappropriate, rate of readmission within 30 days with the same diagnosis, rate or number of unexpected complications or transfers
- *Medical knowledge:* Rate of compliance with new knowledge as it emerges and is approved by the clinical department or service line, compliance with evidence-based pathways, fulfillment of professional continuing medical education requirements
- *Practice-based learning:* Rate of improvement as documented in performance feedback reports, willingness to bring new information to the clinical department or service line as it becomes available, compliance with updated evidence-based pathways
- *Interpersonal and communication skills:* Number of validated professional conduct issues, rate of compliance with administrative requirements, rate of compliance with formal handoff protocols or consultation requests
- *Professionalism:* Number of incidents involving timeliness of response while on call, number of 30-day suspensions for failing to update EHRs, number of validated professional conduct issues
- *System-based practice:* Number of delayed operating room starts due to practitioner being late, average risk- or severity-adjusted cost per case, risk- or severity-adjusted length-of-stay index (actual versus expected)

Exhibit 5.1 provides examples of service line metrics, and Chapter 6 discusses performance metrics and their reporting in greater depth.

Use Performance Results to Inform the Strategic Planning Process

To bring the process full circle, the performance results inform the next strategic planning cycle. Whether actual performance fails to meet expectations or exceeds them, it is worthwhile to take stock. Were the objectives too low or too high? Were the goals and objectives the right ones to get the organization where it needs to be? Were the governing board's expectations aligned with management and medical staff performance? Has the external or internal environment changed to render some of last year's goals and objectives obsolete? How do we want to proceed?

Many organizations use a dynamic strategic planning process that enables updates and modifications mid-course to acknowledge the impossibility of predicting or anticipating political, economic, regulatory, or legal issues that may have a seismic impact on organizational performance. When strategy changes, performance expectations may have to shift as well, and the performance management system may have to adjust its goals and metrics accordingly.

Exhibit 5.1: Sample Service Line Metrics

1. Quality outcomes
2. Mortality and morbidity indexes
3. CMS Core Measures
4. Surgical Care Improvement Project measures
5. Safety measures
6. HCAHPS scores or patient loyalty measures
7. Cost per case (contribution margin, net income)
8. Average length of stay
9. Case mix index
10. Market share
11. Market growth (one- and five-year rates)
12. Percentage of total gross revenue ÷ net revenue
13. Percentage of total discharges
14. Ancillary revenue

Any medical staff member who is unable to voluntarily agree to adhere to the principles contained within the medical staff professional code of conduct shall be deemed to voluntarily resign from the medical staff without access to procedural rights.

Privileging criteria establish performance expectations, metrics, and targets that must be met for a physician to be eligible to request and be granted clinical privileges. Examples of performance metrics to be considered at appointment and reappointment include the following:

+ Number of validated behavior incidents per a defined time frame (green, yellow, and red targets; see explanation in the next paragraph)
+ Number of validated issues of noncompliance with evidence-based, medical staff–approved treatments and approaches per a defined time frame (green, yellow, and red targets)
+ Number of validated issues of noncompliance with administrative requirements based on federal, state, and accreditation regulations per a defined time frame (green, yellow, and red targets)

A red performance indicator reflects poor performance *and* poor leadership and should be addressed as both an individual and a systemic performance issue. The credentials committee may require that any candidate for appointment or reappointment with a red indicator take part in a formal improvement plan (with measurable goals, defined time frames, and specific consequences and accountabilities) as a condition of the committee's support. The key with successful performance management (as discussed in the next chapter) is that ideally, no reappointment applications should appear before the credentials committee or MEC with any red indicators if performance issues have been addressed appropriately by physician leaders over the normal course of the appointment cycle. Similarly, no new application should be presented to the medical staff without performance metrics from a professional reference or prior healthcare organization that would preclude the medical staff from making objective and evidence-based privileging decisions.

Both acute and chronic behavioral issues should be addressed proactively through the credentialing and privileging process and should not be left to management to handle in lieu of or absent effective physician leadership. It often requires special training or coaching from management or a reputable outside source to enable physician leaders to perform this essential leadership function.

the basis of a failure to perform up to the bylaws' standards of behavior and ethics.

- *Wieters v. Roper Hospital, Inc.* (2003): The court upheld the hospital's decision to suspend a surgeon on the basis of disruptive conduct, which the surgeon claimed was discrimination against legitimate concerns regarding the quality and safety of care.
- *Blau v. Catholic Healthcare West* (2003): The court upheld the hospital's decision to suspend a physician on the grounds that he did not work well with others.
- *Miller v. St. Alphonsus Regional Medical Center* (2004): The court upheld the hospital's decisions to deny a surgeon's request for membership and privileges on the basis of a significant history of disruptive and noncollegial behavior and conduct.
- *Catipay v. Humility of Mary Health* (2006): The court upheld the hospital's decision to suspend a physician on the basis of sexual harassment and disruptive behavior.

The ideal process for addressing professional conduct issues with a physician is presented in Chapter 9. The remainder of this section discusses the critical role of credentialing and privileging in managing this challenge.

Professional Conduct Issues and Credentialing/Privileging

As mentioned in earlier chapters, strategic medical staff development planning (MSDP) and credentialing and privileging form the foundation for any performance management system. In terms of professional conduct, MSDP describes the types of personal and professional characteristics the organization seeks for building its medical staff.

Credentialing criteria describe the specific characteristics physicians must exhibit to be eligible for membership on the medical staff. The following statements are examples of these criteria:

All members of the medical staff must be willing to work collaboratively and respectfully with others at all times, even during times of disagreement.

All members of the medical staff must support the medical staff's professional code of conduct as a condition of appointment and must annually sign an agreement to abide by its principles.

SUMMARY

Performance management is not a destination; it is a continual process. As many improvement experts point out, the rate of improvement has little to do with specific techniques or methods but rather lies in the number of improvements an organization is willing to make over the shortest period of time (i.e., rapid cycle improvements) (Butler and Caldwell 2008). Alignment of the organization and medical staff's strategic plan is key to enabling the medical staff and management to work toward shared goals and objectives in a mutually beneficial way.

REFERENCES

Atchison, T. A., and J. S. Bujak. 2001. *Leading Transformational Change: The Physician-Executive Partnership*. Chicago: Health Administration Press.

Burroughs, J. 2013. "Physician Relationship Management—The Foundation for All Physician Alignment Strategies." *Synergy* 41 (6): 16–17.

Butler, G., and C. Caldwell. 2008. *What Top-Performing Healthcare Organizations Know: 7 Proven Steps for Accelerating and Achieving Change*. Chicago: Health Administration Press.

The Economist. 2008. "The Hawthorne Effect." Published November 3. www .economist.com/node/12510632.

Kaplan, R. S., and D. P. Norton. 1992. "Using the Balanced Scorecard as a Strategic Management Tool." *Harvard Business Review.* http://hbr.org/2007 /07/using-the-balanced-scorecard-as-a-strategic-management-system/ar/1.

Levitt, T. 1983. *The Marketing Imagination.* New York: Free Press.

Mack, K. E. 2012. "Physician Integration Strategies: Advanced Lessons from Successful Organizations." Presentation at American College of Healthcare Executives Cluster program, Anchorage, AK, August.

Zolnierek, K. B., and M. R. Dimatteo. 2009. "Physician Communication and Patient Adherence to Treatment: A Meta-analysis." *Medical Care* 47 (8): 826–34.

CHAPTER 6

Creating Performance Indicators
and Targets Collaboratively

A hospital CEO was asked what her key strategic organizational objectives for the coming year were, and she responded, "Enhance service, reduce operating costs, and fully digitalize our infrastructure." When she was asked what financial incentives she offered her contracted physicians, she said, "Work RVUs [relative value units], much like other organizations." When asked what work RVUs had to do with service, operating costs, or information technology infrastructure, she paused, reflected, and stated, "I guess we have a disconnect between our aspirations and our incentives."

In the traditional quality assurance world of healthcare delivery, physician performance was assessed by the absence of egregious or negative information. The assumption was made that if no significant negative information came to light about him, the physician was competent and therefore eligible for reappointment or any reasonable new privilege requested; no further measurement or action was necessary. Furthermore, if the physician generated significant revenues, lower performance outcomes and standards were tolerated. It was virtually impossible politically for the organized medical staff to perform further focused review or take any constructive form of corrective action.

Of course, the absence of negative information does not necessarily imply a high level of performance or even competence. The Joint Commission (2013, MS.06.01.05, p. 28) stated in 2007, "The decision to grant or deny a privilege(s) and/or renew an existing privilege(s) is an objective, evidence-based process." In other words, the assessment of a practitioner's current clinical competence must be based on systematic measurement and analysis of that measurement and not on assumption or the absence of negative information.

This regulation sets the stage for answering many questions that had previously plagued medical staffs attempting to evaluate colleagues' performance, such as the following:

♦ How do we know if a new practitioner is competent based solely on certification, a few handpicked professional references, and the absence of malpractice cases?
♦ What do we do about performance concerns that emerge through the grapevine?
♦ How do we address performance issues that involve direct competitors assessing one another?
♦ How do we evaluate potentially biased professional references?

For Joint Commission–accredited organizations, these and other assessment-related questions are addressed through ongoing professional practice evaluation (OPPE) and focused professional practice evaluation (FPPE). Specifically, every Joint Commission–accredited organization is required to collect data on the following metrics:

♦ Operative and clinical procedures
♦ Patterns of blood and pharmaceutical usage
♦ Requests for tests and procedures
♦ Length-of-stay patterns
♦ Morbidity and mortality data
♦ Use of clinical consultants
♦ Other relevant criteria

Organizations not accredited by The Joint Commission must create their own systematic process by which the medical staff establishes, measures, assesses, and manages performance in a credible way. The Healthcare Facilities Accreditation Program (HFAP 2009, 03.02.02) states that, through a quality assessment and performance improvement process (QAPI), "The medical staff provides leadership and actively participates in the review of clinical work. All medical and surgical services performed in the hospital shall be evaluated as they relate to appropriateness of diagnosis and treatment." Required QAPI functions include the following:

♦ Medication therapy
♦ Infection control

- Surgical or invasive and manipulative procedures
- Blood utilization
- Data management
- Discharge planning and utilization review
- Utilization management
- Complaints regarding medical staff–related issues
- Restraint or seclusion usage
- Mortality review

Det Norske Veritas (DNV 2008) mandates that

the organization shall evaluate all organized services and processes, both direct and supportive, including services provided by any contracted service. . . . Those functions to be measured at a minimum must include the following:

- Threats to patient safety
- Medication therapy/use
- Operative and invasive procedures
- Anesthesia/moderate sedation
- Blood and blood components
- Restraint use/seclusion
- Effectiveness of pain management system
- Infection control system
- Utilization management system
- Patient flow issues
- Customer satisfaction
- Discrepant pathology reports
- Unanticipated deaths
- Sentinel events
- Adverse events
- Critical or pertinent processes
- Medical record delinquency
- Physical environment management systems

Standard QA-2, "Collection & Use of Data," of the Center for Improvement in Healthcare Quality (CIHQ 2013) states:

The organization shall collect, analyze and use data to monitor the effectiveness, safety, improvement in health outcomes, and quality of care and services provided.

A. The organization prioritizes its efforts to focus on those processes and/or care areas that are high-volume, high-risk, or problem-prone.

- The organization identifies the specific processes and/or care areas that will be monitored based on the incidence, prevalence, and severity of known or potential problems.
- The organization determines the specific indicators and/or metrics that will be measured for each process or care area identified.

B. Data will be collected on at least the following:

- Medical errors and adverse events;
- Significant medication errors and adverse drug reactions;
- Use of blood and blood components;
- Confirmed hemolytic blood transfusion reactions;
- Significant discrepancies between pre-operative and post-operative diagnosis in pathology findings;
- Adverse events involving the use of anesthesia along the continuum (i.e. moderate sedation to general anesthesia);
- Adverse events

Finally, organizations accredited directly through their state department of health under the terms of the Centers for Medicare & Medicaid Services (CMS) Conditions of Participation must ensure that the "granting of medical staff membership and privileges, both new and renewal, is based upon an individual practitioner's meeting the medical staff's membership/privileging criteria that must include (at minimum) individual character, competence, training, experience, and judgment" (CMS 2009, §482.12(a)(6)). In addition, these organizations must collect data on the following measurements:

- Quality and safety outcomes
- Specific quality and safety events
- Case review of surgical procedures
- Blood utilization
- Medication safety
- Utilization management
- Restraint and seclusion
- Discharge planning

Taken together, the implication is that (1) every organization with an organized medical staff must measure performance in a systematic way for every practitioner granted clinical privileges, and (2) the organization as a whole must collect data for proscribed areas and activities. No requirement dictates that every organization collect data for every privileged practitioner regarding every required aspect of performance activity, only that current clinical competence be assessed in a systematic way.

The challenge for most organizations is that regulators and accreditors state clearly *what* data they require but do not articulate *how* to gather and report those data, leaving each organization to operationalize quality assessment activities on their own. Ideally, the process should be designed and carried out by the organized medical staff with the support, guidance, and expertise of management. The contributor text that follows and the remainder of the chapter offer insight and recommendations regarding this important activity.

John J. Nance, JD, cofounder of the Orca Institute, aviation commentator for ABC News, and patient safety expert, describes how the medical staff can significantly contribute to the creation of a culture of safety.

How the Medical Staff Can Support a Culture of Safety
The universal requirement for achieving a culture of safety in healthcare is the understanding that zero unintended harm is not only attainable but also, in terms of ethics, the only acceptable goal. However, when the attitude prevails in an organization that zero harm will never be achieved, the underlying corrosive cynicism supports the status quo as effectively as it eats away and dissolves the best efforts and programs thrown at the problem.

People tend to cling to established methods if they do not believe that change can produce improvement. When an American hospital maintains that its true client is the physician and its physicians have been trained as autonomous scientists whose ethos requires rejection of methods or procedures "not invented here," little change, and even less improvement, results. When, however, physicians challenge the status quo and lead the process of revolutionary improvement, the entire medical staff can catch fire with the same deeply felt determination.

Indeed, nothing short of that fervor works. But with an average of 22 to 30 patients per hour perishing from avoidable medical mistakes and infections in US hospitals (OIG 2010), how can any physician justify *not* demanding better?

(continued)

In his book *Inside the Physician Mind*, Bujak (2008) makes the key point that physicians are led by a critical mass and not by consensus, which means that only a small group of physicians determined to improve safety rates can form the nexus of a revolution. Moreover, when physicians on the front line—not their chief medical officer or CEO—are the change agents, who accept the opportunity to inspire belief in zero harm, the rest of the clinical team tends to follow. Is it any wonder that the philosophical effectiveness of physicians determined to embrace true improvement in patient safety is at least an order of magnitude higher than the impact of top-down directives and endless programs originating from the C-suite (Bujak 2008)? This is exactly how clinical bundles took root and began saving thousands of lives a few years ago. Physicians drove the belief that central line infection disasters could be completely eliminated. This willingness was echoed by staff members who did what was necessary, accepting standardization of best practices over maverick autonomy. In other words, first comes the belief in the shared vision; *then* comes the achievement.

This sequence was also seen in the airline industry's approach to striving for zero fatal accidents in US commercial aviation. Until the airline industry embraced the philosophy that zero accidents was possible, and until the airline captains and CEOs signed on and led the charge, little improvement was made. Even as late as 1988, an airline industry–generated cynicism was pervasive, such that the occasional fatal accident was seen as just a cost of doing business. When, in 1989, the concept of zero accidents as an achievable goal gained ground, the performance of the industry began to improve markedly, and as of this writing (July 2014), 12 years have passed with only six major airline accidents occurring in the United States. Furthermore, 2011 marked the first year in aviation history with no fatalities from a commercial airline flight anywhere in the world (AirDisaster.com 2014). Thus, zero believed can lead to zero achieved.

All the noble efforts to eliminate inadvertent medical harm will continue to fall short until we truly believe in zero harm and until the natural leaders of healthcare—our physicians—accept their pivotal role in leading the charge. Simply put, no other approach will work.

ONGOING PROFESSIONAL PRACTICE EVALUATION

OPPE is the continuous measurement and assessment of clinical performance and conduct for all practitioners granted clinical privileges through the organized medical staff. The term *practitioner* includes not only physicians and dentists but also podiatrists, psychologists, advanced practice professionals (e.g., advanced practice nurses, physician assistants), and any other professionals (e.g., chiropractors) identified by the governing board—at the recommendation of the medical executive committee (MEC)—to be granted clinical privileges.

According to The Joint Commission (2013, MS.08.01.03, pp. 38–39, EP1–3), "OPPE information is factored into the decision to maintain existing privilege(s), to revise existing privilege(s), or to revoke an existing privilege prior to or at the time of renewal. Furthermore, there is a clearly defined process in place that facilitates the evaluation of each practitioner's professional practice: the type of data to be collected is determined by individual departments and approved by the organized medical staff, and information resulting from OPPE is used to determine whether to continue, limit, or revoke existing privilege(s)." (Although healthcare organizations not accredited by The Joint Commission are not required to perform OPPE as described, this approach is considered a best practice absent specific operational guidance from CMS, HFAP, DNV, or CIHQ.)

Chapter 5 provides the steps for operationalizing this standard to create a credible OPPE program. Here, we describe the OPPE process in detail.

Classify Performance Metrics and Indicators

Performance metrics and indicators are classified in three ways: as reviews, as rules, and as rates. (For purposes of this discussion, we use the word *indicator* to refer to both an indicator and a metric.)

Review Indicator
Indicators related to reviews must be analyzed each time a defined event is triggered. A typical example is the unexpected death of a low-risk or low-acuity patient, which usually calls for a peer review evaluation to determine the cause of death, whether it could have been averted, and whether the care provided can be improved for similar cases going forward.

Rule Indicator

The rule indicator measures the number of incidents over a period of time and triggers a peer review evaluation when the defined number is reached. Using the earlier example of number of validated incidents of unprofessional conduct per year, the medical staff might decide that the consequences for triggering this indicator should be as follows:

Violations per Year	Action
0–2	Provide feedback to practitioner.
3	Have practitioner meet with department chair to discuss and develop a voluntary improvement plan.
4	Have practitioner meet with peer review committee to discuss and develop a mandatory improvement plan.
5	Have practitioner meet with MEC; communicate final warning.
6+	Have practitioner meet with board of trustees and impose corrective action (e.g., some loss of membership or privileges).

As performance improves, the number of violations triggering a consequence may be reduced until so few violations occur that the rule indicator can be discarded altogether, having served its function successfully.

Rate Indicator

A peer review rate indicator evaluation is triggered when a critical rate of performance excessively declines or increases and is defined as some variant of a numerator divided by a denominator, such as a percentage, percentile, ratio, or fraction. This type of indicator is used to measure a specific activity that the medical staff would like to improve for a significant number of practitioners.

One example is the risk- and severity-adjusted primary cesarean section rate per population per period. Unlike a rule indicator, which triggers a consequence based on an absolute number (a numerator without a denominator), a review indicator triggers a specific consequence based on the variance of the rate from an expected or normative value (a numerator *and* a denominator). In this example, the expected primary C-section rate might be 15 to 25 percent (depending on the population observed). Thus, the further the rate is from expected performance, the more significant the consequence. Consequences might be defined as follows:

Rate of Incidence (%)	Action
0–14	Have practitioner meet with department chair to validate and evaluate data.
15–25	Provide practitioner with feedback and commendation.
26–30	Have practitioner meet with department chair to validate and evaluate data.
31–35	Have practitioner meet with department chair to create a voluntary improvement plan.
36–40	Have practitioner meet with peer review committee to create a mandatory improvement plan.
41–45	Have practitioner meet with MEC; communicate final warning.
46+	Have practitioner meet with board of trustees to impose corrective action (e.g., loss of membership or privileges).

Obviously, these percentages would be significantly larger for a high-risk obstetrical population, which is why risk- and severity-adjusted data are more accurate and meaningful than raw data are.

Prioritize and Weight Performance Indicators

Not every performance indicator is equally important in terms of the strategic goals and objectives of the medical staff and organization. Therefore, indicators should be weighted to emphasize importance and priority.

Each performance level is multiplied by the relative weight of its indicator, where the sum of all the weights equals 1.0. Say the leadership team has identified ten performance indicators with two targets and three performance levels each—level 3 represents excellent (green), level 2 represents satisfactory (yellow), and level 1 indicates the need for follow-up (red). If all ten indicators are equally important, each indicator is weighted at 0.1 (10 indicators × 0.1 = 1.0). However, if the indicators are weighted differently according to relative importance, the performance level (1–3) is multiplied by the relative weight of its indicator, and the total score should fall between 1.0 and 3.0. A theoretical feedback report is shown in Exhibit 6.1.

Exhibit 6.1: Sample Feedback of Performance Indicators

Indicator	Performance Level Weights and Scores
Indicator 1 (relative weight 0.1)	Performance level green (3) = $3 \times 0.1 = 0.3$
Indicator 2 (relative weight 0.05)	Performance level green (3) = $3 \times 0.05 = 0.15$
Indicator 3 (relative weight 0.2)	Performance level yellow (2) = $2 \times 0.2 = 0.4$
Indicator 4 (relative weight 0.05)	Performance level red (1) = $1 \times 0.05 = 0.05$
Indicator 5 (relative weight 0.1)	Performance level green (3) = $3 \times 0.1 = 0.3$
Indicator 6 (relative weight 0.15)	Performance level yellow (2) = $2 \times 0.15 = 0.30$
Indicator 7 (relative weight 0.05)	Performance level yellow (2) = $2 \times 0.05 = 0.10$
Indicator 8 (relative weight 0.1)	Performance level green (3) = $3 \times 0.1 = 0.3$
Indicator 9 (relative weight 0.1)	Performance level yellow (2) = $2 \times 0.1 = 0.2$
Indicator 10 (relative weight 0.1)	Performance level red (1) = $1 \times 0.1 = 0.1$
Total relative weights = 1.0	Total multiplied weights and scores = 2.20

Average score = Total multiplied weights and scores ÷ total relative weights = 2.20

Create Individualized Feedback Reports

This phase is where all of the pieces of the puzzle are assembled into a well-organized, easy-to-interpret document, often in dashboard or scorecard format.

First, several points about individualized feedback reports are worth noting:

- Volume data should be separated from performance data. Volume only influences rate indicators where it serves as the relevant denominator.
- Performance levels should be color coded, easy to interpret, and clear to all participants. Hence, medical staff leadership and management should design the format together.
- As much of this process should be automated as possible. Many vendors provide software support to print individualized and consolidated feedback reports from electronically abstracted data, and this capability should be included in the electronic health record infrastructure through the use of customized performance software.
- Most indicators are not review indicators, which are criteria for peer review each and every time. Aggregate data—rule and rate indicators—are both more efficient to collect and more accurate in assessing individual and aggregate performance than are review indicators. They only trigger a peer review when a predefined target is reached.

Exhibit 6.2 is a sample physician feedback report illustrating these elements. Overall, the physician profiled in the exhibit should be commended for a strong feedback report. An area to explore for further improvement is his utilization of ancillary services to reduce the length of stay and overall cost of care without compromising quality outcomes.

Consolidate the Feedback Reports for the MEC and Governing Board

Once individual feedback reports are generated, a consolidated feedback report for the entire medical staff can be created to provide the MEC and the governing board with a summary of its overall performance. This report does not include all of the data found in individual feedback reports but highlights key generic measures shared by many of the medical staff members, particularly those measures relevant to the organization's strategic organizational goals and objectives. An example of a consolidated medical staff feedback report is shown in Exhibit 6.3.

Consolidated reports should be compiled monthly and distributed to the MEC, which develops a variance report and a plan to lead its members to meeting the strategic goals and objectives approved by the board. Feedback reports are an effective management and governance tool for promoting performance transparency and holding the medical staff accountable to the governing board in a measurable and meaningful way.

Create and Implement an OPPE Policy and Procedure

Once consensus is reached on an OPPE process to follow, a policy and procedure to do so are developed by management and modified and approved by the medical staff and governing board to guide leaders on OPPE implementation. Typically, an OPPE policy summarizes the steps for documenting, collecting, collating, analyzing, and acting on performance data for all practitioners granted privileges through the medical staff process. It also provides guidance on which leader or committee structure

1. is accountable and provides oversight for each step in the process,
2. determines the performance indicators used in the credentialing and privileging process,
3. determines when FPPE is triggered, and
4. addresses the integrity and credibility of performance data and the OPPE process overall.

Exhibit 6.2: Sample Individualized Physician Feedback Report for a Hospitalist

Physician Feedback Report
Provider: 007   Specialty: Hospitalist Service   Time Period: May–December 2013

Activity:
Admissions = 324
Consultations = 122

Patient care	Indictor Type	Satisfactory Score	Excellent Score	Score	Performance Level	Specialty or Hospital Average
Risk-adjusted mortality index by medical DRGs	Rate	1.1	0.9	1.0	Satisfactory	1.0
Risk-adjusted morbidity index by medical DRGs	Rate	1.1	0.9	0.9	Excellent	1.0
Peer review cases rated < appropriate	Rule	3	1	1	Excellent	2
Procedures (CT) not meeting criteria	Rate	5%	2%	6%	Needs follow-up	4%
Medical knowledge						
CME credit fulfillment	Rate	95%	100%	100%	Excellent	98%
Compliance bundle with evidence-based practices	Rate	90%	98%	99%	Excellent	96%
Performance on simulated case scenarios	Rate	80%	95%	98%	Excellent	90%
Practice-based learning						
Rate of conversions on feedback reports from reds/yellows to green	Rate	75%	90%	95%	Excellent	85%

Compliance bundle with CPOE and automated order sets	Rate	90%	96%	99%	Excellent	94%
Interpersonal and communication skills						
Compliance bundle with administrative responsibilities (e.g., completion of electronic records)	Rate	95%	99%	98%	Satisfactory	97%
Patient satisfaction scores	Rate	75th percentile	90th percentile	92nd percentile	Excellent	82nd percentile
Colleague satisfaction scores	Rate	80th percentile	92nd percentile	95th percentile	Excellent	86th percentile
Professionalism						
Validated incidents of unprofessional conduct	Rule	3	1	0	Excellent	2
Validated incidents of delayed responsiveness	Rule	3	1	1	Excellent	2
Systems-based practice						
Risk/severity-adjusted LOS	Rate	5.3 days	4.2 days	4.8 days	Satisfactory	4.7 days
Risk/severity-adjusted cost per case	Rate	$10,600	$8,400	$9,600	Satisfactory	$9,400
Compliance bundle with patient safety initiatives	Rate	80%	95%	96%	Excellent	88%

Note: CME = continuing medical education; CPOE = computerized provider order entry; DRG = diagnosis-related group; LOS = length of stay.

Exhibit 6.3: Consolidated Feedback Report for the Medical Staff

Medical Staff Feedback Report
Number of Providers: 553   Time Period: May–December 2013

Activity:
Total admissions
for period = 14,300
Total consultations for period = 6,400

	Indictor Type	Satisfactory Score	Excellent Score	Medical Staff Goal	Medical Staff Mean Performance
Patient care					
Risk-adjusted mortality index by medical DRGs	Rate	1.1	0.9	0.9	1.0
Risk-adjusted morbidity index by medical DRGs	Rate	1.1	0.9	0.9	1.0
Peer review cases rated < appropriate	Rule	3	1	1	2
Procedures (CT) not meeting criteria	Rate	5%	2%	2%	4%
Medical knowledge					
CME credit fulfillment	Rate	95%	100%	100%	98%
Compliance bundle with evidence-based practices	Rate	90%	98%	100%	96%
Performance on simulated case scenarios	Rate	80%	95%	95%	90%
Practice-based learning					
Rate of conversions on feedback reports from reds/ yellows to green	Rate	75%	90%	90%	85%

Indicator	Type				
Compliance bundle with CPOE and automated order sets	Rate	90%	96%	96%	94%
Interpersonal and communication skills					
Compliance bundle with administrative responsibilities (e.g., completion of electronic records)	Rate	95%	99%	99%	97%
Patient satisfaction scores	Rate	75th percentile	90th percentile	90th percentile	82nd percentile
Colleague satisfaction scores	Rate	80th percentile	92nd percentile	92nd percentile	86th percentile
Professionalism					
Validated incidents of unprofessional conduct	Rule	3	1	1	2
Validated incidents of delayed responsiveness	Rule	3	1	1	2
Systems-based practice					
Risk/severity-adjusted LOS	Rate	5.3 days	4.2 days	4.2 days	4.7 days
Risk/severity-adjusted cost per case	Rate	$10,600	$8,400	$8,400	$9,400
Compliance bundle with patient safety initiatives	Rate	80%	95%	95%	88%

Note: CME = continuing medical education; CPOE = computerized provider order entry; DRG = diagnosis-related group; LOS = length of stay.

Ideally, most of the process should be driven bottom-up, with the medical staff quality committee or peer review committee and MEC overseeing and encouraging the rank-and-file practitioners to document data that are relevant and important to their specialty-specific and generic medical staff improvement strategies.

Performance intervention by the peer review committee or MEC should be rare and considered a potential failure of the OPPE process. OPPE should enable every privileged practitioner to meet or exceed all performance expectations for every appointment cycle.

FOCUSED PROFESSIONAL PRACTICE EVALUATION

As discussed earlier in the book, FPPE is a concentrated and time-sensitive process for evaluating the current clinical competence of those practitioners

- who are new to the medical staff,
- who would like to perform procedures outside of their existing core privileges, or
- whose performance leads to questions about the practitioner's conduct or privilege-specific competence.

Overview of FPPE

A key element of FPPE is proctoring. The role of the proctor is primarily observational and, under ordinary circumstances, does not include direct participation in the care provided or procedure performed. Several proctors should be engaged for each practitioner to ensure a fair assessment is undertaken.

Assessments should be based on an objective scoring protocol that covers predetermined criteria in each dimension of performance. An example of a standard evaluation form is shown in Exhibit 6.4.

Once the evaluation is completed, the proctor should share his scoring and comments with the practitioner so that she is not surprised when they are reported to her department or service line director. This approach serves a dual purpose: It provides direct and honest feedback to the practitioner in a timely way and holds the proctor accountable to both leadership and the individual being proctored to ensure that the assessment is fair, balanced, reasoned, and credible.

At that time, the director makes a determination whether to terminate the proctoring process and release the physician to practice independently. The decision is based on both the organization's policy and the director's professional judgment. Professional judgment may be particularly important when the proctored physician's performance is strongly positive or negative. The policy should permit some latitude for judgment to conserve medical staff resources and, more so, to address any patient safety concerns. As one might expect, strongly positive ratings can mean fewer cases proctored, and strongly negative ratings might signal the potential need for more proctoring over an expanded period with an increase in the scope and number of cases. Egregious errors noted by the proctor may be cause for the medical staff to cease the proctoring process altogether and reconsider the credentialing and privileging application for the practitioner.

Similar to the OPPE feedback report, an FPPE report can be created. It reflects a shorter time frame (one to two months versus eight months for OPPE) so that physician leadership can address performance issues in a timely way.

The intention behind the proctoring process should be to provide an objective observational assessment of clinical and professional skills while offering collegial support and empathy. Experts may experience difficulty—and sometimes even feel psychological pain—when being scrutinized by other experts. A little compassion helps build trust and lays a solid foundation for strong professional relationships once the initial evaluation ends and the practitioner has gained some tenure with the staff.

FPPE for Practitioners New to the Medical Staff

Most high-risk professional fields (e.g., aviation, military, nuclear) apply a structured and rigorous vetting process to applicants and new recruits to ensure their professional competence and the public's safety. When a physician or another type of practitioner applies for medical staff membership, the organization has only the evidence of accredited training program completion; a few, often biased, professional references; board certification or eligibility for certification; and the presence or absence of medical negligence cases, Office of Inspector General sanctions, or National Practitioner Data Bank reports on which to form an impression of the candidate.

In the past, organizations either took leaps of faith on or declined applicants based on this limited information and, for those granted membership, awaited quality outcomes that either confirmed or contradicted the initial impression. This evidence-free process placed both patients and the organization at risk. Imagine a new pilot for an airline taking charge of a flight based solely on her previous

Exhibit 6.4: Sample Proctoring Evaluation Form

Type of review: ☐ Prospective / ☐ Concurrent / ☐ Retrospective

Practitioner:

Proctor:

Date assigned:

Privilege(s):

Medical record no.:

Date due:

Element	Exemplary	Satisfactory	Needs Improvement	Unsatisfactory	No Information/ Not Applicable
Patient care (medical and procedural)					
Use of diagnostic testing					
Use of medication and therapies					
Appropriate and timely consults					
Appropriate resource use (admissions, length of stay, tests)					
Abnormal lab results recognized/followed up					
Complications recognized and managed appropriately					
Patient care outcomes					
Documentation completeness (H&P, progress notes)					
Patient care (procedural only)					
Procedural indications appropriate					
Intra-operative care conforms to accepted practices					

Procedure justifed by findings/pathology			
Documentation completeness (Consents and OP Report)			
Medical knowledge			
Use of clinical guidelines/evidence-based medicine			
Interpersonal/communication skills			
Clarity/legibility/compliance of records			
Ability to work with members of healthcare team*			
Rapport with patients/family*			
Professionalism			
Timely medical record completion			
Plans for follow-up documented			
Ethical standards in treatment			
System-based practice			
Abides by facility medication use policies*			
Abides by facility patient safety and operations ⋯icies*			

on medical record documentation and any incident reports associated with this case.

P = history and physical.

professional record and the opinions of a few of her professional colleagues or friends.

Now, wise healthcare organizations put potential medical staff members through a credible vetting process that is designed around the answers to two fundamental questions:

1. Which essential skills, procedures, and behaviors should be evaluated to determine current clinical and professional competence?
2. How many skills, procedures, and behaviors should be evaluated to ensure a valid and reasonable assessment?

The challenge is that the answers to these questions vary according to clinical specialty, prior experience of the applicant, the rigor of the training or performance program, and the reliability of the professional references. A good approach is to evaluate performance from a cross section of representative OPPE indicators from each performance dimension (e.g., patient care, medical and clinical knowledge) that are most likely to provide a reliable initial assessment and represent both cognitive and procedural competence.

Specifying the number of diagnoses made, procedures performed, or tests conducted for evaluation provides a reasonable starting point. However, leaders need to be flexible so that neither too many nor too few activities are required. Say, for example, a 20-year-veteran orthopedist comes to the organization with stellar references and a strong reputation. During the first few procedures he performs, he demonstrates excellent technique, skills, judgment, bedside manner, communication, and teamwork. There should be no obligation to keep evaluating him just to reach the standard threshold number and types of procedures set forth by the FPPE process, as he is clearly a high performer. On the other hand, a practitioner who comes to the organization straight out of training, lacks confidence, displays uncertain technique, and is tentative in her judgment may require an extended FPPE to make sure she is competent and secure in her professional role before recommending her to independent practice.

Another way to improve the efficiency of FPPE is to minimize the use of concurrent assessment, where a practitioner is physically present to evaluate another's competence. Concurrent assessment may be necessary—and in fact prudent—for the first few cases or procedures but should be limited thereafter whenever possible. For example, many medical directors proctor a new practitioner on his first day, speak to patients and staff to receive immediate feedback during his course of FPPE, and make themselves immediately available to the practitioner until he is clearly functioning in a capable and predictable way. Similarly, a surgical director may scrub in with a new surgeon on that practitioner's early significant cases to assess her overall operative management technique and get a sense of her professional demeanor.

Once leadership has determined that the new practitioner is on solid footing, later cases or procedures can be evaluated using prospective review (evaluation prior to treatment) and retrospective review (evaluation following treatment). *Prospective review* is seen frequently in training settings and more rarely in the practice environment. It is a way for a proctor to assess an individual's anticipated performance by sitting down with the practitioner and requesting an overall plan to assess, diagnose, and treat the condition or conditions. *Retrospective review* comes into play when the proctor is ready to evaluate the practitioner by reviewing the patient's chart or discussing the treatment with the practitioner, staff, and patient after it has taken place.

Concurrent review as described earlier may be necessary if the practitioner is tentative or provides inaccurate information. The proctor requests to see orders she has written and may guide the practitioner prior to implementing treatment plans.

Some organizations conduct FPPE *preemptively*, such that the training program begins in advance of the practitioner joining the organization so that it can complete the process once the practitioner is on staff. Finally, the organization can enter into *reciprocal arrangements* with other facilities to share FPPE processes. These programs facilitate completion of proctoring by engaging experts in specific procedures from other organizations to proctor members of the medical staff.

Other ways to conduct FPPE proctoring can take advantage of technology, including the following:

- *Tele-proctoring*—Long-distance electronic proctoring is often available for ancillary practitioners (e.g., radiologists, pathologists) and should be considered for practice settings (e.g., intensive care unit [ICU], psychiatric facility) in which no specialty-trained proctor is immediately available. For instance, some remote ICUs require a new practitioner to present a case to an intensivist in a tertiary setting prior to beginning nonemergent treatment, which can be accomplished via web conference or other electronic means.
- *Procedure recording*—Recording procedures that new medical staff members perform is helpful for assessing their ability to perform surgical cases in which the proctored portion of the case represents a small part of the procedure. For instance, when evaluating a coronary artery bypass graft procedure, the proctor may want to evaluate the bypass itself and the distal vascular anastomosis but not focus on the opening or closing of the thoracotomy, which may take significant time. Recording the surgery allows the proctor to select the

segments of the video that show the practitioner's technical and cognitive competence in the essential aspects of the case.

- *Simulation*—The technical capability to simulate procedures may be in the future for some hospitals, but the future is now for a number of large systems that have built sophisticated and comprehensive simulation laboratories. Here, proctors can assess new members of the staff as well as permit existing practitioners to continually expand and refine their skills. As with simulations in the commercial airline industry, medical practitioners are expected to successfully complete a rigorous simulation assessment prior to operating or managing complex problems on patients to ensure their cognitive and technical competence. This technology will likely assume a dominant role in prospective proctoring in a short time nationwide.

All of these techniques should save both the proctors and the organization time and resources without sacrificing accuracy in assessments.

FPPE for Practitioners Embarking on New Areas of Practice

For existing medical staff who wish to take on additional procedures, FPPE is a privilege-specific evaluation that is far more limited in scope than are evaluations for recent entrants to the field or new members of the medical staff. For example, emergency physicians who seek to expand their practice to utilize ultrasound in the emergency department undergo proctoring that focuses on the specific new skill or technique, the knowledge required to practice it, the judgment to react appropriately to various situations, and the management of cases in the new privilege granted.

Challenges arise when no one on staff is qualified to proctor the practitioner. Options for overcoming this obstacle include the following:

- Preemptive proctoring at a training facility followed by monitoring from a visiting or outside proctor at the physician's organization to complete the FPPE process
- Reciprocal proctoring at a regional facility by practitioners who possess the necessary skills and background to proctor, followed by monitoring at the physician's organization by a visiting or outside proctor to complete the process
- Tele-proctoring (ideally in real time) with a regional medical center once a visiting or outside proctor has determined that it is safe to subject patients to procedures performed by the practitioner
- Simulation training followed by proctoring from a visiting or outside proctor

Many organizations face the same privileging and proctoring challenges. A healthcare organization might consider seeking out other similarly sized facilities for a customized solution that meets its unique needs.

FPPE for Practitioners with Questionable Competencies

FPPE should not be initiated until concerns are validated. It is not uncommon for questions to be raised only to find that the information is biased, skewed, or not supported by objective and reliable data. For instance, an emergency physician may be perceived to order too many CT (computed tomography) scans when in fact her volume is higher than everyone else's and her actual rate of CT scans is lower. A surgeon may be perceived to have a high complication rate until the data reveal that the acuity of his patients is much higher than for other surgeons and, in terms of the risk- or severity-adjusted morbidity index, his complication rate is lower.

If the concern is validated, a narrowly focused review (both ongoing and retrospective) should be launched to define the scope and depth of the issue. For instance, if a surgeon is found to have a higher-than-expected rate of perforation of the bowel during colonoscopies, a good first step is to conduct a retrospective review of all her colonoscopy cases over a specified period and compare the results with other local surgeons and national benchmark data.[1] If the rate is still deemed unexpectedly high following risk and severity adjustment, a proctor may be assigned to evaluate the practitioner's performance to make a professional judgment as to why the performance in question is an outlier. This step should lead to some form of improvement plan that is expected to result in normalization of the performance. In rare instances, the practitioner's privileges may need to be modified voluntarily or involuntarily to ensure patient safety.

FPPE Challenges

Typical challenges that arise as a part of the FPPE process include the following:

◆ *Inevitable conflicts and conflicts of interest.* The Joint Commission requires each medical staff to create a policy that addresses conflicts and conflicts of interest so that they do not adversely influence clinical and leadership decisions. The best approach to avoiding this issue is to use multiple proctors for each practitioner whenever possible to ensure a fair and balanced assessment. Personality conflicts in particular should be resolved so that the individual being proctored does not feel that the proctor wants her to fail.

- *Need for intervention.* In rare instances, proctors must intervene during a procedure to avoid patient injury or harm. The FPPE procedures should be flexible enough to permit the proctor to take over performing the treatment when he determines that patient safety demands it, and the proctor must always be qualified to exercise the clinical privilege to be able to do so.

- *Liability concerns.* The medical staff is generally covered under the board's directors and officers indemnification policy as long as (1) OPPE and FPPE are defined properly as a part of the medical staff's peer review process and (2) proctors or other leaders do not bill the patient for any aspect of the care provided. Physicians should be educated as to the scope and coverage of this policy to both reassure and inform.

- *Communication with patients and staff.* Under the Health Insurance Portability and Accountability Act, every patient has the right to be informed about every individual involved in his care. To ensure that the proctoring process adheres to this rule, staff should be prepared to communicate, openly and clearly, the role and responsibility of each individual caring for the patient. It may be necessary to consider using a script (e.g., "Dr. H is an important part of our healthcare team") so that the patient has confidence that the proctoring process in no way diminishes the credibility of the attending's professional standing.

- *Surveyor-specific proscriptions.* Some accreditation surveyors tend to interpret standards in a rigid and proscriptive way and communicate their opinions to clients as accreditation fact. Organizations should respectfully ask the surveyor to demonstrate opined operational details in the accreditation manual. If the surveyor cannot do so, ask her to explain the intent of the standard so that the organization can fulfill it in a customized and pragmatic way. If all else fails, organizations can contact the accrediting body directly for advice and direction.

FPPE Policy and Procedure

As with OPPE, once physicians and managers agree on an FPPE process, it should be memorialized in FPPE policy and procedures that are approved by the MEC and governing board. The document should cover the scope of the FPPE program, roles and oversight responsibilities of physician leaders, the specific scope and process for each clinical department and service line, proctoring and scoring methodology, rights and responsibilities of participants, and the specific challenges mentioned throughout the chapter. This policy should be considered a living document and modified periodically with input from both the medical staff and management to ensure a cohesive and coordinated process.

SUMMARY

Effective performance management is not an accident; it is a habit established by physicians and managers working in tandem to ensure that a reliable and resource-sensitive approach is in place. Organizations that handle physician performance management well experience fewer safety events, improved outcomes, higher patient loyalty, and lower costs than do organizations with loose or vague performance policies. Importantly, the process helps the organization establish a trusting bond between the medical staff and management as they face the challenges that lie ahead.

NOTE

1. National benchmark data can be found in the literature; on specialty society websites; or through the Agency for Healthcare Research and Quality, the National Committee for Quality Assurance, the National Quality Forum, specialty societies, and other quality and government organizations.

REFERENCES

AirDisaster.com. 2014. "Accident Database." Accessed August 21. www.air disaster.com/cgi-bin/database.cgi/.

Bujak, J. 2008. *Inside the Physician Mind: Finding Common Ground with Doctors.* Chicago: Health Administration Press.

Center for Improvement in Healthcare Quality (CIHQ). 2013. *Accreditation Standards for Acute Care Hospitals.* Round Rock, TX: CIHQ.

Centers for Medicare & Medicaid Services (CMS). 2009. "Appendix A: Survey Protocol, Regulations, and Interpretive Guidelines for Hospitals." *State Operations Manual.* Baltimore, MD: CMS.

Det Norske Veritas. 2008. *National Integrated Accreditation for Healthcare Organizations (NIAHO^SM) Interpretive Guidelines and Surveyor Guidance,* Revision 7. Cincinnati, OH: DNV Healthcare Inc.

Healthcare Facilities Accreditation Program (HFAP). 2009. *Accreditation Requirements for Healthcare Facilities.* Chicago: HFAP.

Joint Commission. 2013. *Hospital Accreditation Standards.* Oakbrook Terrace, IL: Joint Commission.

Office of Inspector General (OIG). 2010. *Adverse Events in Hospital: National Incidence Among Medicare Beneficiaries.* Published in November. http://oig .hhs.gov/oei/reports/oei-06-09-00090.pdf.

CHAPTER 7

Moving Peer Review from Quality Assurance to Performance Improvement

An unusually large number of intensive care unit cases had been referred to peer review, citing the poor performance of several physicians. One member of the peer review committee suggested that these physicians undergo additional clinical training to ensure that they were competent to care for seriously ill patients. Another member of the committee asked, "Does the problem lie with incompetent physicians, or with our organization, which is small enough that our physicians will never achieve the clinical volume necessary to maintain competence?"

An effective peer review process generates the interest and desire among the medical staff to participate fully in the organization's continuous performance improvement process. Constructive, fair, transparent, and credible, with a high degree of integrity and consistency, the ideal peer review mechanism provides strong, actionable performance data for all privileged members of the medical staff. It is cost-effective, demonstrating a calculable return on investment (ROI) through its impact on quality, safety, service, and efficiency. As such, a well-functioning peer review process should be seen by medical staff members as a benefit of being part of the organized medical staff.

The traditional peer review process did not live up to this standard. Many medical staffs expressed frustration with peer review, noting that it was often negative, arbitrary, subjective, and riddled with politicized bias and conflicts of interest.

Much of this sentiment grew out of medical staffs' long experience with peer review: Individual physicians came up against an autonomous and powerful department chair whose motivations seemed as much political and economic as clinical. Worse, traditional peer review approaches failed to result in positive action or improvement, leaving medical staff members feeling that peer review was a futile and wasteful exercise.

Fortunately, new, transparent, and objective models of peer review are emerging. They lead to measurable improvement opportunities because they are designed to answer the question, "How can we use peer review to provide better care tomorrow than we did yesterday?"

Increasingly, organizations now implement a centralized multidisciplinary peer review (CMPR) structure made up of a broad cross section of clinical specialties. This approach follows a standardized process of gathering and analyzing objective criteria for case peer review and is the focus of the chapter. Later, a sample form is provided to help the CMPR committee document cases using a rating system.

PEER REVIEW DEFINED

Peer review is the measurement, assessment, and improvement of practitioner performance (individually and in aggregate) on the basis of multiple sources of data (e.g., the peer review assessment itself, reimbursement claims analysis, the results of proctoring). It encompasses all performance levels (not merely negative outliers) and focuses on moving all practitioners to a higher level of performance on a continual basis.

The definition is important because it emphasizes analysis and improvement and not merely the categorization of performance. It also acknowledges that practitioner performance is complex, entails far more than technical skills and knowledge, and requires multiple sources of data to provide a full and credible assessment.

For organizations accredited by The Joint Commission, peer review is part of ongoing performance practice evaluation and focused performance practice evaluation, as discussed in Chapter 6.

CMPR COMMITTEE STRUCTURE

Organization

Typically, 7 to 11 physicians, representing a broad spectrum of clinical specialties, serve on a CMPR committee. They should be respected clinicians, have high ethical standards, and be committed to serving the medical staff in driving continuous performance improvement. The individuals serving on the committee should be known for fairness, solid analytic thinking, and mature professional and clinical judgment.

Committee members are delegated by the medical executive committee (MEC) and board to serve and may receive fair market value compensation for committing their time, careful consideration, and dedication to high-quality committee work, as long as a job description is in place and performance standards are established and met. They should serve staggered terms of office to maintain continuity and ensure an adequate level of experience at all times. Their terms should exceed the traditional one- to two-year terms of medical staff officers and members of the MEC to help stabilize leadership throughout the medical staff. The specific clinical specialties represented are not important, as long as the committee recognizes when external input is required for a specific case.

The vice president of medical affairs (VPMA) or chief medical officer (CMO), chief nursing officer (CNO), and medical staff services professional often serve as ex-officio members of the CMPR committee. They have no voting rights but provide support and guidance. Ad hoc committee seats may be created at any time and with any members of the medical staff, or any suitable physicians outside of the medical staff, who have specialized expertise, at the discretion of the peer review committee, to address technical clinical issues beyond the scope of practice of the committee's core membership.

CMPR super committees may be established for larger systems. They typically are made up of the chairs of each member hospital's CMPR committee and its VPMA or CMO. CMPR super committees are discussed in more detail later in this section.

Scope and Functions

The CMPR committee reviews only individual or aggregate cases that meet MEC-recommended, board-approved criteria. As discussed in Chapter 6, these criteria are developed from established review, rule, and rate indicators and targets for both external and internal peer review. See Chapter 6 for a complete discussion of peer review criteria and their development.

In the process of fulfilling its peer review duties, the CMPR committee performs the following functions:

- Oversees quality initiatives of all clinical departments and service lines on behalf of the MEC
- Selects and deselects, in an ongoing way, performance indicators or metrics and targets on behalf of the MEC
- Ensures the credibility and integrity of all practitioner performance improvement plans
- Ensures the credibility and integrity of performance data with the support of the quality staff and executive management
- Ensures compliance with the medical staff's strategic quality plan

Managing Conflicts and Conflicts of Interest

Taking a thoughtful approach to peer review (or any medical staff function) allows the medical staff to address conflicts and conflicts of interest in a proactive and transparent manner. Neither conflicts nor conflicts of interest can ever be completely eliminated; however, they should be mitigated and managed so that decision making is as consistent and fair as possible.

From a peer review standpoint, one recommended practice is to separate potential conflicts of interest into absolute and relative conflicts. An *absolute conflict of interest* may exist when a physician is asked to review his or her own work or the work of a spouse. This situation might occur when a physician leader is the chair of a department, the medical director of a service line, or a member of the peer review committee. A physician whose case is under review should be treated as any other member of the medical staff and should not be present during any phase of review except to provide input as requested by the committee.

A *relative conflict of interest* exists when a physician's partner, competitor, employee, employer, or associate is under review. These situations cannot be avoided, as everyone on the medical staff has an economic and political relationship with everyone else on the staff. Therefore, they need to be adjudicated on a case-by-case basis, tapping the committee's understanding of the individuals involved and their ability to maintain objectivity and sound clinical judgment during the review.

About Super Committees

The super CMPR committee reports to a systemwide super MEC (made up of the presidents of each member hospital's medical staff and its VPMA or CMO), which in turn reports to a corporate systemwide board. A CMPR super committee's functions are different than those of a hospital-level centralized committee. Instead of performing routine, criteria-based peer review, it focuses on the following activities related to systemwide issues:

- Develops systemwide quality initiatives that are consistent with the corporate strategic and quality plan
- Selects and deselects systemwide performance indicators/metrics and targets on behalf of the super MEC that are consistent with the corporate strategic and quality plan
- Serves as a source of external peer review when external peer review criteria are triggered locally and the super CMPR committee can provide the clinical expertise for an appropriate review (The only exception is when the system seeks an unbiased outside expert to testify for a hearing, an appellate review, or civil litigation proceedings.)
- Ensures the credibility and integrity of each organization's peer review process
- Ensures the credibility and integrity of systemwide performance data and data collection systems
- Ensures compliance with the corporate strategic and quality plan

APPLYING THE CMPR MODEL

A customized approach to CMPR is built by taking the following steps:

1. Create board-approved criteria for both internal and external peer review.
2. Develop a procedure for screening cases.
3. Establish case follow-up procedures.

In this section, we explore these steps in terms of how to perform CMPR.

Identify Cases That Meet Preexisting Peer Review Criteria

Quality management staff review the individual or aggregate case(s) to determine if they meet the criteria for physician peer review. If the case qualifies for review, a quality management staff member initiates a peer review case-rating form. An example of a case-rating form is provided in Exhibit 7.1. This procedure should be undertaken within one week of the case being identified.

To carry out this function, members of the quality management staff are provided with a list of all review, rule, and rate indicators that trigger peer review and continually monitor clinical activities throughout the organization to identify cases that meet the criteria. These cases may come to the attention of the quality management staff through direct referrals, chart review, abstraction through the coding and billing process (e.g., searching ICD-9-CM or ICD-10-CM codes for significant complications, unexpected procedures, or transfers to a higher level of care), legal review, or other means. Ideally, cases that might warrant peer review should be noted in the identification process within one month of that patient's care being provided so that quality issues may be addressed in a timely way.

If a quality concern comes to the peer review committee independent of the quality management department's process, it does not meet current peer review criteria, and the committee agrees that the creation of criteria to address the concern is not a priority at that time, the case should be referred back to relevant clinical department chairs or service line medical directors for decentralized review.

Peer Review Case-Rating Form

The peer review case-rating form not only documents the findings of a case review but also ties the results back to the medical staff's and organization's strategic goals and objectives. It is completed in three stages, as illustrated in Exhibit 7.1 and explained here.

Quality management staff complete the first stage (above the first heavy black horizontal line) of the form. This section of the form documents the identification and confirmation of a peer review case (or aggregate cases under rule or rate criteria) and notes the key elements that triggered the physician review.

Assign Physician Reviewers

A member of the quality management staff assigns a physician reviewer for routine cases that do not require subspecialty-specific technical expertise, such as compliance or communication issues. When cases require subspecialty-specific technical

Exhibit 7.1: Sample Peer Review Case-Rating Form

MR #:_____ D/C Date: _____ Referral Date: _____ Provider #: _____

Referral Source: Check the corresponding box

Screen or abstract	RM	HIM	Med staff	Nursing	Management	External	Other _____

Quality screen date: _____ Date submitted for physician review: _____

Review/rule/rate criteria:

Elements of the case that trigger the above criteria:

Key issues for physician reviewer:

To be completed by physician reviewer(s)

Reviewer: _____ Date: _____
Significant conflict of interest? Yes __ No __ Potential: _____

		Overall Practitioner Care: Check One
	1	Exemplary
	2	Appropriate
	3	Questionable
	4	Controversial
	5	Inappropriate

If practitioner care rated questionable (3), controversial (4), or inappropriate (5), please check the relevant issue(s):

		Physician Care Issues: Check All That Apply
	A	Diagnosis and treatment (patient care)
	B	Clinical judgment and decision making (patient care)
	C	Technique and skills (patient care)
	D	Planning and disposition (patient care)
	E	Supervision: house physician or APP (patient care)
	F	Clinical knowledge (medical knowledge)

(continued)

	G	Timely/clear communication (communication/interpersonal skills)
	H	Responsiveness and timeliness (professionalism)
	I	Follow-up and follow-through (professionalism)
	J	Evidence-base or policy compliance (system-based practice)
	K	Other:

If Overall Practitioner Care rated **Exemplary** or **Appropriate**, provide a **brief description** of the basis for findings:

If Overall Physician Care rated **Questionable, Controversial,** or **Inappropriate**, provide a brief description of the basis for findings:

Nonpractitioner care issues:

Systemic issues:

Nursing issues:

Educational opportunities:

Committee Review:

Is physician response needed? Yes _____ No _____ (Care exemplary or appropriate, no issues or concerns)

Practitioner response: Letter ___ Committee appearance _____

Specific practitioner issues to be addressed:

Additional information/input required, and source:

COMMITTEE FINAL SCORING:

		Overall Practitioner Care: Check One
	1	Exemplary
	2	Appropriate
	3	Questionable
	4	Controversial
	5	Inappropriate

If practitioner care rated **questionable (3), controversial (4),** or **inappropriate (5),** please check appropriate issue(s):

		Physician Care Issues: Check All That Apply
	A	Diagnosis and treatment (patient care)
	B	Clinical judgment and decision making (patient care)
	C	Technique and skills (patient care)
	D	Planning and disposition (patient care)
	E	Supervision: house physician or APP (patient care)
	F	Clinical knowledge (medical knowledge)
	G	Timely/clear communication (communication/interpersonal skills)
	H	Responsiveness and timeliness (professionalism)
	I	Follow-up and follow-through (professionalism)
	J	Evidence-base or policy compliance (system-based practice)
	K	Other:

Committee Recommendation/Action: Check Any That Apply

	Feedback and collegial discussion with department chair or service line director
	Practitioner voluntary improvement plan
	Practitioner mandatory improvement plan
	Department or service line improvement plan
	Medical staff improvement plan
	Refer to MEC

System issues identified and forwarded to organization quality committee for analysis (please indicate date sent and when response is due):

Nursing issues identified and forwarded to nursing department for review and analysis (please indicate date sent and when response is due):

Cases referred for educational review/discussion by clinical departments/service lines:

expertise or involve potential conflicts, conflicts of interest, or corrective action, the chair of the peer review committee makes the assignment. Some cases may require more than one reviewer if they involve the expertise of multiple specialties or disciplines.

Complete the Physician Review

The quality manager documents for the physician reviewer those issues that are most relevant to the criteria that triggered the review. (The only cases that should be sent to a physician reviewer that do not meet the predetermined criteria are those that the peer review committee feels are so significant that new criteria should be established, approved, and applied to the case at hand.) The physician reviewer conducts the second stage of the peer review and completes the middle section of the case-rating form (below the first heavy black horizontal line and above the second). If the physician does not feel he is qualified to perform the review for technical, political, or economic reasons, he notifies the chair of the peer review committee and a new physician reviewer is assigned.

In the physician review section, the peer reviewer identifies potential conflicts of interest that may preclude a fair analysis and his opinion as to the level of the practitioner's overall care as exemplary, appropriate, questionable (not enough information), controversial (unusual approach that may be appropriate), or inappropriate. If the care is rated questionable, controversial, or inappropriate, the reviewer notes specific issues, such as technique, judgment, decision making, follow-up, or timeliness. He adds a summary qualitative statement in support of the overall case rating, along with the identification of any potential systemic or nursing issues and educational opportunities raised by the case.

This stage of the review should be completed within one to two weeks of being assigned, and the form is then submitted to the CMPR committee for ratification or analysis and further discussion. The case should appear on the CMPR committee agenda at least three days prior to the meeting at which it will be discussed.

Consider the Initial Review Rating

Next, the case is presented to the peer review committee as a part of a consent agenda for ratification. If any member of the committee disagrees with the rating, the case moves from the consent agenda to the meeting agenda for committee discussion. The committee has the right to disagree and overrule an initial rating of exemplary or appropriate if it feels that the care rendered was questionable, controversial, or inappropriate.

If the committee as a whole agrees with the initial rating, it obtains additional information, such as mandatory input from the physician(s) involved and any relevant or substantiating external references or input (e.g., subject matter experts; the professional literature; or external reviewer(s), if conflicts of interest are apparent and irreconcilable or the organization lacks the expertise to make a determination). The committee allows the peer-reviewed physician no more than two weeks to respond; if she fails to do so, she forfeits her opportunity to provide input.

Make the Final Determination

Once the additional information is collated, analyzed, and discussed, the committee determines its final rating, identifies specific issues, and documents a qualitative rationale for its findings. Finally, the committee refers potential systemic issues to the organization's performance improvement committee, nursing issues to the nursing department or chief nursing officer, and educational opportunities to the appropriate department or service line for presentation, review, and discussion.

The third stage of CMPR is thus completed by the peer review committee, which documents its findings in the last section of the peer review case-rating form (below the second heavy black horizontal line).

The final section of this form can be transferred to a spreadsheet to track any action plan and accountabilities that result from the committee's findings. It can then be used to inform future committee agendas so that improvement plans, root cause analyses, and nursing analyses are performed in a timely way. As it is a summary of the CMPR committee's determinations and next steps, the spreadsheet can be used as part of a report to the MEC and governing body to demonstrate the measurable improvements that are generated by the medical staff's peer review process (Marder 2013).

ADDRESSING MEDICAL STAFF CONCERNS ABOUT CMPR

With the emergence of a centralized, multidisciplinary approach to peer review, thoughtful physicians have voiced legitimate concerns. This section presents a number of questions raised by physicians, with responses that should help allay their concerns.

Case Follow-Up Procedures

The CMPR committee may require an individual-level, department- or service line–level, or aggregate-level improvement plan as a result of the case findings. An improvement plan typically specifies terms for achieving measurable improvement, including a specific time frame, the accountable individuals (often practitioners and a leader), and positive and negative consequences of the outcomes.

If the case review uncovers a global or aggregate performance issue, it makes no sense to assign full responsibility to an individual when the performance deficit is likely shared by many. Such systemic issues should be forwarded to the organization's quality or performance improvement committee for discussion or root cause analysis so that systemic improvements can be made and documented.

One organization, as a result of the peer review case cited in this chapter's introductory paragraph, transitioned its intensive care unit to a step-down unit, required more rigorous privileging criteria (e.g., critical care certification) of those caring for patients in this unit, and rotated call coverage. The number of peer review cases referred from this unit dropped significantly as a result.

Similarly, nursing issues should be referred to the director of nursing or chief nursing officer, and cases that offer educational value should be referred to the medical and nursing staff for morbidity or mortality conferences or grand rounds. For high-risk peer review cases, all organizations accredited by The Joint Commission must complete a peer review of sentinel events in an expedited manner. The initial physician review should take place within three days of occurrence, and the complete disposition of the case (including any improvement plans or systemic plan of corrective action) should be completed within 30 days. For all non–Joint Commission accredited organizations, this type of time frame should be considered a best practice.

Otherwise, the peer review committee should hold each other accountable to establish an improvement plan or report of findings within 60 days of making its final determination.

Q: How can practitioners who do not subspecialize in a specific clinical area perform effective peer review within that area of expertise?

A: Most peer review cases result from fundamental systemic or individual performance issues, such as communication skills, interpersonal skills, citizenship, and professionalism. Rarely is a peer review case triggered because a physician fails to execute basic technical or cognitive skills. Most physicians serving on the CMPR committee have the ability to assess the general quality and appropriateness of care. For the rare case requiring specialty or subspecialty technical expertise, someone deemed to have that expertise, either on or off the medical staff, may participate to ensure a qualified analysis is conducted. At no time will any practitioner who lacks sufficient technical knowledge be asked to review a case that requires technical expertise.

Q: *Doesn't moving peer review out of a department or service line undermine the primary purpose of these bodies, to oversee and improve the quality of care?*
A: Although peer review is now performed outside of the traditional departments and service lines, these bodies retain responsibility for performing morbidity and mortality conferences and discussing interesting and informative cases that have a beneficial impact on quality, safety, service, and cost. Furthermore, the peer review committee will turn to the department or service line for input on performance improvement plans if a related performance issue is identified.

Q: *Won't a centralized peer review system create unnecessary redundancies if a case is reviewed by both the department or service line and the centralized committee?*
A: The CMPR committee follows a clearly defined process with predetermined criteria for internal and external peer review, uses a standardized scoring methodology, and conducts systematic follow-up to ensure that performance improvement plans are consistently carried out. Departments and service lines are free to examine any kind of quality issue they recognize as important, whether formally or informally.

Q: *What kinds of checks and balances will be in place to ensure that everyone receives a fair and unbiased review through the centralized process?*
A: Well-managed CMPR has multiple checks and balances in place, including the following:
1. Individuals who participate on the committee are trained, appropriately compensated, and held accountable for their peer review work.
2. Standardized processes, criteria, scoring, and assessment methodologies are followed to ensure that outcomes are consistent and reproducible.
3. Any peer review case in which the care is initially deemed to be questionable, controversial, or inappropriate is reviewed by the entire committee, which may overrule the initial rating. The committee may also overrule findings of peer review cases in which the care is initially found to be

exemplary or appropriate if it feels that major performance issues were overlooked or ignored. This step minimizes the impact of personal or specialty-specific bias in the process.

4. The process allows for any individual involved in a peer review case to provide input directly to the committee related to cases rated less than appropriate.

5. The CMPR committee has the option of seeking outside input for any case that requires technical expertise beyond the scope of the committee or medical staff and that may involve irreconcilable conflicts of interest or require formal expert input or testimony at a later date.

6. CMPR committee members must adhere to a medical staff conflict-of-interest policy approved by the MEC and board, which does not permit individuals with irreconcilable conflicts to participate in related peer review cases.

7. The peer review process is overseen by the MEC, and the CMPR committee is accountable for ensuring fairness and accuracy. Ideally, the chair of the CMPR committee is an ex-officio member of the MEC and can provide input and address concerns from the viewpoint of the MEC.

8. MECs and boards are authorized to request audits of the peer review process, particularly if concerns regarding potential bias or unfairness are raised by a department or service line leader or staff member.

Q: Can an individual practitioner or leader demand that CMPR take place?
A: Because the centralized process is criteria driven, an individual may only ask for CMPR if the specific case (or aggregate cases) meet any preexisting criteria. This screening mechanism minimizes the impact of economic or political bias on the peer review process.

Q: Should professional conduct, behavior, and potential impairments be handled through the peer review process?
A: Because these areas require specialized expertise, they should be handled in a separate process, discussed in detail in Chapter 9.

EFFECTING THE PEER REVIEW CULTURE SHIFT

Powerful shifts in the culture surrounding medical staff peer review depend on the amount of positive feedback that comes out of the peer review process. In a traditional peer review system, physicians and practitioners only hear about negative performance; positive performance is expected and scored with a "0" (i.e., no adverse outcomes, standards of care met). This scheme creates an unspoken assumption that the primary purpose of peer review is to identify negative outliers (bad apples), cite them (often with letters of sanction), and assume that the remainder of their performance is fine. Not only does this approach ignore the non-negative dimensions of the performance curve but it offers no credit or recognition for outstanding performance, which is what most members of expert cultures strive for as inherent motivation.

Providing feedback and recognition for both appropriate and exemplary performance alters the medical staff and organizational culture by celebrating excellent performance and hardwiring it into systemwide performance and culture. For example, if a general surgeon's rate of risk- or severity-adjusted mortality or morbidity is particularly low, his practice should be studied to identify any best practices that can be shared with other surgeons to improve overall surgical performance. Here, the CMPR committee has not only recognized a high performer but also enabled the medical staff as a whole—not to mention the entire system—to improve its performance.

Recognizing high performance enables the organization to "manage up" its physicians and medical staff to the community and beyond, which reflects positively on the organization, its employees, and its leaders. Practitioners who receive a high number of exemplary reviews may be commended by the MEC and governing board to both stimulate improved performance by "average" performers and communicate to its community that a high level of care is available.

Asking the question, "How can we use the peer review process to improve the quality, safety, service, and cost-effectiveness of our care tomorrow beyond what we provide today?" shifts the entire process to one of constructive problem solving and analysis, which is far more satisfying and productive for physicians and managers than merely identifying negative outliers. It helps demonstrate measurable improvement that drives quality and financial performance and achieves an ROI, not only rationalizing the resources required to perform peer review but, more importantly, demonstrating the organization's commitment to continual improvement.

SUMMARY

A positive peer review process generates individual, aggregate, medical staff, nursing, and organizational opportunities for measurable improvement. Standardization and transparency in that process create fairness; objectivity ensures validity, reliability, and consistency. The CMPR process can serve to highlight excellence, generate

Maria Greco Danaher, JD, shareholder with Ogletree Deakins, Nash, Smoak, and Stewart, PC, writes of the increasing ambiguity regarding the performance and protection of peer review information with regard to employed physicians and practitioners.

Navigating the Maze of Peer Review Information in Federal Employment Cases

In recent years, an obvious shift has been seen in the ways courts address employment-related claims brought by medical staff members. With increasing frequency, peer review and medical credentialing information previously viewed as confidential or otherwise protected is subject to production during litigation.

Under applicable federal and state laws, hospital employees—specifically including employed physicians—generally can bring claims for hostile environment, wrongful termination, or discriminatory treatment against healthcare institutions. In some cases, courts also have extended to independent contractor physicians the rights associated with true employment status, based on peer review procedures (*Salamon v. Our Lady of Victory Hospital* 2008).[1] In addition, hospital bylaws have been successfully cited as the basis of contract-based discrimination claims under federal antidiscrimination laws, further expanding the number of fact scenarios under which such cases can be brought. Counsel for both hospitals and individual physicians must develop an understanding of the legal bases for employment-related cases and increase their awareness of the rationales used by courts to reach decisions in such cases to effectively and accurately advise healthcare clients on these issues.

Production of Peer Review Documents in Employment Cases

Allegations of employment discrimination based on a protected characteristic—most often age, race, gender, and national origin—typically are raised under federal civil rights statutes or under parallel state laws. Such claims may be based on direct evidence, such as the utterance of racial slurs or sexually inappropriate language. Most cases of discrimination, however, rest on indirect evidence, in which inferences of illegal actions must be drawn from witness testimony and relevant documents.

The US Supreme Court has noted that in a claim of discrimination, a plaintiff must be given a full and fair opportunity to demonstrate by "competent evidence" that the reason given for the adverse action against him was simply a cover-up for an unlawful or discriminatory decision (*McDonnell Douglas v. Green* 1973). Courts regularly have held that the need for such probative evidence in discrimination cases outweighs a hospital's or an employer's asserted interest in promoting candor in medical peer review proceedings (*Mattice v. Memorial Hospital of South Bend* 2001[2]; *Sonnino v. University of Kansas Hospital Authority* 2004[3]).

Impact of Federal Rules on Production of Peer Review Information

Because most antidiscrimination cases are brought in federal courts, the Federal Rules of Civil Procedure govern the actions. While most states have enacted statutory privileges restricting the release of peer review information, those state-law privileges generally do not apply in federal court when a case is based on a federal antidiscrimination statute. In fact, every federal court to have considered the issue has declined to recognize an overarching peer review privilege. Instead, the courts rely on the wording of Federal Rule of Civil Procedure 26(b)(1), which includes the broad statement that "Parties may obtain discovery regarding any non-privileged matter that is relevant to any party's claim or defense." Therefore, production of peer review records typically has been ordered if "any possibility" exists that the documents sought may lead to information that is relevant to any claim or defense in a federal discrimination case.

Federal courts have varied in their approaches, but they frequently allow access to certain information that hospital and other healthcare provider entities have historically asserted are subject to peer review privilege. Consider these examples:

- ◆ *Shortened period of "relevance":* In a race discrimination case ultimately decided in 2006, the Fourth US Circuit Court of Appeals resolved an earlier discovery dispute by ordering the defendant-hospital to provide documents pertaining to competency review of similarly situated doctors for a 15-year period in response to a broad request from the plaintiff for all peer review decisions made by the hospital over a 20-year period (*Virmani v. Novant Health Incorporated* 2001).
- ◆ *Redaction of confidential information:* One federal district court ordered production of e-mails and computerized memoranda created or maintained by the hospital and "relating to the plaintiff's credentialing as a member of the medical staff," but it allowed that certain identifying information could be redacted (*Kunajukr v. Lawrence & Memorial Hospital, Inc.* 2008).

(continued)

- *Compilation rejected; protective order applied to peer review information:* A Connecticut district court found that a composite document summarizing performance review outcomes over the relevant period was not an adequate substitute for the actual peer review material sought by a physician claiming race and nationality discrimination. It ordered production of all such documents, subject to a protective order (*Ray v. Pinnacle Health Hospitals, Inc.* 2008).

In these and other cases, courts have found an increasing number of ways to circumvent the application of the historical privileges applied to peer review and credentialing information, including production from a restricted time frame, production with some redactions, and production subject to a protective order. The number of employment-related claims in which peer review or credentialing information is the subject of discovery requests and motions to compel is on the rise, and the willingness of courts to make decisions without full consideration of the health law ramifications of the production of such information continues to expand.

The counsel for healthcare institutions and providers should become familiar with the rationales used by courts to accept peer review information as relevant admissible evidence in various employment cases. The failure of healthcare providers and their counsel to be aware of this trend could create unintended liability from an employment law perspective.

improvement strategies, emphasize the interdependence between the medical staff and other clinical areas of the organization, and spotlight the medical staff's commitment to quality oversight and its continual improvement efforts.

NOTES

1. A federal appellate court decided that a hospital's quality assurance standards and peer review process extended beyond health and safety concerns as well as the plaintiff-physician's specific medical qualifications to the goal of maximizing revenue and in reaction to the physician's complaints of harassment. Furthermore, based on that fact, the physician would demonstrate a genuine issue of fact regarding the hospital's control over her performance.

2. Peer review materials would aid the physician in proving he was qualified for position of anesthesiologist and would support the discrimination claim.

3. Peer review privilege does not bar disclosure of documents in female physicians' disparate treatment claims (*Virmani v. Novant Health Incorporated* 2001).

REFERENCES

Kunajukr, et al. v. Lawrence & Memorial Hospital, Inc., et al., No. 3:05CV01813 (D. Conn. Feb. 14, 2008).

Marder, R. 2013. *Effective Peer Review—The Complete Guide to Physician Performance Improvement,* 3rd ed. Danvers, MA: HCPro.

Mattice v. Memorial Hospital of South Bend, 203 F.R.D. 381 (N.D. Ind. 2001).

McDonnell Douglas v. Green, 411 U.S. 792 (1973).

Ray v. Pinnacle Health Hospitals, Inc., No. 1:07-cv-0715 (M.D. Pa. May 22, 2008).

Salamon v. Our Lady of Victory Hospital et al., 514 F.3d 217 (2d Cir. 2008).

Sonnino v. University of Kansas Hospital Authority, 220 F.R.D. 633 (D. Kan. 2004).

Virmani v. Novant Health Incorporated, et al., 259 F.3d 284 (4th Cir. 2001).

CHAPTER 8

Providing Feedback and Managing Improvement

One physician on staff was responsible for $3 million in operating losses due to the excessive lengths of stay his patients experienced and his inappropriate use of ancillary studies and consultations. The CEO was asked whether she shared this kind of financial data with the physician leadership and the physician in question. She reflected for a few moments and thought aloud, "Maybe we should."

The provision of timely, supportive, and effective feedback is an essential part of the performance management system. Many healthcare organizations collect reams of critical quality, safety, service, and cost data that are never shared in a meaningful way with the stakeholders who must execute the strategic plan on behalf of management.

A good performance feedback process accomplishes the following overarching goals:

1. *It emphasizes what is strategically important.* As mentioned earlier, most physicians have little, if any, knowledge of the organization's strategic plan or their role in executing it on behalf of management. Performance management brings the strategic plan from the boardroom to the clinical setting by asking each clinician to achieve goals and objectives that reflect well on his individual performance and contribute to the success of the medical staff and organization. Performance feedback should never be an exercise in accreditation compliance but instead serve as a framework for strategic execution.

2. *It offers experts the opportunity to self-assess and self-manage.* It is important to leverage the pride and drive of the expert culture to achieve high

levels of performance in a mutually beneficial way. Individuals modify their performance when they know that they are being observed (known as the Hawthorne effect; see Chapter 5), and members of the expert culture are no exception. They care about not only their individual performance but also their relative standing among respected peers. Credible feedback enables them to make a rapid comparison of their performance against peer-established benchmarks, reflect on the causes of any variances, and decide how to self-correct or modify their actions for superior performance.

Interestingly, experts may not openly admit that the feedback was helpful or even desired; however, by their actions, they demonstrate the importance of the data to them personally and professionally.

3. *It supports a dialogue around performance and improvement.* The core function of the organized medical staff is to oversee and continuously improve the quality of care provided to patients. Constructive feedback serves as a foundation for that discussion and should contribute to a culture of continual improvement. The discussion should not be about the identification of negative outliers or what went wrong with a physician's specific performance, but rather how the physician and physician leadership can collaborate to improve the individual practitioner's performance as well as that of the medical staff.

In the vast majority of cases (with the exception of egregious situations and violations) an extensive focus on the past is unhelpful. Instead, it is better to strive to create a desired future state together through constructive and creative dialogue toward identifying factors that led to the individual and systemic performance issues.

4. *It serves as a foundation for effective performance management.* In rare cases, individual performance issues must be managed as what they are—individual performance issues. These usually result from a physician's overemphasis on the importance of individual autonomy and control, lack of desire to follow evidence-based practices, or deviation from established practice and behavioral norms to achieve personal and professional goals.

Providing constructive feedback is the first step in a customized performance management process, which should lead to normative performance and a willingness to work collaboratively with the organized medical staff to improve the quality of care. It is important to document the initial discussion so that if the individual falls back into poor practice behaviors, the performance management process has an established place to progress from, rather than having to revert to a first intervention.

Richard Blakely, MD, chief medical officer, and *Shawn P. Griffin, chief quality and informatics officer of MHMD–the Memorial Hermann Physician Network, describe their journey from using bubble charts for feedback to adopting a sophisticated performance management reporting process, becoming a national leader in physician integrated performance in the process.*

From "Bubble Trouble" to National Leaders

The Crimson Initiative—described by the Advisory Board as "the first physician performance data management platform developed by physicians for physicians" (PR Newswire 2014)—was born out of frustration with what we referred to as "bubble charts." Physicians who were perceived as being poor utilizers (high cost/high average length of stay) were shown a graph on which the physician's inpatient cases were displayed by diagnosis-related group (DRG) as points, or "bubbles." The bigger the bubble, the greater the volume of cases with that DRG. If the bubble was above the x-axis, the cost per case for that DRG was greater than the average. Bubbles to the right of the y-axis indicated a greater-than-average length of stay. So physicians with sizable bubble in the upper right quadrant of the bubble chart were shown their results. But they asked questions that were perfectly reasonable: Over what period of time were these cases from? Which patients, and how sick were they? What was the source of the cost?

Memorial Hermann could not answer most of these questions in a timely manner. Hence, we wanted a tool that would update us in real time and be interactive, visually clear, accesssible by each physician, and capable of showing drill-down data to the level of the individual patient. We were fortunate to encounter two young graduates of the Harvard Business School who were entrepreneurs developing technologic solutions for other industries. Starting from scratch, we worked with them to develop a tool that was able to show physicians detailed risk-adjusted, all-patient-refined DRG information regarding how the quality and efficiency of the care rendered by them compared with that of their peers. We hoped to someday develop a tool that would even yield a quality and efficiency score that could be used for at-a-glance comparisons.

Early work with the tool, called the Oversight Project, focused on decreasing unnecessary resource utilization variation among a group of hospitalists headed by one of our design physicians. This project achieved savings averaging $358 per case through cost reductions and reduced readmissions. It also demonstrated improved quality with Core Measures compliance. This focused effort included multiple meetings with involved physicians to review

(continued)

their performance in a nonjudgmental peer-to-peer interaction. It was this project that led to the first white paper demonstrating the value the new tool could have in a healthcare system.

Our partnership continued as we began developing clinical integration in our network of more than 2,000 physicians. We deployed a new module in the tool to collect claims data and provide our physicians with online access to their office performance on selected Physician Quality Reporting System–based metrics. This "one-stop shop" for physician quality metrics was reinforced by our design of incentives, which rewarded connecting to the data warehouse and performance on the measures. Recognizing the difficulties involved in connecting the disparate electronic medical record systems, we also were the first organization to deploy a manual registry entry tool for the less connected offices to comply with data collection.

Our organization has now progressed beyond clinical integration to accountable care and population health. When we launched our population health strategy, we deployed claims-based population health management tools for disease tracking, risk stratification, and resource efficiency. These tools provided our physicians with insights ranging from the population's makeup to the specific claims level that had previously been restricted to payers. Memorial Hermann Physician Network physicians provide real-world feedback to their development teams, letting them create meaningful physician-level reports to enable our physicians to manage their specific clinical populations. Our organizational partnership provides Memorial Hermann with the leading-edge technology needed for innovation. When a tool or process works for a varied physician network with more than 800 practice locations and representing the most focused subspecialist to the rural general practice physician, that technology vision has survived the furnace of practical tempering.

Our contributions to the platforms continue to grow. And to think that the relationship all started with a small group of visionaries trying to solve "bubble trouble."

SUCCESSFUL PHYSICIAN FEEDBACK TECHNIQUES

Communicating with members of an expert culture requires preparation, care, and a foundation of respect. Physicians assume that their time spent in graduate and postgraduate training and practice has earned them respect. They appreciate dialogue and feedback that is thoughtfully constructed, referenced, and supported. Therefore, providing feedback to physicians can be considered a "crucial conversation."

Crucial Conversations

Patterson and colleagues (2002) prescribe *crucial conversations* when the communication involves legitimate differences of opinion, high stakes, and a charged environment. Physicians may perceive such conversations as a threatening activity that may place their autonomy, independence, and professional standing at risk. They approach these attempts at communication with their deepest values at the forefront and focus on how they will defend their position.

The objective of a crucial conversation is to move beyond the individual's defensive outer layer to a core of shared meaning. A good technique is to avoid addressing the performance issue first. Instead, it is helpful to seek common ground by exploring the "opposing truth" that the individual may be defending. For example, most physicians consider administrative documentation a burden despite its importance in providing excellent patient care and adhering to relevant federal requirements. Physicians respond when any lax health record documentation behaviors are addressed with a primary emphasis on patient safety, effective handoffs, and clear communication.

Crucial conversations take into consideration each party's tendencies and inclinations. The zone of comfort for members of an expert culture typically reflects their need for absolute control and autonomy with a tendency toward a confrontational or adversarial style of communication, extreme discomfort with serving in a follower

---

A Deeper Dive

When communicating with physicians about their role in fulfilling federal requirements, it is best to broach the topic from the physician's perspective and not the hospital's. For example, rather than framing the issue in terms of the hospital's need to prove that it meets the Medicare Conditions of Participation, ask the documentation-deficient practitioner, "Does the delay in completing medical records have an impact on your ability to legally bill Medicare and on your cash flow?" This introduction to the subject can serve as a springboard for a far more fruitful discussion about how physicians and managers can work together to consistently achieve optimum and timely documentation while decreasing the burdens of related activities for both parties.

role, and limited scope of vision primarily focused on their expertise. The manager or physician leader must approach the individual with respect and leverage her inclinations toward developing a mutually beneficial solution. Specifically, seek to solve problems by providing the physician with objective data and relevant insight into operational and financial exigencies as a gesture of cooperation and partnership.

Finally, the foundation of any crucial dialogue between members of collective and expert cultures is trust. It must be earned one conversation and one relationship at a time. Crucial conversations are characterized by the following trust-building features:

1. Respect at all times, even during times of disagreement
2. Appreciative and empathetic listening, so that the individual feels respected and acknowledged
3. Empathy for the complexities of the physician's world, including economic, clinical, and personal pressures
4. A focus on excellent clinical outcomes and operational efficiencies that will benefit patients and physicians
5. Social and political currency accumulated from leadership's sincere efforts to support physicians and remove obstacles from their ability to provide high-quality, efficient patient care
6. Physician relationship management (see Chapter 5) with outreach mechanisms to support physicians' practices and professional needs
7. Humility regarding the interdependent nature of the physician–hospital relationship to avoid invoking the hierarchical relationship

Getting to Yes: Every Conversation Is a Negotiation

H. L. Mencken, the acerbic journalist, is said to have remarked: "For every complex problem there is an answer that is clear, simple, and wrong" (BrainyQuote.com 2014). Confronting an expert with a performance issue that needs to be fixed is not only disrespectful but can be perceived as a setup for conflict. This approach will neither improve performance nor establish trust.

Instead, consider following the insight behind Niels Bohr's famous quote, that the opposite of a deeply held truth is not a lie, but another deeply held truth. It is not enough to address those performance issues; you must come to understand what higher priorities the physician is fulfilling in lieu of complying with administrative processes and regulations.

In their seminal text, *Getting to Yes: Negotiating Agreement Without Giving In*, Roger Fisher and William Ury (1986), of the Harvard Negotiation Project, present a number of essential steps to negotiation that serve both parties' needs while laying the foundation for trust, deeper understanding, and working rapport. These steps are to separate people from the problem; focus on interests, not positions; consider a variety of options before making a decision; apply mutually agreed-on criteria; and have a BATNA (best alternative to a negotiating agreement), or "plan B."

Separate People from the Problem

The first step in any successful negotiation is to treat the other individual with respect, regardless of differences, and search for ways to build mutual respect and understanding. As Fisher and Ury (1986) note, "Never attack an individual but rather attack an issue as a mutual problem to solve." This collaborative approach frames the discussion as problem solving and not proving who is right or wrong.

Focus on Interests, Not Positions

One of the most common errors in working with physicians is focusing on the manifestations of poor performance (symptoms) instead of examining the priorities and interests behind the physician's behaviors (underlying causes). A physician might seek compensation for call coverage not just to make more money but to shore up his private practice, which is failing because its business model is ineffective. A spate of peer review cases from the intensive care unit might be explained not by the individuals' poor performance but by a lack of volume in the unit for physicians to maintain critical care skills.

The underlying issues may be individual, systemic, or both. One ophthalmologist fell behind in updating his patients' medical records. He was not lazy or unconcerned about maintaining up-to-date records. He could not keep pace because his cataract cases were always scheduled for late in the day on Fridays. The medical records personnel were already gone by the time he finished seeing these patients, so the updates for these cases were consistently delayed, which affected the care offered by other attending physicians. This issue was remedied by creating an e-signature function for the electronic health record, which permitted the physician to complete his records in a timely way online and away from the office, regardless of the time of day or day of the week. What had initially appeared to be a performance problem turned out to be a simple systemic fix that satisfied both the physician and the management team.

Consider a Variety of Options Before Making a Decision

When embarking on a crucial conversation or a get-to-yes discussion, it is common for each party to have a fixed idea of the desired outcome. But this dynamic can inhibit the discovery of a more creative approach than either had in mind. To avoid limiting their options, both parties need to check their initial expectations at the door and arrive ready to jointly brainstorm and problem solve. A good discussion often leads to solutions that neither party would have arrived at individually, and the process of getting there can be extremely satisfying.

Once, during a discussion regarding call coverage, an orthopedist complained that he lost $2,500 in revenue when he was forced to cancel three elective procedures to attend to a trauma victim with numerous fractures who, the orthopedist was sure, never intended to pay for the care provided. When the CEO was asked how much revenue the hospital lost when the orthopedist canceled those three cases, she added up the forgone reimbursement based on the assigned ICD-9-CM (International Classification of Diseases, Ninth Revision, Clinical Modification) codes and arrived at a figure of more than $13,000. She looked at the orthopedist, and he looked at her, and they both had the same epiphany: Maybe the problem was the call coverage system, and they both would be better served by hiring a surgical hospitalist to handle cases to avoid similar opportunity costs (a total of $15,500, in this case) caused by disruptions to the elective surgery schedule.

Use Mutually Agreed-on Criteria or Standards

Healthcare performance data are far more objective than the performance assessment measures of the past. Healthcare performance data are not perfect indicators of performance, of course, but if physicians and leaders focus on the patterns and trends that the data suggest, useful information and insights can be gleaned. Any helpful pattern of objective data can temper subjectivity with a constructive exploration and discussion of the meaning behind the trend.

The advantage of using mutually agreed-on criteria and standards as a frame of reference in "getting to yes" dialogues is that it keeps the discussion as objective as possible so that the focus is on the problem to solve and not the individuals involved.

In addition to using criteria and standards, it is helpful to focus on principles shared by the physician and managers as a platform for deeper discussions. These tenets might include optimizing quality, reducing costs, providing high levels of safety and service, and improving access to healthcare. By starting with areas of shared meaning, the discussion can enhance understanding of and respect for the expertise that each party brings to the dialogue.

Plan B

Fisher and Ury (1986) emphasize the importance of having a BATNA (best alternative to a negotiated agreement) as a "plan B"—a fallback position established in advance—for any negotiation. This preparation acknowledges that not every discussion will result in a mutually acceptable solution. Ideally, the BATNA will leave an opportunity to reengage, whether with the same leader or another leader if the chemistry does not seem right.

---

*The following two articles describe how good performance management and positive physician feedback can drive organizational performance. The first article, by **Chip Caldwell, FACHE,** chairman of Caldwell Butler & Associates LLC, describes how the medical staff can contribute to continuous process improvement activities necessary to drive quality and reduce costs. The second contribution, by **Peter A. Stille, CPA, CPM,** president and CEO of Strategic Sourcing Results Inc., describes the essential role of the medical staff in working with management to reduce supply chain costs.*

The Physician Leader's Role in Driving Process Improvement
Chip Caldwell

"Hospitals are entering a fiscal crisis the likes of which we have never seen in our history," stated Tennessee Hospital Association President Craig Becker (Sher 2013). This story line is being repeated throughout the country as state and federal authorities wrestle with the rising cost of Medicare and Medicaid, massive new enrollments as the Patient Protection and Affordable Care Act rolls out, and caring for an aging population while the employed population declines. Indeed, if there has ever been a time when we need "all hands on deck"—clinical administrators, clinical and support service managers, and physicians—now is that time.

Donald Berwick, MD, founder of the Institute for Healthcare Improvement, set out 11 aims to achieve lasting quality improvement in the US healthcare system. The three most crucial objectives are as follows:

1. *Guidelines.* "Guidelines are the answer. We need to standardize [the] care that we give" (Berwick 1996).
2. *Identifiable physician scorecards and dashboards.* Physician performance feedback systems have evolved from printouts with the identities of individual physicians blinded and outlier scores highlighted to highly automated systems that can provide detailed case information for each poor performance encounter.

(continued)

---

3. *Individual pay for performance (P4P)*. P4P initiatives have gained acceptance as a transformational force in clinical practice at the practitioner level.

Indeed, as Berwick suggests, P4P may have ushered in an era of heightened accountability. But why have these approaches generally failed to improve healthcare delivery?

The margin of achievement is wide between low-performing organizations and top-tier organizations. Leaders in poor-performing organizations continue to "rely on much simpler notions of leadership, like empowerment, guidelines, score-carding, or incentive pay design, in which the workforce, clinicians, and others figure out the new models of care delivery" (Berwick 1996).

Leaders at all levels in top-performing organizations—C-suite members, vice presidents, physician leaders, directors, and supervisors—take ownership of the quality improvement system, mastering the following elements of successful organization-wide change models:

1. **Clarity and transparency in the goal-setting process.** Although many low-performing organizations use sophisticated goal-setting tools, such as Lean methodology's A3, their stakeholders often introduce conflicting goals that sideline the original aim as initiatives unfold. Top performers stick to their goals, not by ignoring other issues raised by stakeholders but by suggesting those issues be solved in a follow-on improvement activity. They create the plan, stick to the plan, test changes within the plan, and hardwire successes produced by the plan.

   Role of physician leaders: Physician leaders, and the CEOs who oversee their activities, must ensure that they have an active voice at the strategic planning table, along with their C-suite colleagues. They must insist that strategies assigned to them under their watch be clearly metricized and supported by the organization.

2. **Speed in the use of data.** Low performers ask, "Do we need any more data before moving to action?" The mere suggestion of this option can lead to many additional months of analysis. Top performers, on the other hand, ask the question, "Do we have *enough* data to begin making changes?"

Role of physician leaders: Physician leaders in lower-performing organizations can impede the speed to action, not because they desire slow improvement but because they hold strongly to the belief that action planning cannot begin until every possible angle of analysis has been completed.

3. **Speed of implementation.** An organization that wants to move forward in an effective way does so while collecting any clarifying data. This approach decouples the analysis component of the quality improvement model from the implementation component, whether it be Lean, Six Sigma, the Toyota Production System, or the more traditional FOCUS-PDCA (Find, Organize, Clarify, Understand, Select–Plan, Do, Check, Act). The decoupling decreases time to action and doubles or triples the number of changes effected. Low performers see quality improvement and change as a linear process; top performers see quality improvement and change as a parallel and cyclical process.

   Role of physician leaders: Physician leaders can be the voice of speed to implementation among the C-suite team, Lean experts and quality professionals, and their physician colleagues by demonstrating efficiency and coaching others to adopt a mind-set of agility.

4. **Reliance on rapid cycle testing of change.** Rather than attempt to design the "perfect" care model in a meeting room, top performers get out into the organization and apply small-scale experiments in real-world environments, eschewing the endless debates in meetings about a particular change idea that is raised.

   Role of physician leaders: Physician leaders can become the experts in the use of rapid cycle testing and small-scale experimentation throughout the organization by studying available techniques and participating in demonstrations of their effective use.

5. **Deployment of an organization-wide accountable change model.** Instead of relying on a decentralized project structure to drive change, consider the following steps to an organization-wide model:

   ◆ Centralize projects into one accountability system at the CEO level, rather than managing each project independently at much lower levels throughout the organization.

(continued)

- ◆ Set short assessment time frames for results.
- ◆ Expect to see two changes from each director per month during each 100-day phase. Every director, physician, and manager is expected to change processes within their control, not simply serve as advisers.
- ◆ Schedule monthly check-ins with leaders to report on those changes implemented in the past month. This step helps ensure that changes will be successfully implemented during the upcoming month.

Role of physician leaders: Physician leaders can assert influence in two distinct, but related, tracks in the deployment of robust change models. First, the physician leaders' breadth of responsibility enables them to deploy rapid change models independently to achieve the strategic goals assigned to them. Second, physician leaders can be assertive advocates around the C-suite for the organization to aggressively redesign its existing change models to replicate the success factors outlined in the bulleted list above.

6. **Institutionalization of a culture of change.** Allowing a culture that protects the status quo to prevail stymies any change initiative and wastes precious resources.

7. **CEO as driver of change.** Providing the impetus for change should not be delegated to the CMO or other members of the C-suite.

The following are successful techniques to integrate physicians into the organization-wide change model:

- ◆ *Expect results.* Every member of the medical staff should be held to the same standard regarding improvement outcomes; no one should receive a "bye" based on political or economic standing.
- ◆ *Assign physician leaders to lead operational departments.* The best way for physician leaders to learn the rigors of day-to-day management is not to send them to classroom training but to get them directly into the role of leading one or more departments.
- ◆ *Model a physician-led improvement structure after the operational department's structure.* Physician leaders may be held to the same standard of "two measureable improvements per month" as the department manager.
- ◆ *Teach Lean specialists, quality professionals, and department directors how to work with physicians, as opposed to working for physicians.* This step

probably sounds overly simplistic, but it is worth noting as the culture of many organizations supports—subtly, if not overtly—superior–subordinate relationships at the expense of collaboration among managers, physicians, or both.

- ◆ *Avoid overuse of analytic tools, and rely more heavily on implementation-oriented tools, such as rapid cycle testing and small-scale experiments.* As suggested earlier, the adoption of implementation tools provides physician leaders the opportunity to demonstrate organization-wide leadership.

Physician-driven change may be the most important initiative in the accountable care era. Relying on methods of the past is not an effective route to designing the care system we need for the future. They may be relevant or even necessary, but alone, they are not sufficient.

◆ ◆ ◆

How to Work with Physicians to Optimize Supply Chain Performance
Peter A. Stille

In hospitals, supplies are the second largest expense category, after labor. Many supplies fall into a basket we refer to as "physician preference items," or PPI, which can become costly to a hospital.

Effectively managing the supplies, lab test outsourcing, and pharmaceuticals preferred by physicians is a competitive imperative. In particular, the successful management of physicians' supply preferences can remove millions of dollars from a hospital's cost structure while enhancing patient outcomes through standardized approaches. Hospitals and other healthcare organizations that cannot work with physicians to reduce supply costs will be saddled with an untenable cost structure.

On the other hand, hospitals that position themselves for optimal supply chain performance by working with physicians to develop administrative structures, effective leadership, and a methodical implementation strategy are poised for success in supply chain management.

Designing for Success

Efforts to address PPI must be founded on sound physician relations. One strategy that has proved effective is to establish an oversight committee

(continued)

consisting of physician leaders and hospital administrators to share overall industry trend information, hospital financial data, strategic plans, and the terms of physician compacts or covenants to ensure common understanding and alignment of purpose. Oversight committee meetings on PPI generally include the following key components:

- *Selecting scope and approach.* The committee should establish criteria to determine how to identify specific PPI areas or policies to review. Supply areas that can be directly linked to patient outcomes, net revenue, labor or non-labor costs, and particular physicians tend to benefit most from this review.
- *Defining physician engagement protocols.* The role of individual physicians and physician groups in the improvement effort should be specified, with stakeholder physicians co-developing their supply area's review approach. Agreeing up front on reasonable time commitment expectations from department chairs and practicing physicians facilitates these efforts. Once an area of focus is identified, physician champions for each PPI area are selected. Whether or not to offer physician incentives should be decided early on as well. Next, engagement forms, to define the specific roles and responsibilities of physician members of the oversight committee, and communication about the improvement effort are outlined and finalized with feedback from the full medical staff.
- *Establishing processes for ongoing communication and monitoring.* The committee must identify the metrics it wishes to monitor and establish success milestones to determine progress. The types of communication required for physicians to understand the PPI initiative, its progress, and their role in its outcome should be selected as well. Typically, communication includes introductions to and updates on the review process at department meetings, medical staff memos, newsletters, and letters to individual physicians. Milestones achieved should be communicated to the entire medical staff and celebrated.

Steering Toward Success

To make the overall initiative actionable and to enhance its effectiveness, hospital administrators typically assign overall and area sponsors. These sponsors must be seen by physicians as driving the effort and must be involved in key communication activities. Considering the time required to fulfill this role, the leadership of PPI reviews is often delegated to area champions and supported by formal committees or ad hoc teams.

The role of the sponsor requires setting expectations and a protocol with area champions, structuring a steering committee to monitor progress and navigate barriers, and ensuring that champions are enabled with access to the resources they need.

The speed and success of the area champion's leadership depends on her credibility among the medical staff, time availability, and access to data. The area champion should have an abundance of each.

- *Credibility.* The area champion must have established credibility with the individual stakeholder physicians. For example, presenting a well-prepared introductory meeting will go a long way toward solidifying credibility and sets the stage for the meeting's content to be well received.
- *Workload.* A comprehensive PPI initiative will address more than 100 commodity areas and involve just as many physicians. The time frame for completion is compressed, usually just six months. The amount of work required to support such an endeavor should not be underestimated. One rule of thumb used to estimate the area champion's time commitment is one hour of labor for every $10,000 in annual spending under review. The majority of this time will be split between the area champion and the data or research support staff (typically purchasing managers with the ability to evaluate and communicate on clinical matters).
- *Data.* Hospitals often find it difficult to assemble data that meet the needs of managers and physicians. The best type of information for this initiative is variable cost data by diagnosis-related group linked to actual spending data and identifiable by specific physician. Even analyzing data by physician within the hospital and comparing with industry peers can lead to valuable practice changes without any product evaluation required. The area champion should be prepared to explain how the presented data fit into data from suppliers, healthcare journals, the hospital, or mental simulation models that demonstrate the potential impact of various supply chain decisions.

Short-term gaps in data availability can be filled by internal sources that provide historic variable cost information that may be corroborated externally through commercial databases. Long-term solutions include investing in service line data and financial software with the capability of providing customized drill-downs and dashboard metrics for monitoring.

(continued)

Delivering Success

Aligning resources to achieve goals and navigate barriers is key to a successful implementation. Once the sponsors and area champions are in place, the actual work commences. It includes research, holistic review, and decision making.

- *Research.* With the current state defined, potential new supply solutions must be identified and evaluated. This research can be conducted using information from incumbent suppliers, competitor suppliers, consultants, group purchasing organizations, industry publications, benchmarking reports, government resources, and hospital peers. The organized medical staff's input must be sought as well.

  The information to be gathered must include the total cost of ownership, which takes into consideration any expired products, freight costs, restocking fees for returns, and free products provided on a trial basis; gross margin analysis; capital requirements; service requirements; and, most importantly, patient outcomes. All data should be verified against independent sources.

  Moreover, the area champion and select physicians should evaluate the soundness of the data gathered. For example, is the medical device under consideration patented? Is it approved by the Food and Drug Administration for safety? What safety records are available on industry database alerts? If a competitive advantage is cited with a particular medical device, is this claim documented in a study? If not, why might the manufacturer not document it? If published, is the study found in an established academic, peer-reviewed journal within parameters of a double-blind study?

- *Holistic review.* For both the champion and the physicians, it is important to manage preexisting biases. As solutions are gathered, an open mind is critical. Practicing medicine is a continuing process, not a static event. Discarding options before data are gathered and analyzed does not serve the patient, the doctor, or the hospital. It is the job of the area champion to work with the physicians to present enough valid information for the comfortable expansion of PPI options to consider. Price reduction and standardization may not be the answer.

An unbiased, big-picture perspective should be maintained by the area champion as well. Improvements in patient outcomes, revenues, or productivity may be more valuable than simple, per-unit cost reduction. Increasingly, and with the right incentives and structure, physician collaborations lead to holistic, meaningful discussions surrounding resource consumption, optimal algorithms, clinical pathways, and compliance with established industry guidelines.

◆ *Decision making.* Once data are assembled, reviewed with physicians, and perhaps modified on the basis of their feedback, the time for decisions has arrived. The hospital typically summarizes the options with key financial; quality; and other valued, physician-communicated criteria. Here again, the facts speak for themselves. The area champion should be prepared to accept the outcomes indicated by the information.

In addition, one or more implementation pathways should be identified. If a trial run of a specific supply chain option is required, its timing, sample size, and success criteria must be established prior to its start. Comprehensive patient outcomes and financial information, such as revenue and labor and supply costs, should be reported post-trial using internal evaluation forms— not forms provided by salespeople—at a mutually agreed-on date, with periodic review thereafter. During the trial, all suppliers must be prohibited from counter-detailing or creating counter offers in an attempt to reverse or modify a supply chain decision.

In cases where standardization on one device is preferred financially but consensus for adopting that device is not reached with targeted physicians, decisions should be deferred to area sponsors, physician champions, or the department chair.

Hospital administrators and physicians often bristle at the thought of discussions that lead to changes in PPI. "Do not get involved in how physicians choose to treat patients" is a common refrain. However, evidence-based decisions born of thorough research, deep vetting, and the careful consideration of options is now the standard for medical practice and hospital management. By following the best practices described here, administrators and physicians can optimize their supply chain and achieve fruitful outcomes for the hospital, its physicians, and, most importantly, their patients.

SUMMARY

The good news is that most physicians want to perform the best they can—if the price and obstacles are not too high. Most physicians want to participate meaningfully in their healthcare organization as long as it does not conflict with their business or practice model. Most understand the need to temper self-interest and appreciate and respect both the organization's mission and the need for patient-centric decision making.

The bad news is that the rare physician inappropriately defends independence and autonomy against the best interests of patients and their safety. A few physicians may have undiagnosed psychiatric issues or impairments that hinder their ability to make rational decisions. Those vexing issues and more are addressed in the next chapter.

REFERENCES

Berwick, D. 1996. "Run to Space." Speech delivered at the IHI National Forum on Quality Improvement in Healthcare, December 6.

Fisher, R., and W. Ury. 1986. *Getting to Yes: Negotiating Agreement Without Giving In*. New York: Penguin.

Mencken, H. L. 2014. BrainyQuote.com. Accessed August 7. www.brainyquote .com/quotes/quotes/h/hlmencke129796.html.

Patterson, K., J. Greeny, R. McMillan, and A. Switzler. 2002. *Crucial Conversations: Tools for Talking When Stakes Are High*. New York: McGraw-Hill.

PR Newswire. 2014. "The CRIMSON Initiative—the First Physician Performance Data Management Platform Developed by Physicians for Physicians—Is Now Working with Over 200 Hospitals and Over 25,000 Doctors." Published September 9. www.prnewswire.com/news-releases/the -crimson-initiative---the-first-physician-performance-data-management -platform-developed-by-physicians-for-physicians---is-now-working-with -over-200-hospitals-and-over-25000-doctors-62119882.html.

Sher, A. 2013. "Hospitals Push for TennCare Expansion." *Chattanooga Times Free Press*. Published February 11. www.timesfreepress.com/news/2013 /feb/11/hospitals-push-for-tenncare-expansion/.

CHAPTER 9

Addressing Significant Performance Issues Collaboratively

The impaired physician is a labor of love; the disruptive physician is a labor of law.
—*Spence Meighan, MD*

A physician may be a significant admitter, a generator of revenues, a long-standing informal leader, an opinion maker, and a highly competent technical performer and still demonstrate performance issues. The range of issues is far reaching and includes a pattern of indolent behavior, the early manifestations of impairment, a chronic lack of compliance with administrative or clinical initiatives, a persistent inclination to obstruct important quality and safety initiatives, an inability to work cooperatively or communicate clearly with others, and a history of competitive economic or political behavior that undermines the mission and vision of the organization. Regardless of the benefits a physician brings to the hospital, her performance problems *must* be addressed.

The interventions required are often complex, difficult to manage, and laden with political and economic consequences. Most leaders are reluctant to spend the political currency necessary to "make things right," preferring instead to keep the peace, particularly if a large, heavily political bloc of physicians supports the individual and moves to block managers' decisions. The looming physician shortage, revenue shortfalls, declining market share, rising costs, and the pressure to be perceived as a "physician-friendly" environment are all factors that may lead hospital executives to excuse, enable, and even unintentionally endorse some physician performance issues.

Unfortunately, a failure to act is shortsighted and dangerous. As challenging as they are, these interventions *must* be conducted—in an effective and timely way—to ensure the delivery of safe, high-quality, patient-centric healthcare services.

IMPACT OF PHYSICIAN PERFORMANCE DEFICITS

Poor performance in any of the areas mentioned here are not to be treated as isolated incidents. In reality, they affect the entire hospital's operations, particularly in the following areas:

- Patient safety
- Medical staff environment
- Organizational culture
- Leadership integrity
- Staff safety, morale, and confidence
- Laws, regulations, and accreditation
- Community trust
- Concerns of individual physician impairment

Each of these areas is discussed at length in the following sections.

Patient Safety

Until recently, the medical profession operated on the assumption that technical competence and expertise were the sole relevant factors in achieving high-quality patient outcomes. Physicians considered beyond reproach in terms of their clinical skill were afforded great tolerance for deviant behaviors as long as their actions never adversely affected their clinical outcomes.

This assumption proved to be false. Between 1995 and 2005, The Joint Commission performed thousands of root cause analyses, categorizing the root causes into groups. It found that the most common root cause of unexpected risk to life or limb was not level of technical competency or credentialing—ranking sixth among all root causes identified, with a 20 percent incidence rate—but rather effectiveness of communication, the lack of which led to 68 percent of sentinel events. On July 9, 2008, The Joint Commission released Sentinel Event Alert 40, which states:

> Intimidating and disruptive behaviors can foster medical errors, contribute to poor patient satisfaction, and to preventable adverse outcomes, increase the cost of care, and cause qualified clinicians, administrators, and managers to seek new positions in more professional environments. Safety and quality of patient care is dependent on teamwork, communication, and a collaborative work environment. To assure

quality and to promote a culture of safety, healthcare organizations must address the problems of behavior that threaten the performance of the healthcare team.

Since the publication of the alert, the healthcare profession has come to accept that interpersonal and communication skills have a far greater impact on quality outcomes than technical competence. That conclusion is supported by more than 100 observational and 20 experimental studies, which found that communication and professional conduct can adversely affect patient satisfaction, lower patient compliance rates by as much as 400 percent, increase morbidity and mortality rates for both acute and chronic disease management, lead to higher rates of medical error, and increase the overall cost of care (Zolnierek and Dimatteo 2009).

Medical Staff Environment

Nothing can tear a medical staff apart (and alienate a support staff) faster than allowing a high-performing practitioner to flout legal, regulatory, accreditation, and policy requirements to protect a revenue stream. It pits those who support best practices and compliance with evidence-based approaches against those with great influence by virtue of their revenue generation and premier political status. The hospital suffers significant opportunity cost, as practitioners and staff members quietly refer cases away from problematic individuals and the organization to avoid dealing with the issue directly.

Significant conflicts and conflicts of interest can also emerge, as when referrals are not made based on patient need but political and economic forces. All these situations can place the organization at risk on a number of levels.

Organizational Culture

Culture is not molded from what is written, what is said, what is meant, or what is implied; it is created solely by what is done. An organization that professes high quality and enables poor or marginal performers defines itself as having a culture that lacks integrity. Its leadership compromises the organization's mission, vision, and values in the face of financial exigencies. There is a point at which an organization must live its values or risk forfeiting its high moral and ethical ground. Many organizations have reached that point and made the necessary changes—with outstanding results. Organizational culture issues are covered in greater detail in Chapter 12.

Leadership Integrity

For many years, healthcare systems did themselves a disservice by promoting a management style that emphasized operating and total margins. This error is being rectified somewhat by the evolution of pay-for-value reimbursement methodologies, but the greatest impact on leadership integrity will come by way of the narrow networks that will be developed. In narrow networks, third-party payers, large employers, and savvy consumers preferentially divert large volumes of beneficiaries, employees, and peers, respectively, to high-quality, low-cost organizations. Leaders who operate successfully (i.e., secure long-term gains) within narrow networks will need to address physician performance deficits immediately, even if those actions result in temporary financial setbacks.

Leaders who for years (advertently or not) overlooked poor or marginal performers under fee-for-service are now adopting a different stance: They understand that only those organizations that deliver superior performance will survive—let alone thrive—in a healthcare economy characterized by global competition that will drive market share to high performers and permit average performers to fail. These are transformational leaders. They are doing the right thing for themselves and the organizations they serve.

Staff Safety, Morale, and Confidence

As one might expect, low performers have a significant impact on fellow medical and support staff. According to the Studer Group (2008), performance that leads to decreased patient satisfaction scores (1) undermines staff confidence and morale and (2) doubles or triples turnover rates. Performance issues not only significantly increase costs related to turnover—at 1.5 to 2.5 times the annual total compensation for each staff member replaced—but are directly responsible for increasing medical errors and sentinel events. Length of stay rises 24 percent, and mortality rates increase by 28 percent (Studer Group 2008).

Laws, Regulations, and Accreditation

The Centers for Medicare & Medicaid Services (CMS) Conditions of Participation require that the person responsible for the conduct of the medical staff be a physician, dentist, or podiatrist (CMS 2013). Furthermore, standards of corporate compliance mandate that the medical staff conform to federal, state, regulatory, and accreditation requirements that support superior quality outcomes. Many legal cases have upheld healthcare organizations' right to take corrective action against an individual who places the organization and the patient care environment in "imminent danger" as the result of her poor performance (White and Burroughs 2010).

In terms of accreditation, in 2009, The Joint Commission updated its leadership standards as a follow-up to its 2008 sentinel alert. Standard LD.03.01.01 requires that (Joint Commission 2013):

> Leaders create and maintain a culture of safety and quality throughout the hospital. Safety and quality thrive in an environment that supports teamwork and respect for other people, regardless of their position in the hospital. Disruptive behavior that intimidates others and affects morale or staff turnover can be harmful to patient care. Leaders must address disruptive behavior of individuals working at all levels of the hospital, including management, clinical and administrative staff, LIPs, and governing body members.

Community Trust

It takes hard work and deep commitment over many years to build an organization's reputation, trust, and standing in the community, but just one small oversight can cause years of irreparable harm. The community perceives all healthcare leaders to be fiduciaries of a public trust, who act only in the best interests of patients and the community. Community members experience anger and distress when they perceive that sacred trust to be violated in the name of political or economic expediency and self-interest. Leaders have the unique opportunity among the various stakeholders to leave a legacy of community trust.

Concerns of Individual Physician Impairment

Fully one-third of individuals who manifest chronic behavioral issues may suffer from an undiagnosed and potentially treatable impairment (White and Burroughs 2010). A physician who exhibits poor or marginal performance may be manifesting signs of a psychological, physical, or organic impairment. From a purely collegial and humanistic perspective, helping an individual overcome an impairment while protecting the safety and interest of patients may be one of the highest callings of leadership.

CRITICAL FACTORS FOR SUCCESSFUL PERFORMANCE INTERVENTIONS

A common error in the healthcare field is executing a performance intervention without a solid performance management foundation in place. The stability of this foundation relies on these factors:

- Strategic medical staff development planning to establish board-approved performance criteria
- A solid credentialing and privileging process that can determine whether every practitioner meets medical executive committee (MEC)–recommended, board-approved credentialing and privileging criteria
- Clear and well-articulated performance expectations that are reinforced in all applicable contracts
- Appropriate performance metrics, featuring targets and timely and effective feedback
- Effective initial performance management if expectations deviate significantly from expectations

Following are recommendations for building this platform.

1. Involve the right people at the right time and the right place. Hospital leaders tend to expect titled physician leaders or officers to handle intervention without orientation, training, or support from management. This is an unrealistic expectation and sets all parties up for failure. Physicians who demonstrate chronic performance issues have a well-developed defense technique that expertly eludes accountability and responsibility. Overcoming their defenses requires expertise that is well beyond all but the most subtle and skilled intervention leader.

Choosing the right venue for the intervention is important as well. It may be reasonable to visit the physician in his own setting to perform initial interventions in a respectful and collegial way. A final intervention may be best executed in a formal setting, where the authority of medical staff leadership and the governing body is unmistakable.

2. Inform key members of the organization. The execution of a performance intervention may require ongoing collaboration between the MEC and executive leaders to determine the best approach and the best individuals to perform the intervention(s) on an ongoing basis. This engagement is particularly relevant for employed physicians, who are under dual accountability by virtue of their employment agreement and the medical staff bylaws.

The governing body should be aware of any progressive discipline that is likely to reach the board level so that it can prepare to address the issue in a fair and legally defensible manner. Boards do not like surprises. It is incumbent on medical staff and hospital management to keep the board well informed as necessary. (However, the board should neither micromanage nor become overly involved, particularly if board members have a personal relationship with the physician(s) in question.)

Legal counsel should also be informed if a reduction in membership rights or privileges is likely to occur. The legal team can set the proper groundwork to ensure compliance with the medical staff bylaws and all applicable state and federal laws.

3. Anticipate and realistically think through downstream scenarios. The organization should be culturally aligned to handle any politically and economically challenging intervention. Once organizational alignment is achieved, a realistic downstream assessment must be made to determine the inevitable economic and political repercussions and how the organization will address them. Potential scenarios are a division within the medical staff, the creation of political factions, the loss of a robust revenue-generating practitioner, political fallout in the community, or damage to the organization's reputation and a resulting decrease in market share.

To understand the trade-offs inherent in taking action, assess the opportunity cost of doing nothing. One board refused to address a practitioner's conduct because he was responsible for almost 5 percent of the operating revenue, until the president of the medical staff demonstrated the dramatic opportunity loss. This practitioner was costing nearly triple the amount of his revenues in lost referrals, legal costs, staff turnover, and declining market share and reputation.

An essential component of this activity is an effective communications plan that balances the need for confidentiality for all peer-review-protected activities with the need for key individuals within the organization to understand and prepare for potential changes that may affect their units or departments.

Kenneth H. Cohn, MD, FACS, CEO of Healthcare Collaboration, explains how excellent physician engagement creates the foundation for trust and effective physician performance management.

Optimizing Physician Performance

When I am not invited to sit at the table, I feel like I am on the menu.
—*Upstate New York physician*

According to the Advisory Board Company (2007), engaged professionals strongly agree with the following statements:

(continued)

- This organization really inspires the very best in me.
- I am willing to put in a great deal of effort beyond what is normally expected to help this organization be successful.
- I talk up this organization to my friends as a great organization to work for.

Why don't we see more physician engagement, when most doctors enter medical school to make a difference in patients' and families' lives? One answer may be that our lengthy training has not prepared us for the challenges that have emerged for physicians in recent years (Cohn and Peetz 2003).

Daugird and Spencer (1996) identified 11 distinct losses that the average physician experiences, including financial security, community and social status, independent clinical decision making, collegiality, freedom of choice of specialty and practice location, and power in hospital governance. *Engagement* has a double meaning: as a promise (as in "engaged to marry") and as a battle cry (as in "engage the enemy"). In this contribution, I aim to help healthcare leaders fulfill the promise of engagement and minimize the battle cry of unnecessary conflict.

Enhancing the Promise of Physician Engagement

Hospital and health system leaders who contemplate solving their problems by simply hiring physicians might heed FHN (formerly Freeport [Illinois] Health Network) CEO Michael Perry's advice (personal communication with Dr. Cohn):

> Ninety-five percent of our physicians are employed by or contracted with the system. The high percentage of physicians employed by the system by no means indicates that our physicians are any closer to achieving consensus with administration, and we must be intentional about aligning our organizational goals with those of the doctors. The same skills of communication, aligning strategies and goals, and decision making are needed in our situation as are needed in organizations with fewer employed physicians.

Authentic engagement that enlists physicians as long-term partners rather than transactional customers is a prerequisite for twenty-first-century hospital–physician alignment. The following strategies, tactics, and tools have facilitated authentic engagement at community hospitals throughout the United States:

- *Appreciative inquiry (AI)* is based on the premise that people respond favorably to positive reinforcement and that sharing stories of past successes generates more energy and less defensiveness than analyzing problems and attributing blame. AI may be helpful when root cause analysis becomes mired in finger-pointing. Physicians and hospital leaders can use AI to overcome defensiveness, turf battles, negativism, change fatigue, and slow response time. Physicians can encourage healthcare leaders to incorporate AI into their daily practice by asking people, "What is going well for you?" rather than making problems the focus of rounds (Studer 2004).

- *Healthy competition* derives from the achievement pressure that physicians face to obtain entrance into medical school, residency, and fellowship training. For example, the director of a cardiac catheterization laboratory presented clinical data to encourage his five cardiologists to limit variation, improve outcomes, and cut supply costs, telling them that leadership would reexamine the data in four months, hoping to see progress. If the cardiologists could not reach consensus on how to limit variation and improve outcomes and profitability in six months, he would put names above the individual physicians' data and post them on a bulletin board in the catheterization laboratory, in full view of the entire staff. Within four months, procedure times and outcomes for the entire group were within one standard deviation, and the cardiologists had decreased their vendors to two and cut costs substantially, all while improving outcomes. As one of the cardiologists explained, "None of us wanted to be an outlier, except on the positive side" (Cohn and Lambert 2005).

- *Positive deviance* is a bottom-up approach to organizational change, founded on the premise that solutions to problems already exist within the community. It encompasses intentional behaviors that depart from the norms of a group in honorable ways. For example, Dr. Anthony Cusano at Waterbury (Connecticut) Hospital used positive deviance to cut the number of patient readmissions caused by medication noncompliance from two per month to virtually zero. He arranged for physicians or nurses to contact patients within 24 hours of discharge to converse with the patients about their compliance with the medication orders. Dr. Cusano learned of this solution by studying patients who

(continued)

took their medications correctly and hence avoided readmission. He said, "If communication is the issue, positive deviance showed us that it is also the answer. To me, this was a beautiful thing" (Cohn, Thieme, and Feldman 2006).

Drs. Jon Lloyd and Sandeep Jain, working with hundreds of healthcare professionals at the VA Pittsburgh Healthcare System, reported a 50 percent decrease in MRSA (methicillin-resistant *Staphylococcus aureus*) surgical site infection rates within 15 months of implementing positive deviance training practices (Singhal and Greiner 2007). Jerry Zuckerman, MD, noted: "A true cultural transformation has occurred from within, with support from leadership that demonstrated faith in its people, which manifests in a growing sense of ownership among staff and patients of the implementation of hundreds of small solutions" (Lloyd, Buscell, and Lindberg 2008). Positive deviance bridges the gap between what healthcare workers know and what they do. A surgical intensive care unit director commented, "What we're seeing is just a whole culture change. People really want to be part of a team. People who used to be very quiet are coming forward. This has let them bloom."

◆ *Structured dialogue* is a process that helps a group of practicing physicians articulate their collective *patient-centered* self-interest. For example, structured dialogue can help physicians improve physician–physician communication, understand more fully the complexity of hospital operations, and articulate clinical priorities for their communities. Unlike hospital-centric change efforts, the structured dialogue process is led by a medical advisory panel (MAP) of high-performing, well-respected clinicians, who review and recommend clinical priorities on the basis of presentations made by the major clinical sections and departments. The MAP's report contains a statement of the direction in which the hospital and medical staff should be heading, rather than a list of capital-intensive budget items. In return for giving physicians a say in clinical priority setting, the hospital is able to enlist physicians to attend meetings where the hospital can outline its priorities.

A CEO of a 400-bed northeastern hospital stated, "The MAP process works because, in the process of discovery, practicing physicians [whom the hospital does not employ] begin to think and act as owners." A West Coast nephrologist commented at the beginning of a structured dialogue process, "I never felt that any physician could really influence what a hospital was doing or where it was going. . . . I quipped that for this process to work, the hospital would have to undergo a cultural enema, in that decision-making processes and operations would have to become significantly more transparent, efficient, and timely for physicians to feel that their ideas mattered. . . . The reason for my change in behavior stems from the feeling that I am making time count and that we are truly making a difference."

◆ *Virtual gain-sharing* is a way for hospitals to share savings with physicians without violating the Stark laws. For years, administrators at a West Coast community teaching hospital tried unsuccessfully to negotiate with orthopedic surgeons to reduce the number of vendors and types of prostheses used in joint replacement surgery. Vendors bypassed hospital administrators to work directly with surgeons, leaving the hospital to pay the difference between the cost of the implant and the Medicare reimbursement. As a result of a presentation to the MAP, cardiologists [who had consolidated their vendors to two] and an orthopedist who was a member of the MAP prevailed on the other orthopedic surgeons to standardize their processes and consolidate vendors. All but one orthopedic surgeon agreed to a single vendor and unified operative approach, which saved the hospital approximately $1.2 million during the first year of the contract (Cohn and Allyn 2005). Hospital leaders shared some of the savings by purchasing a new fracture table and imaging system for the orthopedic surgery unit.

Minimizing the Battle Cry of Unnecessary Conflict

Conflict is inevitable in rapidly changing environments. Collaborative or healthy conflict raises interesting questions, provokes new lines of discovery, aids in understanding others' positions, and displays openness to new ideas (Roberto 2005). However, top-down strategies provoke skepticism, dismissed as flavor-of-the-month innovations that quickly fade out of favor. Physicians prefer to be inspired rather than supervised. Structured dialogue demonstrates that when physicians are treated like adults, they behave like adults. When physicians perceive that hospital leaders only pretend to invite their opinion, they may react with feelings of betrayal and anger. These reactions can impede subsequent efforts to collaborate. Hospital leaders should direct their dialogue to advisory groups of physicians that respect their time and are willing to create an action plan with deadlines and an accountable individual responsible for performance (Cohn 2009).

(continued)

In the long run, physicians are more receptive to adopting initiatives and making necessary process adjustments when they have a shared vision with hospital leaders than when confronted with, "We need to do more with less" or "Because of some unforeseen development, we need you to work harder." One physician dismissed such directives as, "We screwed up; now you need to work harder."

Discussion

The increased focus on population health in particular demands new partnerships, roles, and expectations to deliver high-quality, cost-effective care to the members of our communities. To smooth the way to hospital–medical staff collaboration, first, propose a compact or social contract that spells out expectations for both physicians and hospital leaders. Tracking the fulfillment of these expectations increases transparency and builds, or rebuilds, trust.

Second, provide meaningful data that support efforts to improve outcomes. Information is best shared frequently and across areas of responsibility rather than distributed within silos, to be used primarily in peer review battles.

Third, optimize physician performance by researching and adopting field-tested strategies, tactics, and tools that facilitate dialogue and treat physicians as valued partners. Occasionally, trusted outsiders may be brought in to help both parties gain perspective on the national and global economic trends—rather than any perceived local incompetence—that are causing many of their difficulties.

Conclusion

Although complete alignment between physicians and hospital leaders may be difficult to attain, authentic engagement can improve clinical and financial outcomes for both groups. A virtuous cycle of increased collaboration, increased revenues, decreased expenses, and improved patient outcomes facilitates heightened recruitment and retention and culminates in outstanding processes that lead to the provision of cost-effective, coordinated care.

CHALLENGES OF COLLABORATING ON PERFORMANCE ISSUES

As demonstrated in this chapter, trust, culture, and communication are necessary ingredients for launching and managing a solid performance management feedback program. But skill, perseverance, and patience are needed to overcome particular challenges. The following paragraphs discuss such challenges and the efforts required to meet them.

Challenge 1: Chronic Noncompliance

Physicians may exhibit chronic noncompliance related to clinical, quality, safety, service, administrative, legal, regulatory, or accreditation issues. The typical road-block to overcome is the practitioner's defense of independence and autonomy under a guise of patient safety. When leaders deal with noncompliance superficially, by addressing the manifestations of the problem rather than its root cause, patients may get caught in the cross fire: A practitioner fails to respond while on call. A member of the medical staff does not provide adequate documentation so that peers can effectively manage her patients after hours. A physician refuses to follow evidence-based protocols or pathways. A privileged member of the staff does not adhere to medical staff bylaws or rules and regulations. These issues must be addressed in a timely and effective way before patients get hurt and the credibility and integrity of physician leadership are questioned.

Adequate Reason

Certainly, the mechanism for addressing noncompliance must be embedded in the performance management system, often through a rule-based indicator, as described in Chapter 7, so the physician understands that the medical staff considers this to be of importance and not "merely" a management concern. However, the most important step is to gain the offending physician's buy-in for the modification by bringing her to understand why her noncompliance is a problem and why she must modify her approach or behavior. It is important to impress on her that correcting her noncompliance issue will better serve her interests.

Charles Dwyer (1992), in presenting his American College of Physician Executives (now American Association for Physician Leadership) course entitled "Power and Influence," said, "Never ask anyone to engage in behavior that serves your interests until you have given that individual adequate reason to do so."

Demonstrating adequate reason affords a strong and single-minded individual the perspective to consider a revised course of conduct.

The approach should be customized to reflect where the practitioner sits on Maslow's (1943) hierarchy of needs. Some practitioners react positively to clinical data showing poor performance, recognizing the need to do their best for the patient. Others respond to concerns that their perceived standing on the medical staff will be compromised. Still others only pay attention to warnings when their personal security and professional standing are threatened. Thus, *adequate reason* means that which is important and influential to a specific individual; it is not a generic approach that works effectively with everyone.

The reason for compliance must resonate with the physician. Hence, it is important to explore those factors that carry genuine value to the physician to know how to proceed. One physician responded effectively to chronic medical records incompletion when he was asked if he was billing for care in which the documentation was incomplete. When he realized that this was a fraud and abuse issue under the False Claims Act, he understood that it was in his personal self-interest—independent of the interests of the hospital—to complete the records.

Examples of adequate reason in terms of a practitioner's position on Maslow's hierarchy of needs are found in Exhibit 9.1.

Exhibit 9.1: Customizing Noncompliance Feedback to Maslow's Hierarchy of Needs: Examples

Evidence-based medicine, patient safety, service excellence, superior outcomes, pride in one's work, personal achievement, self-fulfillment

Perception of colleagues and peers; professional standing and reputation; leadership role on the medical staff; respect of management, staff, and board

Adverse clinical outcomes and patient safety events; patient complaints and liability; loss of referrals; potential loss of membership and privileges; potential loss of professional status and security; potential loss of family, friends, and colleagues

---

Pick Your Issues Wisely

Of course, as with any feedback activity, leaders need to determine which compliance protocols to enforce and which might be left alone. The following paragraphs provide guidelines for making these determinations.

Enforce issues that matter. Not every issue is equally important. At one organization, the leadership tried to convince a highly generative neurosurgeon—her gross revenue stream in this particular year was $4.8 million—to complete her medical records. She claimed she was far too busy taking care of her patients to focus on administrative details. A thoughtful executive offered to hire a nurse practitioner to assist the neurosurgeon on rounds and handle her administrative responsibilities. The neurosurgeon gladly accepted, and management was rewarded with an appreciative and energetic neurosurgeon who increased her productivity to $5.4 million. In addition, the medical records were up to date and far more complete, which significantly improved the organization's revenue cycle performance for that physician. Frequently, a systemic solution can end an unnecessary and nonproductive conflict to the satisfaction of both parties.

Prioritize compliance issues. With myriad compliance issues to contend with, leaders find it helpful to prioritize the issues in terms of which can be managed (as in the example above), which require an urgent solution, and which simply must be enforced (e.g., "red rules"). The easiest approach is to hardwire a solution into the operational system or process. A common example is the often uneven process of dating, timing, and validating physician orders. This activity can be automated through the implementation of a computerized provider order entry system. As with the concept of picking issues that matter, noncompliance may be seen as an opportunity to address a systemwide problem manifested by noncompliance.

When intervention is necessary, get everyone on board first. Say a practitioner consistently fails to respond when on call. A useful first step is to facilitate a discussion of on-call professional standards of conduct and performance at the medical staff level. Then the medical staff can create a rule-based indicator and targets with specific consequences for each validated incident of noncompliance so that each individual practitioner is responsible for the consequences that ensue. This approach takes the pressure off physician leaders to address noncompliance without the benefit of a process and sends a clear peer-to-peer message on the importance of this specific issue to the staff.

Remember your BATNA, or "plan B" fallback plan. On rare occasions, persistent noncompliance is so significant that it must be addressed, up to and including some form of corrective action. One example of significant noncompliance is chronic falsification of medical records to support up-coding. Falsifying records carries financial and clinical integrity concerns as well as potential legal action under the

False Claims Act, which may put the entire organization at risk. Leadership has no choice but to provide corrective feedback in these situations and, if necessary, take some form of definitive action to help the physician understand the serious nature of her missteps.

Challenge 2: Chronic Behavioral Issues

Behavior in the care environment that was once tolerated is no longer acceptable. Unfortunately, in the waning days of fee-for-service reimbursement, some healthcare organizations continue to enable chronic behavior violators. The good news is that they are becoming fewer every year with the shift in reimbursement methodology and organizations' attitudes regarding culture and its impact on performance.

As a rule, physicians who exhibit egregious behaviors (e.g., aggravated battery, rape) are dealt with expeditiously and definitively. However, a select few chronic offenders have the technical competence and sense of entitlement to take advantage of management's and physician leadership's weakness. Addressing the behavior of these individuals requires an assertive and well-defined process to (1) assess them for undiagnosed and potentially treatable impairments and (2) restrict the offending behavior.

David Marx, CEO of Outcome Engenuity and creator of the just-culture concept, advocates balancing individual and systemic accountability by dividing human factors into three categories: human error, at-risk behavior, and reckless behavior. He recommends that managers attempt to correct negative behaviors according to the definitions outlined in the chart that follows (Marx 2014):

Human Factor Category	Management Approach
Human error	Rare or episodic offender
At-risk behavior	Chronic offender
Reckless behavior	Egregious offender

In this section, each category is explained in detail, followed by a discussion of the management approach recommended for that category.

Human Error
Human error is a product of our current healthcare system design as well as behavioral choices. It often arises at times of change in systemic and personal situations, processes, procedures, training, design, and environment.

Managing the rare and episodic offender: Most good practitioners have the rare bad day, which is often triggered or exacerbated by an unanticipated systemic failure. Rare and episodic offenders tend to have good insight into these occurrences and are fairly easy to manage in these situations. Approaching the feedback with sincere consolation, a search into the causality of the systemic failure, a blameless apology for the failure, and a search for cost-effective solutions generally suffices. It is important not to mislabel these practitioners as anything but good physicians who were unable to successfully adapt to a systemic problem at a single moment in time.

At-Risk Behavior

At-risk behavior is an act performed when the offender believes that any risk associated with it is insignificant or justified.

Managing the chronic offender: A rule indicator should already be in place that sets a defined number of validated behavioral occurrences, moving the individual from a rare and episodic offender to a chronic offender. At-risk practitioners demonstrate a well-established pattern of dysfunctional behavioral choices that have an adverse impact on the environment of care.

Chronic offenders should be managed by removing the incentives that enable at-risk behavior and introducing incentives that promote healthy behaviors (thereby increasing situational awareness). The overarching approach is to assess, diagnose, rehabilitate, and retrain these individuals in terms of their impact on patient care, the care delivery environment, communications, and the standing of the practitioner on the medical staff.

This process can begin with a referral of the chronic offender to a behavioral event review committee (BERC). This ad hoc committee is made up of behavioral experts (e.g., psychiatrists, psychologists, psychiatric social workers, addiction specialists, primary care practitioners with special training) who are skilled at assessing, diagnosing, and treating behavioral issues. As part of this process, the BERC should determine whether the individual suffers from a potential impairment (e.g., depression, bipolar disorder, chronic addiction) that may require further evaluation by the medical staff wellness, health, or advocacy committee. It also should assess the need for a fitness-for-work evaluation to discover any psychiatric, cognitive, physical, or organic issue that would preclude the practitioner from exercising his clinical privileges safely. (See Chapter 4 for a detailed discussion of impairment and fitness-for-work concerns.)

Once a diagnosis is made, the medical staff leadership and practitioner work together to develop a behavioral contract and improvement plan to address the issue. It should include measurable goals and objectives, a defined time frame for improvement, established accountabilities, and the positive and negative

consequences of the outcome. Ideally, no progressive discipline is needed if the practitioner is willing to assume responsibility for the behavioral pattern, demonstrate
sufficient insight into the consequences of the behavior, and indicate a willingness
to work with physician leadership to adapt and successfully modify the behavior.
Of course, a small number of physicians may require progressive discipline, up to
and including corrective action or reduction in membership or privileges, if these
measures prove ineffective.

Reckless Behavior

Reckless behavior is characterized by a person's conscious disregard for substantial and unjustified risk. Examples of this type of misconduct include aggravated
battery, rape, endangerment of self or others, having a patient encounter while
intoxicated, or any action that places patients and the patient care environment in
imminent danger.

Managing the egregious offender: Reckless behavior is an immediate concern and
must be addressed with urgency. Egregious offenders are primarily managed with
remedial and punitive action (Marx 2014)—correcting the behavior and facing
punishment exhibiting that behavior. Such a significant response must move along a
clearly defined chain of command—up to and including the chair of the governing
board, along with legal counsel—in a carefully rehearsed and constructed manner.
This process is discussed in Chapter 10; suffice to say here that the offending individual's exit from the organization—if that is the outcome—needs to be managed
in a fair and legally defensible manner.

Challenge 3: Potpourri

A number of other commonly encountered performance issues may require feedback or corrective action. They include the following:

◆ Disruptive competition in violation of corporate or governance conflict-of-
   interest policies
◆ Disruptive conflict and political factionalism meant to undermine leadership
   and detract from its initiatives
◆ Chronic fraud and abuse issues (e.g., up-coding, fictitious documentation)
◆ Chronic safety issues (e.g., poor communication, poorly executed hand-offs,
   unwillingness to work in a team)
◆ Chronic obstructionism (e.g., blocking important quality and safety initiatives
   to demonstrate political clout or autonomy)

SUMMARY

Addressing performance issues requires a customized approach based on the practitioner's level of understanding and progression along the spectrum of Maslow's hierarchy of needs. Framing the practitioner's understanding of the "why" from the perspective of respected colleagues is crucial to a successful outcome. Failure to address these issues in an effective and timely way can lead to poor patient care outcomes; a stagnant, undermining culture; and an expensive and politically divisive corrective action process. That process is covered in detail in the next chapter.

REFERENCES

Advisory Board Company. 2007. "Achieving Breakthrough Engagement: Lessons from High Performing Organizations." Washington, DC: Advisory Board Company.

Centers for Medicare & Medicaid Services (CMS). 2013. "Conditions of Participation Survey Procedures." §482.22(b). Baltimore, MD: CMS.

Cohn, K. H. 2009. "Changing Physician Behavior Through Involvement and Collaboration." *Journal of Healthcare Management* 54 (2): 80–86.

Cohn, K. H., and T. R. Allyn. 2005. "Making Hospital-Physician Collaboration Work." *Healthcare Financial Management* 59 (10): 102–8.

Cohn, K. H., and M. J. Lambert. 2005. "Engaging Physicians in Hospital Operations." In *Better Communication for Better Care: Mastering Physician-Administrator Collaboration*, by K. H. Cohn, 46–51. Chicago: Health Administration Press.

Cohn, K. H., and M. E. Peetz. 2003. "Surgeon Frustration: Contemporary Problems, Practical Solutions." *Contemporary Surgery* 59 (2): 76–85.

Cohn, K. H., D. Thieme, and A. Feldman. 2006. "Taking a Proactive, Collaborative Approach to Malpractice Issues." In *Collaborate for Success: Breakthrough Strategies for Engaging Physicians, Nurses, and Hospital Executives,* by K. H. Cohn, 119. Chicago: Health Administration Press.

Daugird, A., and D. Spencer. 1996. "Physician Reactions to the Health Care Revolution. A Grief Model Approach." *Archives of Family Medicine* 5 (9): 497–500.

Dwyer, C. E. 1992. *The Shifting Sources of Power and Influence.* Tampa, FL: American Association for Physician Leadership.

Joint Commission. 2013. "Rationale for LD.03.01.01." In *2013 Hospital Accreditation Standards.* Oakbrook Terrace, IL: Joint Commission.

———. 2008. "Behaviors That Undermine a Culture of Safety." *Sentinel Event Alert,* Issue 40. Published July 9. www.jointcommission.org/assets/1/18/SEA_40.PDF.

Lloyd, J., P. Buscell, and C. Lindberg. 2008. "Staff-Driven Cultural Transformation Diminishes MRSA." *Prevention Strategist,* Spring issue. Accessed December 20. www.positivedeviance.org/pdf/publications/staff%20driven%20cultural%20transformation%20diminishes%20MRSA.pdf.

Marx, D. 2014. "Getting to Know Just Culture." Published February 18. https://www.justculture.org/getting-to-know-just-culture/.

Maslow, A. H. 1943. "A Theory of Human Motivation." *Psychological Review* 50: 370–96.

Roberto, M. A. 2005. *Why Great Leaders Don't Take Yes for an Answer: Managing for Conflict and Consensus.* Upper Saddle River, NJ: FT Press.

Singhal, A., and K. Greiner. 2007. "'When the Task Is Accomplished, Can We Say We Did It Ourselves?' A Quest to Eliminate MRSA at the Veterans Health Administration's Hospitals in Pittsburgh." Accessed December 19, 2008. www.lean.org/FuseTalk/Forum/Attachments/Positive%20Deviance%20Pittsburgh%20VA%20MRSA%200709041.pdf.

Studer, Q. 2004. *Hardwiring Excellence: Purpose, Worthwhile Work, Making a Difference.* Gulf Breeze, FL: Fire Starter Publishing.

Studer Group. 2008. "The Impact of Low Patient Satisfaction Scores on Staff Turnover and Patient Outcomes." Gulf Breeze, FL: Studer Group.

White, D., and J. Burroughs. 2010. *A Practical Guide to Managing Disruptive and Impaired Physicians.* Danvers, MA: HCPro.

Zolnierek, K. B., and M. R. Dimatteo. 2009. "Physician Communication and Adherence to Treatment: A Meta-analysis." *Medical Care* 47 (8): 826–34.

CHAPTER 10

Taking Corrective Action

Imminent Danger . . . Danger exists that could reasonably [be] expected to cause death or other serious physical harm immediately or before the imminence of such danger can be eliminated.

—Section 13: Procedures to Counteract Imminent Dangers, Occupational Safety and Health Act of 1970

With the exception of rare and egregious adverse events, actions to correct performance or behavioral issues are not likely to include reduction of membership or privileges. If the medical staff's performance management system works properly, constructive improvement plans are all that should be required.

The Ritz-Carlton Hotel Company considers the termination of an employee to be a human resource sentinel event. Leadership performs a root cause analysis to determine how its performance management system failed so that it can be immediately corrected to maintain a more positive and proactive performance management culture.

Many medical staffs that undergo the corrective action process—with its attendant costly and politically divisive fair or judicial hearing, appellate review, and civil litigation—can avoid it completely by placing greater emphasis on its performance management process.

Exhibit 10.1 reviews the key components of a medical staff performance management system and the most likely sources of failure for each step.

NEED FOR CORRECTIVE ACTION

Patient harm caused by a breach of safety barriers cannot be permitted. Leaders must act when such penetrations occur, even when it is difficult or politically

Exhibit 10.1: Medical Staff Performance Management System Steps and Likely Sources of Error

1. *Strategic medical staff development planning*—lack of attention to key competence and noncompetence (or economic) credentialing and privileging criteria
2. *Credentialing and privileging*—lax application of credentialing and privileging criteria or enablement of chronic performance issues, particularly at reappointment
3. *Negotiating and establishing key performance expectations*—lack of medical staff buy-in to a culture of accountability; failure of physicians to recognize the authority of the organized medical staff to oversee and manage professional performance or to hold professional colleagues accountable
4. *Executing employment and professional services contracts*—lack of attention to or emphasis on specific performance expectations in contracts
5. *Negotiating and establishing performance metrics or indicators and targets*—lack of attention to key strategic performance issues when creating performance metrics or indicators and targets
6. *Offering timely and constructive feedback*—lack of performance improvement plans or contracts that are time-limited with specified accountabilities and consequences
7. *Managing chronic performance issues*—lack of accountabilities, time-limited consequences, or progressive discipline
8. *Taking corrective action*—absence of meaningful corrective action when an egregious action occurs or the entire performance management system has failed

---

contentious to do so. The litmus test of true leadership is whether a leader has the personal character and strength to do the right thing when that action is not in her self-interest or the immediate interest of the organization and community as a whole.

Health Care Quality Improvement Act

Most medical staff bylaws have a section that covers investigations, corrective actions, hearings, and an appeals plan, which outlines the process to follow in case corrective action is considered. This section of the bylaws is derived from the Health Care Quality Improvement Act of 1986 (HCQIA), which was informed by a legal case, *Patrick v. Burget et al.*—whose outcome had a devastating impact on the peer review process as it was practiced at the time—that was argued before the US Supreme Court in 1988 and resulted in the bankruptcy of the Astoria (Oregon) Clinic (see sidebar on page 213).

Patrick v. Burget et al. and the HCQIA

Timothy Patrick was a general surgeon in competition with the Astoria Clinic, located in Astoria, Oregon. He was known to perform high-risk surgeries only to abandon the cases postoperatively, turning them over to primary care physicians who did not feel qualified to manage critically ill patients. The result was a number of unnecessary deaths.

The Astoria Clinic sought to terminate Dr. Patrick's medical staff membership and privileges not through Columbia Memorial Hospital, also located in Astoria, where Dr. Patrick's membership and privileges originated, but through the clinic itself. Dr. Patrick sued the Astoria Clinic for alleged violations of the Sherman Antitrust Act, contending that the Astoria physicians used the peer review process to limit competition rather than improve the quality of care.

The Oregon Court of Appeals sided with the Astoria Clinic under Oregon's state-action doctrine, which granted physicians state-level prosecutorial immunity to perform peer review. However, the US Supreme Court disagreed, ruling that the state did not actively supervise the peer review process to prevent potential abuses and thus it did not meet the federal government's active-supervision test for peer review immunity protections. The Supreme Court reversed the appellate court's decision, resulting in treble damages against the Astoria Clinic (*Patrick v. Burget et al.* 1988).

This case sent a chill throughout the country, and many medical staffs refused to perform peer review without the guarantee of immunity protections. In response, the US Congress passed the Health Care Quality Improvement Act of 1986, which provides healthcare entities with qualified federal immunity protections for conducting good-faith peer review if the resultant actions are taken

1. in the reasonable belief that it is in the furtherance of quality healthcare,
2. after a reasonable effort to obtain the facts of the matter,
3. after adequate notice and hearing procedures are afforded to a physician or dentist, and
4. in the reasonable belief that it was warranted by the facts after meeting the first three requirements.

These four criteria emphasize the importance of performing peer review and professional review activities in good faith, without malice, and in the best interests of patient care. Conflicts of interest should be disclosed, identified, and properly managed.

To be covered by the HCQIA in terms of prosecutorial immunity, organized medical staffs must take specific actions during peer review to address the clinical competence or professional conduct of a physician or dentist that affects, or could affect, the health or welfare of a patient or the patient care environment. To protect the public from incompetent physicians moving from state to state without detection, the HCQIA also created the National Practitioner Data Bank (NPDB), which requires a healthcare entity to report physicians or dentists whose practice or conduct may have an adverse impact on patient care if they have been

- suspended or terminated for more than 30 days (even if on a precautionary basis; see explanation later in this chapter),
- involuntarily restricted in their membership rights or clinical privileges, or
- permitted to resign while under, or in lieu of, a formal investigation.

A report to the NPDB triggers a practitioner's right to a fair or judicial hearing and appellate review by the governing body (as mentioned in an earlier chapter, restriction of membership or clinical privileges may not automatically trigger this right depending on bylaws language). Healthcare entities must query the NPDB at the time of medical staff appointment, reappointment, and consideration of new privileges for existing members.

Issues of licensure and certification actions of a licensing board, healthcare-related criminal convictions, and exclusions from federal or state healthcare programs arising from fraud or abuse convictions were traditionally reported to the Healthcare Integrity and Protection Data Bank. This organization merged with the NPDB, which, effective May 6, 2013, is responsible for all of these functions.

All of the deemed-status accrediting organizations require due process rights for physicians, dentists, and those approved by the medical staff and governing body as consistent with federal law. These rights are centered on the concept of a fair or judicial hearing and appeals process. Appendix 10.1, at the end of this chapter, provides excerpts from the US healthcare accrediting bodies for medical staff due process rights.

DUE PROCESS FOR TAKING CORRECTIVE ACTION

Three main steps are involved in taking corrective action in adherence to due process rights as mandated by the accrediting bodies: an investigation, a fair or judicial hearing, and an appellate review.

Nonphysician/Nondentist Due Process Rights

Interestingly, no federal requirements are in place to provide a fair hearing or appellate review for nonphysicians or nondentists. Any due process rights afforded to podiatrists, psychologists, advanced practice providers, and others serving on the medical staff are at the discretion of the medical staff and governing body. The healthcare entity is responsible for reporting nonphysician/nondentist members of the medical staff to the NPDB under circumstances similar to those described in this section for physicians and dentists. Issues that do not directly lead to involuntary reduction in membership rights or clinical privileges do *not* require reporting to the NPDB. These include letters of reprimand; probation; monitoring; proctoring; continuing education; leaves of absence; and voluntary relinquishment of membership rights or privileges or administrative/automatic suspensions due to failure to meet bylaws obligations, such as professional or Drug Enforcement Agency registration, board certification, liability coverage, and medical records completion.

Conduct an Investigation

An investigation should be initiated by the medical executive committee (MEC) to determine if sufficient evidence exists to recommend some form of corrective action to the governing board. The MEC should draft a formal resolution to make clear to the practitioner and the organization that an investigation has begun. This is an important step in terms of the HCQIA; if the practitioner resigns any of her membership rights or clinical privileges while under or in lieu of an investigation, a report must be made to the NPDB, which triggers procedural rights (i.e., a fair or judicial hearing and an appellate review).

The formal resolution leads to a certified letter (return receipt requested) being sent to the practitioner involved that informs her of the investigation, the need for her participation, and the legal consequences of taking any form of voluntary reduction in membership rights or clinical privileges during the investigatory process.

An ad hoc investigation committee of five to seven members is usually appointed, which includes an expert representative from the relevant clinical specialty, to evaluate the practitioner's current clinical competence and professional

Many medical staffs use the term *investigation* in their bylaws, rules and regulations, and policies when they actually mean *look into* or *evaluate*. Similarly, they may indicate *corrective action* to mean *improve* or *correct*. This word usage may be problematic from a legal perspective. It is best to use *investigation* or *corrective action* when intended, to be consistent with the legal connotations deriving from HCQIA to avoid an unnecessary report to the NPDB.

conduct. In a small organization, it may be best to invite an outside peer from the same clinical specialty to participate if any concern arises regarding the perception of conflict or conflict of interest. The committee should review all relevant information, including the following:

- Ongoing professional practice evaluation data
- Focused professional practice evaluation data
- Reports from peers or proctors
- Appointment and reappointment files
- Relevant complaints or reports
- Relevant legal claims, actions, or settlements
- Eyewitness reports
- Reviews by the direct supervisor (e.g., medical director, department chair) and administrative liaisons (e.g., nurse managers, vice president for medical affairs [VPMA] or chief medical officer [CMO], chief nursing officer)
- External reviews by licensure bodies or agencies
- Internal or external peer review reports
- Interview with the practitioner under investigation

The interview by the investigatory committee—which some medical staffs' bylaws inappropriately make optional—is particularly important, as it indicates the degree of insight or self-awareness that the practitioner has into her performance issues, which informs the committee as to the practitioner's potential for improvement and ongoing accountability. A medical staff physician who openly acknowledges chronic performance issues leads to a more optimistic appraisal, whereas total denial of responsibility and accountability yields the opposite.

Following its review of the materials listed earlier, the investigatory committee may request the practitioner undergo a fitness-for-work evaluation (see Chapter

4) if physician leadership is concerned that the performance issues have become secondary to some form of potential impairment.

On occasion, the investigatory committee may seek an external peer review analysis, particularly if

♦ litigation seems likely and the medical staff may require an expert witness to testify,
♦ the committee is divided and an outside opinion could help break the deadlock, or
♦ either no one on the medical staff has the requisite technical skills to evaluate the care provided or those who are available are direct economic competitors with an irreconcilable conflict of interest.

Once the investigation is completed, the ad hoc investigatory committee should provide the MEC with its recommendations, along with documentation of fact finding to support its conclusions. It should not be permissible for the committee to conclude "no opinion" or an "inconclusive" determination, as the governing body relies on this committee and the MEC to determine whether or not a practitioner may safely exercise the clinical privileges delineated. The MEC may either concur or disagree with the committee's recommendations; however, the board is entitled to a definitive opinion as to whether or not corrective action is warranted based on the findings of fact presented.

If some form of corrective action is recommended by the MEC, the practitioner in question is entitled to either a fair or judicial hearing with an appellate review by the board (if a physician or dentist) or procedural rights as authorized by the medical staff bylaws. For nonphysicians and nondentists, these procedural rights might be set out in a two-step process that may include a review by the MEC with the opportunity for the practitioner to appeal this review to executive management or the board.

In some states (e.g., Oregon), the organization is obligated to report any professional review action to the state licensing body for independent review and analysis, even if the corrective action is less than 30 days' duration (Oregon Medical Board 2014).

Precautionary Suspension or Restriction

If physician leaders perceive that a practitioner has a clinical competence or conduct issue posing an imminent danger, whether to specific patients or the patient care environment, they may decide to institute a precautionary suspension of that practitioner's membership rights and privileges or a restriction of specific privileges.

Generally, the president of the medical staff, the VPMA or CMO, the CEO, or the chair of the board may act as a designated agent of the governing body to do so. It is important that this action not be taken by a perceived direct economic competitor so that no appearance of conflict of interest will be raised during procedural rights or a civil litigation later on.

Some states permit an administrative "time-out" of less than 14 days without triggering the reporting requirement or loss of federal immunity under the HCQIA. If applicable and appropriate, it may be used to protect patients, emphasize the importance of the performance issues to the practitioner, and avoid unnecessarily triggering any form of procedural rights.

As soon as feasible, the MEC should meet with the practitioner to confidentially convey the rationale for the chosen action, assist the medical staff in reassigning the practitioner's patients, and work with management and the board to resolve the matter in a timely and efficacious way in the best interests of good patient care.

As an aside, some medical staff bylaws claim that neither a precautionary suspension nor the suspension of a practitioner granted temporary privileges triggers procedural rights. These claims result from misconceptions and should be discussed with legal counsel skilled in healthcare issues.

Conduct a Fair or Judicial Hearing

Once procedural rights are triggered, the practitioner in question is notified by certified mail (return receipt), usually by the CEO acting on behalf of the governing body, of her right to request a fair or judicial hearing. The practitioner typically has 30 days from notification to either request or waive her hearing rights. If a hearing is requested, the CEO, upon consultation with the president of the medical staff, arranges for the following:

1. The time, date, and location of the hearing
2. A proposed list of witnesses
3. Findings of fact that triggered the corrective action
4. The organization of the hearing panel

A fair or judicial hearing panel can be organized in several different ways. The following paragraphs highlight two formats: a hearing panel that includes a chairperson or presiding officer, and a single hearing officer.

Hearing Panel

The hearing panel is generally made up of between three and seven physicians, none of whom may be direct economic competitors. Depending on the performance issues, it may or may not be necessary for the hearing panel members to practice in the same clinical specialty. Employment at the organization itself does not exclude physicians from serving on the panel, so potential conflicts of interest should be anticipated and managed proactively. Panel members should commit to being present for the entire hearing (some medical staffs do not require this) to preserve the integrity of the process and ensure a fair decision.

The chairperson of the panel may either be assigned by the CEO and president of the medical staff or voted by other panel members and is responsible, with support from legal counsel, for ensuring that the process is conducted according to the bylaws. In lieu of a chairperson, the organization may assign a presiding officer, typically an attorney skilled in such matters who can oversee and manage the hearing, ensure a fair process, maintain decorum, and participate in questioning but not vote or serve as an advocate for either side. (Neither the legal counsel for the organization nor the legal counsel for the medical staff should serve in this role to avoid inevitable conflicts of interest.)

Hearing Officer

Some organizations appoint a hearing officer in lieu of a hearing panel. The individual selected is an attorney or other individual trained in managing fair or judicial hearings, who orchestrates the entire hearing process, including the examination and cross-examination of witnesses, and makes a final determination and recommendation to the MEC. This person may not advocate for any party involved and may not be a direct competitor of the practitioner. (Again, the legal counsel for the medical staff, the hospital, or the healthcare system should not serve as a hearing officer.)

A best practice is to conduct a pre-hearing conference prior to the regular hearing, at which time all parties may convene to resolve procedural questions, selection of potential witnesses, questions surrounding evidence or findings of fact, and the role that attorneys for either side will play. Generally, attorneys should function in a supportive role, as fair or judicial hearings are considered collegial functions and not subject to formal legal rules of evidence or procedure.

The hearing consists of the following activities:

- Examination and cross-examination of witnesses
- Introduction of evidence and exhibits (e.g., findings of fact)
- Representation of both sides by counsel

◆ Submission of a written statement (or post-hearing memorandum) at the conclusion of the hearing

The burden of proof is typically on the practitioner to demonstrate with a preponderance of evidence (>50 percent) or in a clear and convincing (>75 percent) way, where the burden-of-proof categories are

1. beyond a reasonable doubt (criminal cases) (>99 percent of evidence),
2. clear and convincing (civil cases) (>75 percent of evidence),
3. preponderance of evidence (civil cases) (>50 percent of evidence), and
4. arbitrary and capricious (civil cases) (<5 percent of evidence; the court must follow due process in arriving at this decision).

With a preponderance of evidence or evidence that is presented in a clear and convincing way, the findings of fact do not support the decision to take corrective action. The burden of proof is generally not arbitrary and capricious, as it would only require the MEC to prove it did not act in malice or bad faith, despite any lack of viable evidence or findings or fact, or beyond a reasonable doubt (>99 percent), which is the typical standard in criminal cases.

The HCQIA requires that the fair or judicial hearing be recorded (typically by a court reporter), and good legal practice provides that witnesses be sequestered prior to, during, and immediately following the hearing to avoid potential conflicts and conflicts of interest.

Once both sides have concluded the presentation of their position, the hearing panel or hearing officer makes a final determination and recommendation to the MEC within three weeks. The MEC may either agree or disagree with the findings in its final recommendation to the governing board.

Conduct an Appellate Review

Either the practitioner in question or the MEC may appeal the hearing panel's or officer's decision to the board within a prescribed period of time (e.g., two weeks). Generally, an appeal is made if either party does not believe the hearing's decision was based on or supported by the following:

◆ Prescribed procedure or intent outlined in the medical staff bylaws
◆ Findings of fact or other evidence presented
◆ Desire of the medical staff to support a fair and unbiased hearing

The review is organized by the chairperson of the board with support from the CEO and legal counsel. It may be conducted by a review panel of three or more board members or by the entire board under the leadership of the chair.

Generally, no new evidence or findings of fact are reviewed by the board unless the party introducing them can demonstrate that they were unavailable or failed to be reviewed during the original hearing. The appeals process is shorter than the hearing, usually a matter of several hours. During this time, each party makes a formal presentation to the panel or the board, with time allotted for questions and discussion, followed by a summation by each party. The board may permit witnesses to testify for either side and to be questioned by members of the board. The board or appeals panel may affirm, modify, or reverse the decision recommended by the hearing panel or officer or by the MEC, and a decision by the full board is final.

James Hogan, Esq., healthcare legal counsel with Hall, Render, Killian, and Lyman PC, describes some of the legal nuances of managing an investigation and a fair/judicial hearing.

Legal Issues to Avoid When Conducting an Investigation and a Fair Hearing
Practical considerations arise in both the investigative and hearing aspects of peer review processes. In the investigative phase, three questions frequently arise.

First, there is no legal prohibition limiting competitor participation in the investigation of a fellow physician. In determining how to proceed, bear in mind that the goal is to obtain qualified, knowledgeable opinions to inform the process. Therefore, peer review investigations frequently include participation by potential competitors, as they are the most accessible source for qualified opinions on the issues under review. As long as the participating physicians commit to remaining objective, they may be included in the process. Alternatively, an organization may retain an independent, outside expert opinion. The trade-off for the potential for increased objectivity is the additional time and expense involved in obtaining that opinion. If the reviewers are on the medical staff, it could be argued that they are competitors and biased. If they are outside experts from a large academic medical center, the argument could be made that the reviewer lacks familiarity with local practices and expectations. In either approach, the focus should be on retaining reasonably qualified physicians to provide an accurate, objective assessment.

(continued)

A second issue is which cases, and how many of them, should be reviewed. In some cases, the need for a quick response results in only problematic cases being reviewed. The affected physician may then argue that the cases were cherry-picked to present him in the most negative light. If a larger sample is used, the physician may argue that the overall percentage of significant issues is relatively low. To address these concerns, case selection should be guided by the objective of the investigative process: obtain the best, most well-informed opinion given the relevant facts and circumstances.

Third, many medical staff bylaws are silent as to when affected physicians should be notified of an investigation. There is no reason not to inform them sooner versus later. Additionally, the affected physician is not entitled to participate in all of the investigative proceedings. It is appropriate and consistent with the goal of ensuring the reviewers have complete information for the investigative body to meet with the affected practitioner before proceeding to a recommendation on corrective or adverse action.

Once hearing rights accrue, a number of additional considerations must be weighed. For example, there is no right to discovery under the HCQIA. The affected physician cannot depose witnesses, compel production of documents, or take other procedural actions unless such rights are provided under the medical staff bylaws or state law. Further, the federal law does not afford the practitioner the right to participate in selection of the hearing committee members. That right usually rests solely with the organization. However, the affected physician should be given the chance to object to a member(s) on the basis of economic competition or bias. Unlike the investigative phase, here the affected physician has the right to expect actual competitors to be excluded from service on the hearing committee.

Medical staff counsel frequently recommends use of a pre-hearing agreement with the affected physician. This document identifies in advance how certain procedural issues will be addressed, including the following:

◆ Which side has the burden of proof
◆ How discovery rights, if any, are defined
◆ Which side goes first
◆ The practitioner's opportunity to object to hearing committee members
◆ The basis for objections to evidence or witnesses
◆ The proper role of attorneys in the fair and judicial hearing process

The more of these issues that can be resolved prior to the hearing, the more efficient the proceeding will be. To reduce the likelihood of disputes over these issues, best practice is to ensure they are also affirmatively addressed in the medical staff bylaws. That way, the pre-hearing agreement is merely summarizing the processes already stated there.

The overarching goal of the peer review investigative and hearing process is to ensure that when all is said and done, the medical staff, the hospital, and the participants qualify for immunity under state and federal law. As noted in the HCQIA, to accomplish that goal, peer review actions, including investigations and hearings, must be taken

1. in the reasonable belief that the action was in the furtherance of quality healthcare,
2. after a reasonable effort to obtain the facts of the matter,
3. after adequate notice and hearing procedures are afforded to the physician involved or after such other procedures as are fair to the physician under the circumstances, and
4. in the reasonable belief that the action was warranted by the facts known after such reasonable effort to obtain facts and after meeting the requirement of paragraph 3.

Hospital legal counsel can be invaluable in helping structure the process to satisfy these requirements. In summary, following the medical staff bylaws, the requirements of HCQIA, and applicable state law, as well as focusing on obtaining accurate, objective, and complete information at every stage of the process, provides the greatest comfort that all participants will qualify for relative immunity and result in a well-informed and fair decision.

Once a final determination is made, the results are communicated to the CEO, the MEC, and the practitioner in question. If the determination is adverse to the practitioner, a report is filed with the NPDB, the state licensing body, and any third party determined by state law, licensure, or contract agreement.

REFLECTIONS ON CORRECTIVE ACTION

Although the procedures discussed in this chapter are fair, they are contentious, politically divisive, and expensive to stage. The average fair or judicial hearing and appellate review can easily cost more than $500,000, and many run into the millions. In addition, leadership is not permitted to speak freely with physicians, staff, and the public regarding the performance issues in question due to peer review confidentiality protections, whereas the practitioner in question may say whatever he chooses. This rule often creates political factionalism and division within the organization and the community, actions that do not support the community's trust or the protection of patients (which is the intent of the corrective action process).

As a result, 90 percent or more of serious performance management issues are resolved through some form of legal settlement to eliminate the performance issue from the organization and avoid triggering procedural rights. Although this use of settlements avoids the issues described in the paragraph above, it may also raise moral or ethical concerns as practitioners of questionable competence or conduct may be permitted to slip away, only to appear at another organization to place other patients at potential risk.

SUMMARY

At times, physician leadership, management, and the board feel strongly that a potential risk to the public is greater than the economic and political hardships to be endured by the organization and that federal and state reports are indicated and necessary to protect patients from potential harm. This decision should be made thoughtfully and collaboratively.

Either way, every effort should be made to address performance issues early in a supportive and collegial way to avoid the procedures outlined in this chapter in all but the most egregious and unavoidable circumstances so that (1) the public can be protected and (2) only practitioners who are truly able to practice competently and professionally are permitted access to the organization and its medical staff.

REFERENCES AND ADDITIONAL RESOURCES

Center for Improvement in Healthcare Quality (CIHQ). 2013. *Accreditation Standards for Acute Care Hospitals,* MS-8. Round Rock, TX: CIHQ.

DNV Healthcare. 2008. *National Integrated Accreditation for Healthcare Organizations,* 7th revision, MS.14. Cincinnati, OH: DNV Healthcare.

Healthcare Facilities Accreditation Program (HFAP). 2009. *Accreditation Requirements for Acute Care Facilities,* Standard 03.01.22. Chicago: HFAP.

Joint Commission. 2014. *2014 Hospital Accreditation Standards,* MS.10.01.01. Oakbrook Terrace, IL: Joint Commission.

Oregon Medical Board. 2014. "Rights, Regulations, & Responsibilities: A Handbook for Physicians Practicing Medicine in Oregon." Published in January. http://www.oregon.gov/omb/licensing/Documents/mddodpm /mddo-physicianshandbook.pdf.

Timothy A. Patrick v. William M. Burget et al., 108 S. Ct. 1658 and 486 U.S. 94 (1988).

APPENDIX 10.1: EXCERPTS OF ACCREDITATION REQUIREMENTS FOR MEDICAL STAFF DUE PROCESS RIGHTS

The Joint Commission (2014):

The organized medical staff has developed a fair hearing and appeal process addressing quality of care issues that has the following characteristics:

- Is designed to provide a fair process
- Has a mechanism to schedule a hearing of such requests
- Has identified the procedures for the hearing
- Identifies the composition of an impartial hearing committee of peers
- With the governing body, provides a mechanism to appeal adverse decisions as provided in the medical staff bylaws

Healthcare Facilities Accreditation Program (2009):

The hospital must have a fair hearing plan for medical staff members and allied health practitioners (AHPs). The process may be different for AHPs and medical staff members, and the hospital may choose to include or exclude AHPs from access to the mechanism. Those involved in the peer review activities shall not have an economic interest in or a conflict of interest with the subject of the peer review activity. Excluded individuals include those with blood relationships, employer/employee relationships, or other potential conflicts that might prevent the individual from giving an impartial assessment, or that may give the appearance of bias for or against the subject of the peer review. The fair hearing process outlines the circumstances under which a practitioner may request (or waive) this mechanism.

DNV Healthcare (2008):

The medical staff bylaws shall provide a mechanism for management of medical staff corrective or rehabilitative action. This documented action may result from unprofessional demeanor and conduct and/or this behavior is likely to be detrimental to patient safety or the delivery of quality care or is disruptive to organization operations. Any officer of the medical staff, the CEO, or any officer of the board may initiate this corrective or rehabilitative action.

Center for Improvement in Healthcare Quality (2013):

Fair Hearing Process:

The medical staff must develop and implement a fair hearing and appeal process to address any adverse decisions regarding appointment, reappointment, denial, reduction, suspension, or revocation of privileges to a practitioner.

Note: The medical staff and the organization are given latitude to develop and implement this process. The standard is not prescriptive as to how the fair hearing and appeals process is constructed.

A. The fair hearing and appeal process must assure that the safety of patients and the quality of care rendered by the practitioner is not adversely affected.

B. The fair hearing and appeal process must conform to any State law and regulation.

C. The fair hearing and appeal process is made available to any practitioner who is a member of the medical staff or has been granted clinical privileges (with the exception of temporary privileges).

CHAPTER 11

Effective Models of Medical Staff Integration and Alignment

A chief operating officer was planning to work with key physicians to reduce supply chain operating costs. When asked how aligned her medical staff was, she stated, "Not very. We have very independent physicians still holding onto their autonomy and professional independence." When asked how she intended to reduce supply chain costs with an unaligned staff, she responded, "We'll cross that bridge when we get there."

In order to achieve world-class quality, safety, service, and cost-effectiveness in healthcare delivery, complete integration and alignment of the medical staff, and each individual physician within it, must take place. It is impossible to standardize evidence-based practices, simplify operational processes, develop high service and performance standards, and work in a coordinated fashion with management and the board under a cottage industry model where each physician is given the opportunity to practice medicine according to his unique perspectives and needs. This would be equivalent to enabling each member of the senior management team to function within her unique organizational mission, vision, and strategic plan and expecting coordinated and high-performing results.

That is not to say that an organization can achieve outstanding results in a purely democratic and egalitarian system without visionary leadership. The magic occurs when visionary leadership meets a completely integrated and aligned organization in which each member embraces the vision in a deeply personal and committed way so that the end result is greater than the sum of the organization's parts.

The process to achieve integration and alignment is evolutionary.

Cultural alignment (the relationship) leads to economic alignment (the contract), which leads to clinical alignment (at-risk contract):

CULTURAL ALIGNMENT		ECONOMIC ALIGNMENT		CLINICAL ALIGNMENT

This chapter covers the steps to securing meaningful physician and medical staff integration and alignment. It includes examples of approaches that are being used by successful organizations.

CULTURAL INTEGRATION AND ALIGNMENT

Cultural integration and alignment is fundamental to any successful attempt to bring physicians into an organization in a coordinated and functional way. It answers the question: Will this individual be successful in this organization and be able to work harmoniously with other high-performing individuals? Interestingly, most organizations ignore this essential step completely and wonder why they struggle with unaligned and disruptive behavior. The answer lies in the traditional discounted fee-for-service model, in which the perceived need for revenue at any cost transcends quality. Often, highly generative physicians are tolerated even though

---

A Deeper Dive

Ways in Which Physician Integration and Alignment Efforts Fail

Many attempts to integrate and align physicians and the medical staff fail because an effective model of alignment is not followed. Some tactics that have proved unsuccessful are the following:

- Buy physicians' practices and employ the physicians without any form of partnership or alignment.
- Pay physicians for call coverage rather than addressing the failing business model of private practice or creating a more comprehensive alignment approach.
- Attempt a business venture with high-revenue-generating practitioners who are not interested in or capable of engaging in meaningful professional or business partnerships.
- Attempt to align with clinicians who are unwilling or unable to standardize their practice according to evidence-based approaches or learn new ways to provide cost-effective care.
- Attempt to treat physicians as "regular employees" because management is not able to share influence or authority.

they may have a significant adverse impact on quality and safety, communication, staff recruitment and retention, or the ability to grow and develop clinical services.

Disruptive behavior will not work in the new pay-for-value era, which requires physicians to work in an interdisciplinary and collaborative fashion to standardize evidence-based practices and thereby achieve high levels of quality, safety, and service.

Some elite healthcare organizations (e.g., Mayo Clinic, Cleveland Clinic) have taken cultural integration and alignment seriously by operating under a closed staff model, in which physicians are offered the opportunity to apply for medical staff membership or privileges by invitation only, with the requirement that they undergo a rigorous screening process to ensure that their skills, temperament, and values are consistent with those of the organization. Furthermore, once on staff, physicians are afforded no guarantee of tenure, and any physician whose approach or values are no longer consistent may be "invited" not to reapply without recourse to procedural rights or appeal.

Most organizations do not have the luxury of being as exclusive as those organizations. However, even small stand-alone hospitals will come to realize that keeping an open staff that welcomes all comers, regardless of temperament or organizational fit, is no longer a tenable strategy. The description of Hill Country Memorial Hospital's journey in Chapter 12 is illustrative of an organization with a poor culture that needed to greatly improve its performance by including cultural values and standards as a part of its criteria for membership and employment, leading to a significant initial staff turnover on its journey to excellence.

The best way to lay the foundation for this approach is through the strategic medical staff development planning process described in Chapter 2 or with physician relationship management (PRM) as discussed in Chapter 5.

Ken E. Mack, LFACHE, former president of Ken Mack and Associates, discusses the importance of addressing the engagement and alignment of self-employed physicians with their healthcare organizations.

Life Support
Although the majority of hospitals and health systems appear to be rapidly moving to physician employment as their preferred model of physician integration, supporting those physicians who wish to remain independent can bring many potential benefits.

Until we move on from the current discounted fee-for-service reimbursement model to a pay-for-performance model, the employment of physicians is not

(continued)

---

the panacea for managing and controlling physician performance. Managing a diverse group of physicians is complicated and can be expensive. As physician reimbursement continues to drop, the subsidy required to employ physicians can exceed $200,000 per physician per year.

A wide range of tactics that do not violate the Stark anti-kickback legislation can be used to aid physicians who desire to remain in private practice. The foundation for any monetary exchange is having a physician relations management program (see Chapter 5) to determine what can and should be done to assist these physicians. The key to a PRM program that meets the needs of independent physicians is ongoing communications. Assign each physician to an account manager—a member of the hospital's management team who is responsible for guiding the physician through the PRM process. The account manager ensures that the physician and organization maintain meaningful communications by making quarterly visits to the physician's office.

Goals to work toward when implementing a PRM program include improved communication, efficient and effective problem solving, and an ongoing commitment to identify ways to partner with physicians in mutually beneficial ways. The more beneficial the program is to the physicians, the greater is the likelihood that they will remain in private practice and support the organization's strategic and operational goals.

Some means by which an organization can support private practice include the following (see Chapter 5 for additional discussion):

◆ Clinical co-management
◆ Joint ventures for real estate, surgery centers, equipment timeshare ancillaries, and imaging centers
◆ Medical management of the organization's self-insured employee population
◆ Management of captive malpractice and healthcare insurance plans
◆ Oversight and management of information technology services
◆ Enterprise partnerships
◆ Physician service leases
◆ Management services organizations and similar cooperative arrangements

When working with physicians, whether employed or self-employed, it is important to build a foundation of trust. Physicians will not remember what you said or what you meant. They will remember what you did for them or to them. PRM is the bridge that leads to trust, which feeds into a successful physician integration and alignment effort.

PRM is a management function that can drive a significant return on investment (ROI). Organizations such as St. Ann's Hospital in Columbus, Ohio, and Oklahoma University Medical Center in Oklahoma City that invest in the process by meeting with key physicians quarterly, working through common challenges, and creating collaborative partnership opportunities see an ROI of between 400 and 500 percent, as measured by monthly inpatient or outpatient revenue, total admissions, average length of stay (LOS), case mix index, adjusted cost per case, core/safety measures, Hospital Consumer Assessment of Healthcare Providers and Systems scores, physician engagement scores, and other metrics (Mack 2012). Important questions that are posed by assigned management to physicians include, "What is the one thing that our organization can do to improve your/your patient's experience at _____?" Asking this question gives management the opportunity to obtain important insights into market leakage to competing organizations, practice management challenges, physician referral patterns, and market demand.

The ultimate goal of this strategy is to build trust and to change culture by forging strategic relationships that are essential for long-term organizational performance. The flipside is that you can identify early on those physicians who do not present as potential partners because they demonstrate the need to preserve autonomy, a lack of organizational fit, or differing fundamental perspectives or values, and thus avoid a nonproductive investment of time and resources to secure a nonviable relationship.

Attaining fundamental trust and understanding between both parties supports any attempt to create a successful alignment strategy and ultimately determines whether the potential for effective partnership is possible and achievable.

ECONOMIC INTEGRATION AND ALIGNMENT

Once the decision is made to invest in a professional partnership, leadership's attention can be turned to determining what model of economic integration and alignment to use.

Physician Employment

By far, the most common economic partnership model is physician employment. The prevalence of this approach dominates all other models because of the following factors:

- Falling physician reimbursement, which will continue under the Patient Protection and Affordable Care Act (PPACA) by 6 percent per year for three years, except for general surgery and primary care
- Climbing overhead costs, particularly as IT meaningful use requirements are fully implemented
- Rising cost of capital due to market consolidation
- Lack of contracting leverage with third-party payers and large employers
- Lack of cost-effective revenue cycle and practice management support

The rate of increase in physician employment is striking. Estimates range from 45 percent (Vaidya 2013) to as high as 75 percent (Beaulieu-Volk 2012) for 2014. Few recent physician graduates seek private practice—with rates as low as 1 percent in 2012, according to a Merritt Hawkins (2012) survey—in response to the failure of the independent-ownership business model. As a result, physician employment is not only the most prevalent hospital–physician alignment framework but also the fastest-growing alignment trend. Accenture found that 5 percent of independent physicians seek employment every year; currently, fewer than 33 percent of physicians remain independent (Accenture 2014).

Employment can take many forms, and employed physicians can work at a variety of care delivery sites, such as hospitals, hospital-owned multispecialty group practices, clinical service lines, or the hospital's clinical institute. In general, however, regardless of whether their physicians are employed or are aligned through some other kind of strategic agreement (discussed in a later section), many healthcare organizations lose money when using a physician alignment model that emphasizes employment for the following reasons:

- Lack of a business model or plan
- No downside risk in physician compensation
- Revenues calculated according to Current Procedural Terminology (CPT) or International Classification of Diseases, Ninth Revision, Clinical Modification (ICD-9-CM) codes without accounting for ancillary or downstream revenues
- Overallocation of indirect labor and supply chain costs
- Lack of strong physician leadership
- Lack of aligned incentives (e.g., for achieving cost-effectiveness)
- Lack of alignment with strategic organizational goals and objectives

Success Factors for Physician Employment
The most important success factor for physician employment is the presence of well-trained and *aligned physician leadership* to oversee and manage employed

physicians. Unfortunately, many organizations never make the investment in professional physician leaders, relying instead on voluntary rotating leaders from the organized medical staff, who typically demonstrate wide variation in performance. As discussed in Chapter 1, leadership has a calculable ROI through performance, which has a direct impact on the organization's financial performance. Physicians seek to be led by respected physician colleagues who have personal insight and knowledge regarding the challenges and pressures confronting physicians.

High-performing organizations view employment as a *strategic partnership* and not as an employer–employee hierarchical relationship. For instance, governing boards rarely, if ever, treat the organization's CEO as an employee (although, technically, he is) but rather as a strategic partner with whom the board can develop corporate strategy and work through the myriad complex governance, managerial, and medical staff issues that inevitably arise. Similarly, a wise CEO looks to physicians for advice on clinical issues, operational efficiencies, evidence-based clinical and functional practices, service initiatives, and ways to achieve cost-effectiveness. Physicians who are treated as respected partners return the favor and collaborate with managers as trusted colleagues who bring essential operational and financial knowledge and perspective to clinical decision making.

With mutual respect comes accountability. Mature partners place themselves and each other "at risk" through *aligned risk contracts* to accomplish strategic goals and objectives. The traditions of providing physicians with salary guarantees and minimal productivity expectations and compensating physician leaders for hours spent at meetings neither support the organization nor treat physicians as bona fide members of the leadership team. Aligned risk contracts bring a "downside" contingency to employed physicians' compensation. This type of agreement holds those few individuals accountable who fail to meet minimum expectations while presenting a strong "upside" to capable physicians willing to work toward stretch goals in a meaningful and constructive way. An example of an aligned risk contract for an emergency physician/medical director is provided in Exhibit 11.1.

This compensation model offers a win–win scenario for physicians and the organization. The hospital can calculate an ROI for its emergency medicine department that works toward optimizing quality, safety, service, and cost-effectiveness; reduces throughput times; optimizes clinical documentation improvement (CDI) initiatives; participates actively in medical staff functions and leadership activities; and supports management and staff in a positive and mutually beneficial way.

These opportunities can only be realized by having *aligned performance metrics or targets* in place that are transparent, created in collaboration with physicians, supported by management, and consistent with the organization's strategic plan. The best way to disseminate performance data is to make it available 24/7 so that each

Exhibit 11.1: Example of Aligned Risk Contract Terms for Emergency Physician and Medical Director of the Emergency Department

50% Base (10th percentile of MGMA compensation, or approximately $150,000)
10% Quality program (2% bonus for each 20% compliance with evidence-based pathways and algorithms)
10% Patient satisfaction (2% for every 10th percentile above 30th percentile)
10% Physician satisfaction (2% for every 10th percentile above 40th percentile for hospital survey of other physicians)
10% Corporate compliance (e.g., medical records completion) (2% for every 10th percentile above 50th percentile compliance)
10% Overall evaluation (based on aggregate performance and organizational alignment)

100% = Top potential compensation (90th percentile of MGMA compensation, or approximately $350,000)

Note: MGMA = Medical Group Management Association.

---

physician can access her information at any time and compare it with internal peer data and national benchmarks. To do so requires a fully integrated IT system that can report, analyze, and format ongoing and focused professional practice evaluation data. This crucial capability should be a high organizational priority.

As indicated in the earlier list, it is imperative to create a viable *business plan* that takes into account all projected revenues and expenses for the program. What makes this task interesting is the definition of what constitutes *revenue* and *expense*. Are revenues a reflection of net collections from CPT or ICD-9 codes, or do they reflect a percentage of downstream ancillary and inpatient revenues? Do expenses include direct variable costs, or do they encompass a percentage of fixed and indirect allocated costs? Do both up- and downside compensation incentives have predicted ROIs so that compensation models are appropriately aligned with the business plan, or are estimates based on arbitrary or negotiated figures?

Many employment models are informed by management's perception of what the market requires rather than a sustainable business model. This approach benefits neither physicians nor the organization in the long term. Regardless of how a business plan is created, the full impact of physician employment should be analyzed from a systemic perspective, taking into account all downstream revenues and all up- and downstream costs so that a careful financial analysis can be made.

Non-employment Economic Alignment Models

Many physicians (particularly those nearing the end of their career) may not be compatible with an employment model because of their deeply ingrained values of independence and autonomy. Nonetheless, hospitals need to engage and align with those individuals who are capable of partnership and collaboration to help the organizations meet the economic pressures of delivering high-quality care at low costs. Thus, other models may be more suitable for these individuals and may even serve to transition them to future employment.

Co-management Agreements

An increasingly popular non-employment model is co-management. Aligning with a hospital under a co-management agreement enables physicians (whether employed or not) to partner with management to oversee the quality, safety, service, cost-effectiveness, marketing, and branding of defined services. This type of relationship requires physicians to work interdependently with nurse and executive leaders to broaden the scope of their responsibilities into operations, marketing, and finance.

Many intangible benefits for both parties can be gained through co-management agreements, including the following:

- Enhanced communication and transparency between physicians and management
- Increased likelihood of engagement through highly leveraged and aligned at-risk compensation models
- Deeper mutual understanding and respect for the complexities of clinical and operational practice
- Unlimited opportunities for joint business ventures

As with service lines and clinical institutes, most co-management practices are overseen by clinical and operational leaders in a dyad (physician + nurse) or triad (physician + nurse + executive) leadership format that permits areas of individual and shared responsibility. For example, physician leaders may be responsible for the quality and coordination of care by physicians and privileged practitioners, supply chain standardization of physician preference items (e.g., implants, stents), medical staff development (see Chapter 2), research or education, and physician communication. Nursing leaders may be responsible for the quality and coordination of nursing services, operations, capital budget, staffing, and nursing performance monitoring. An administrative leader may be responsible for the business plan, operating plan or budget, business analytics, and performance analysis and monitoring. Together, the three leaders share responsibility for the clinical service with its attendant business or strategic plan, compensation model development or oversight, marketing or branding, and overall clinical coordination. As physicians become more experienced and sophisticated in their leadership roles, they typically take on increasing operational and financial responsibilities that may culminate in oversight responsibilities for multiple service lines through an executive management position.

As in employment arrangements, the key to successful co-management agreements is to place a significant percentage of total compensation at risk for meeting collaborative strategic goals and objectives and to create a culture that supports shared clinical and operational decision making. Not every physician or manager is capable of working in a co-management model, and thus most service lines and clinical institutes evolve to a semi-open or closed model in which individuals must meet eligibility criteria before they are considered for participation.

Co-management agreements may exist in a variety of business models, including clinical practice ownership and management, joint ventures, leasing arrangements, enterprise ventures, equity models, accountable care organizations (ACOs), patient-centered medical homes (PCMHs), and management services organizations, to name a few. The principles remain constant: shared oversight, leadership, and accountability for quality, operational efficiency, and financial performance.

Certain legal issues must be addressed in these agreements to avoid potential Stark, anti-kickback, civil monetary penalty statute violations, and inurement issues. A particular area of concern is the perceived tying of specific compensation to the creation of a better payer mix, value of referrals, limiting services, LOS, or access for financial reasons. These potential issues should be addressed with legal counsel throughout the contracting process.

Leasing Arrangements

The hospital or healthcare entity typically receives reimbursement that is 10 to 15 percent higher than physicians normally receive in their practices due to contracting leverage, not-for-profit or critical access status, and economies of scale. Leasing permits healthcare organizations to contract physician services either directly under an employment or co-management agreement or indirectly through a leasing entity (typically a limited liability corporation [LLC]) to secure those services that benefit the organization. In so doing, the hospital brings physicians and management together to manage the cost and quality of the services.

Among the many potential benefits to physicians of these arrangements are the following:

- Enhanced revenue stream
- Preferred reimbursement and contracts
- Preferred referrals from the contracting entity or hospital

- Access to corporate benefits, if consistent with federal law, Internal Revenue Service (IRS) regulations, and human resources (HR) policy
- Access to IT and lower overhead costs (e.g., through a group purchasing organization or ancillary contracts)
- Retained control of their private practices if desired, with no restrictive covenants

Management benefits by not having to take on the additional costs of employment and by expansion of the scope of services provided. In addition, the hospital can augment its facilities and staff with physician practices to better manage flow and bottlenecks during volume surges. For instance, an ultrasound department may be able to lease ultrasound services from an ob-gyn and her ultrasound technologist to handle overflow cases or to see patients on weekends or holidays, when it may be more expensive for the hospital to do so.

Organizations may also lease the services of a practice's managers, medical director, or call coverage team in a mutually beneficial way.

In compliance with these contractual arrangements, and consistent with federal law, IRS regulations, and HR policy, physicians who provide leased services to the organization of more than a set number of hours (e.g., 32) per week may have access to corporate benefits such as the following:

- Liability coverage at reduced rates through a captive insurance plan
- Health, disability, or life insurance
- Participation in a 403(b) (retirement plan for tax-exempt organizations) or 457(b) (nonqualified, tax advantage–deferred compensation plan for governmental and certain nongovernmental employees) plan
- Participation in deferred compensation or supplemental executive retirement plans

As with co-management and employment agreements, the quid pro quo is alignment with the organization's strategic quality, safety, service, and cost-effectiveness initiatives through aligned risk contracts that are heavily weighted with incentives.

Joint Ventures

Due to tightening Stark restrictions and the prohibition of new physician-owned hospitals under the PPACA, the number and types of joint ventures between physicians and hospitals are in decline. However, two fundamental models are worth mentioning: the equity-for-profit model and the contractual (virtual) model. The *equity-for-profit model* consists of joint ownership or investment in a healthcare entity that offers unique facilities or services with control in proportion to the percentage of investment. The investment can be made in cash, hard assets (e.g., physical plant), fair market valuation of an existing business, or financing. Often, management provides investment capital, and the physician practice contributes an existing facility (e.g., imaging center, ambulatory surgery center) and its hard assets. This model offers the ideal level of alignment, but it comes with multiple legal challenges, including Stark and anti-kickback legislation restrictions, double taxation of retained earnings (depending on the legal structure), state certificate-of-need requirements, and capital calls (further investment requirements) to meet future needs.

The *contractual (virtual) model,* which is currently growing in prevalence, is not a joint venture in the traditional sense but rather a contractual relationship (e.g., timeshare with lease, co-management, ACO, PCMH) and partnership between the healthcare organization and physicians, with joint oversight responsibilities.

Because most healthcare organizations have access to lower-cost capital funding and are dependent on physician-generated services to produce revenue, the type of investment in any joint venture reflects the interdependent nature of the relationship and the necessity to combine areas of expertise to optimize quality and reduce costs.

The corporate structure of joint ventures can vary according to the degree of physician leadership, investment, ownership, equity, and participation. They are often formed as LLCs or limited partnerships but can also be C or S corporations, depending on the state where the organization is located, financing parameters, and tax considerations.

The primary purpose of a joint venture is to achieve enhanced partnership and communication between management and physicians; the business structure merely provides the scaffolding for it (Wofford and Messinger 2013). Joint ventures often contain transfer, buy-back, and unwind arrangements to protect the parties in the event that the partnership dissolves.

Innovative Alignment Models

University Hospital in Cleveland, Ohio, exploits what it calls the *enterprise model* of alignment with its physicians by creating partnerships based on shared clinical and economic goals. For example, a single medical office building may house a number of physicians, each with unique contractual relationships to the hospital. The arrangements are customized to the needs of the physician consistent with organizational need. This innovative approach to PRM recognizes that each physician has different professional goals, different tolerances for risk, and varying levels of desire to invest in and partner with an organization rich in resources.

An extension of PRM is the *physician sales team,* which visits key physician offices regularly to explore partnership opportunities and ways in which the organization can earn more referrals by focusing on physician concerns. In this way, important information is mined regarding market leakage; quality, safety, and service concerns; practice management challenges; and operational inefficiencies, which, once addressed collaboratively, feed into a foundation of trust and collaboration. ROI is easy to calculate using data on incremental revenues, referrals, and elective procedures, and the sales force is highly motivated by commission-based incentives.

Marketing co-ops are joint investment schemes in which organizations, physician groups, pharmaceutical and medical device companies, and corporate partners combine resources to uncover untapped demand through market research and data mining. For instance, in one cardiology service line, 62,900 targeted adults received information regarding cholesterol screening (at a cost to the organization of $251,600) that led to a 3 percent response rate (1,887 adults) with screenings performed (cost: $52,836). Of the adults screened, 55 percent (1,038) were found to be at risk and underwent further evaluation (cost: $9,342), of whom 35 percent (363) converted to an office appointment. Of the 363 adults, 55 percent (200) converted to an inpatient or outpatient procedure with total revenues of $6,749,536. This initiative resulted in an acquisition cost of $1,569 per converted adult with an ROI of 21:1 (Mack 2012).

Similarly, many potential patients and customers don't return with potentially treatable issues because they are busy and don't remember to follow up with their practitioner, thus creating untapped revenues. According to the Leapfrog National Survey of Corporate Health Promotion Programs, the average ROI for existing or active patients with reminders is 5:1 and the average ROI for inactive patients with reminders is 13:1. This provides a natural way for physicians and an organization's marketing or community outreach department to partner for mutual benefit (Leapfrog Group 2012).

Many large systems bring high-performing physicians together with executive and board leadership to form a *physician or leadership council* or "kitchen cabinet" to advise leadership at the highest levels on potential issues, such as

- strategic partnerships,
- business ventures,
- strategic medical staff development,
- capital purchases, and
- operational challenges.

Physicians may be chosen to participate on the basis of quantitative (e.g., gross revenues, number of admissions/referrals, clinical performance) and qualitative (e.g., demonstration of formal and informal leadership, communication skills, organizational commitment) criteria and represent the small influential segment of the medical staff that has a significant impact on organizational strategy. Physicians may be compensated for their time at fair market value (FMV) based on consulting agreements to offset the opportunity cost of leaving their practices to contribute to organizational strategic planning and thinking. An example of a highly successful physician leadership council is that at Scripps Memorial Hospital in La Jolla, California, which is part of the Scripps Health system based in San Diego. It meets monthly and provides leadership with important internal intelligence that enables the organization to make effective strategic business decisions with early physician buy-in and support.

Smaller healthcare organizations may consider forming *specialty referral panels* for when patients require care beyond the scope of service of its regular providers. A specialty referral panel enables the organization to align with regional specialists who demonstrate high-quality, low-cost care delivery through various contractual relationships (e.g., services lessor, subcontractor, consultant, director) to improve outpatient management and ensure follow-up in order to reduce preventable readmissions, simplify transfers (particularly after hours), increase access, and provide marketing assistance and credibility.

Again, all parties can experience a calculable ROI: Specialists are often aligned with larger tertiary centers that gain an increased referral base and healthcare network. Smaller organizations benefit from improved responsiveness of "circuit riders" (specialists who cover multiple small hospitals), better cross coverage, consultative services for primary care, and a decline in unnecessary readmissions and emergency department visits resulting from improved continuity of care.

CLINICAL INTEGRATION AND ALIGNMENT

Once the economic relationship is established, the final essential step toward alignment is to develop mutually beneficial quality, safety, service, and cost-effectiveness goals and objectives. The process to create these goals and objectives is described at length in chapters 5 and 6. This section covers the various structures that form the clinically integrated organization.

Governance Structure

Physician participation on the governing board is essential to provide clinical, physician, and medical staff–related expertise. The presence on the board of a chief medical or nursing officer or a member of the quality staff alone is insufficient to provide the kind of insight the board needs to develop a robust and meaningful quality agenda. That being said, several important issues surrounding physicians serving on the governing board must be addressed:

- Some physicians may perceive governing board membership or participation as an opportunity to advocate for self- or constituent interests. Any physician who serves on the board must understand that her fiduciary obligation as a board member requires undivided loyalty to the mission of the organization. All potential conflicts must be disclosed and managed. Physicians (or other board members) who cannot or will not participate in this spirit should not be eligible for board membership or participation.
- Some municipalities do not allow membership of "economically interested parties" on the governing board. For instance, many municipal or public boards do not permit anyone directly employed by an organization to serve as a voting member of the board. Meetings must be public, and many board members must be elected or politically appointed by the community and thus are essentially political positions; their selection is not based on clinical or operational expertise. This process may restrict the participation of physicians or healthcare executives on boards, which may undermine the board's ability to effectively oversee the quality of care.

  Several workarounds are available to overcome this challenge. One is to invite physicians and executives to participate in board-related functions through subcommittees, task forces, and advisory boards to develop the content, policies, and oversight monitoring approaches the board uses. Another is to create a not-for-profit foundation with expert clinical participation to advise the board and to provide expert input behind the scenes. This is particularly relevant in states that have corporate practice of medicine acts that prohibit physician employment. A third option might be to create a medical foundation managed and governed by physicians to provide employment for executive leaders who oversee clinical operations, enabling a more collaborative governance structure in municipalities that limit governance participation. This model is executed with great success at St. Elizabeth Community Hospital in Red Bluff, California (see Chapter 12).
- Boards require quality expertise, and most physicians have applied clinical expertise but may or may not be expert in such quality techniques as Lean, Six Sigma, failure mode and effects analysis, root cause analysis, or flow management. Thus, physician participation may be necessary yet insufficient to ensure that the board can provide a high level of quality oversight.

Once these issues are resolved, the governing board can take advantage of physician participation in several ways. For example, many boards now have a *quality committee* to develop a quality plan consistent with the organization's strategic plan. The quality plan provides the framework to operationalize quality initiatives throughout the organization. Again, quality expertise is essential here, as most board members with nonhealthcare experience lack the background to guide this essential initiative.

The *joint conference committee* is a collaborative governance body made up of board, management, and medical staff officers and provides a forum for governance, management, and physicians to discuss potentially controversial and complex topics so that they can be processed before presentation to the full board. This is an excellent venue for leaders in the three major healthcare leadership structures to come together and reach accord in a proactive way that minimizes conflict and increases understanding between the groups.

Management Structure

Traditionally, the senior management team meets in "huddles" or meetings to develop operational strategy through the creation and oversight of an operations plan and to foster leadership collaboration and communication. Including *physician leadership on the executive management team* may seem like a counterintuitive approach to foster physician engagement and alignment, but in fact it accomplishes the following:

- Provides key formal and informal physician leaders with operational insight into the complexity and interdependency of operational efficiency and the clinical activities of physicians.
- Provides physician leaders with insight into legal, regulatory, and accreditation requirements that depend on physician compliance.
- Supports accelerated buy-in of key physician leaders to operational initiatives and requirements.
- Enables physician leaders to roll out operational initiatives to physicians from a physician perspective. This activity is more challenging for a chief medical officer or vice president of medical affairs to do as he is perceived as a member of the management team by most physicians and therefore an outsider.
- Fosters improved communication between all members of the executive team and physician leadership (particularly the chief operating, information, and financial officers) to support better collaboration for operational, IT, and

financial initiatives, respectively, the success of which depend on physician approval and support.

Perhaps the most significant change is cultural, as management sends a powerful message to physicians and the medical staff that they are an integral part of the organization's ability to achieve mutually beneficial quality and cost-effectiveness results.

Some organizations create a *nurse–physician council* made up of representative leaders that works to improve nurse–physician relations, operations, and communication. This ad hoc group meets on an as-needed basis to discuss the following topics:

- Communication protocols between physicians and nurses, such as formalized handoffs, SBAR (situation, background, assessment, recommendation), and red/yellow/green messages for high-/medium-/low-priority situations.
- Code-of-conduct standards for collaborative management
- Evidence-based approaches to commonly encountered situations that require nurse–physician interaction
- Politically charged issues to design mutually acceptable approaches
- Strategic goals and objectives, consistent with the organization's strategic plan, that affect the clinical team
- The need for a nurse–physician compact to memorialize important resolutions and agreements

This body complements the dyad/triad service line or clinical institute approach and brings nurses and physicians together in a way that goes far beyond the

---

Kathleen Bartholomew, RN, *an international consultant, author, and member of the Orca Institute, explains new ways in which the medical and nursing staffs can work together to achieve alignment.*

How the Medical and Nursing Staff Can Work Together for Alignment
As in any culture, physicians and nurses do not perceive the self-imposed separation in their daily working relationships. A great relationship is like a professionally choreographed and performed dance. If no one challenges the status quo and everyone knows her place, everything is fine. The greatest impediment to collegial and interactive physician–nurse teams, therefore, is our own perceptions that *we already have teams.*

(continued)

Our language and behaviors confirm what statistics validate: Less than 15 percent of physician–nurse relationships have been described by Buerhaus (2005) as "excellent," and only 25 percent are "very good." Furthermore, more than 32 percent of physicians and nurses in defined organizations have witnessed disruptive behaviors that could link to adverse events (Rosenstein 2011). Clearly, there is significant room for improvement.

Professional roles are deeply ingrained. Until we address the very DNA of our profession by training physicians and nurses together, only incremental strides can be made in creating the radically new partnership that focuses on "our patient."

In order to create a new culture, formalized structures, such as a physician leadership institute, need to be put in place to support and nurture collegiality by leaders who realize that the ROI for education and time far surpasses the initial cost. Without these structures, excellent physician–nurse relationships are unlikely because physicians and nurses historically work in silos and lack a comprehensive understanding of each other's roles.

The groundwork for these structures is a medical staff and nursing code of conduct that specifically addresses professional conduct between members of the caregiving team. *Until an organization has the same rules for all roles, substantive cultural change will never happen.* Trust is the foundation for teamwork and, therefore, the bedrock of alignment.

An acknowledgment of the distance we must individually and collectively travel to attain physician–nurse culture change is the first step. To align for the patient's benefit, we must connect on an unprecedented human level and form meaningful relationships that reach beyond our traditional roles. Only when the hierarchy is completely flattened and both physicians and nurses *perceive, feel, and act* like equals will a community of caregivers emerge that is worthy of our patients' trust.

traditional chief nursing officer–chief medical officer alliance and elevates cultural expectations of the two major clinical groups.

Medical Staff Structure

Traditionally, the medical executive committee (MEC) represents the interface between management and the organized medical staff. Recently, many medical staffs have created *medical advisory committees* to work directly with management on operational and financial projects that optimize quality and reduce costs. These collaborative ad hoc bodies are made up of physicians and managers interested in working together to create solutions to complex operational challenges that require medical staff and management support. Typical projects may include the following:

- Redesigning process flows to make them more efficient, reliable, and cost-effective
- Creating CDI solutions to optimize reimbursement/revenue cycle and reduce costs
- Creating service initiatives to drive patient and stakeholder loyalty and drive margin
- Operationalizing service lines and clinical institutes
- Developing ACOs and PCMHs
- Designing and simplifying operational approaches to accreditation standard compliance to improve clinical outcomes and drive down costs
- Developing population health initiatives to horizontally integrate care, reduce preventable readmissions, improve long-term outcomes, and lower the overall cost per case
- Operationalizing important IT initiatives (e.g., electronic healthcare record systems, health information exchanges) to improve care, minimize disruption, and reduce costs

As with physician councils, many organizations compensate physicians for consultative services based on an FMV analysis, and physicians appreciate the opportunity to participate with management to develop and improve operational initiatives that have significant organizational impact.

With the increasing number of advanced practice providers (APPs) on the medical staff who assume increasing responsibilities for managing routine conditions and for providing first-line call coverage, many medical staffs include an *APP advisory committee* as a subcommittee of the MEC to address APP-related credentialing, privileging, and peer review issues. This is another way that these important clinical specialties become increasingly integrated into the medical staff structure and bring acknowledgment of their unique knowledge and clinical expertise. Some medical staffs have gone so far as to support their inclusion as voting members of the medical staff with full political rights (e.g., active staff) in order to better engage and align nonphysicians and nondentists with important medical staff strategic initiatives.

Nonmedical Staff Structure

Service lines and clinical institutes require collaborative structures to oversee clinical quality, operating efficiency, and financial performance. To that end, many have created *joint operating committees (JOCs)* or *management oversight committees (MOCs)* to do so. These permanent leadership structures typically divide membership into groups of physicians and managers and provide input to the executive management team on the structure, processes, and desired outcomes of collaborative clinical entities. As discussed in Chapter 1, service lines and clinical institutes will replace most clinical departments because of their ability to provide better quality outcomes at a lower operating cost and offer more effective leadership. Therefore, the JOCs/MOCs will become the new oversight bodies for clinical operating units and will manage at-risk employment, co-management, leasing, professional services, and joint venture contracts. JOCs/MOCs will create for each relevant service line and clinical institute the following:

- Strategic, operating, business, and marketing plans
- Operating and capital budgets
- Compensation plan
- Quality plan with approval of specific metrics or targets on which incentive-based compensation is allocated
- Performance dashboard or scorecard consistent with the organization's strategic plan
- Recruitment and oversight performance measure of relevant medical directors

In short, this body becomes the new management oversight body for clinical operating units and reports directly to executive management for operating and financial performance and to the MEC for medical staff–related functions. Because work on this committee is a management (and not a medical staff) function, all members are paid on the basis of FMV, with appropriate incentives for management services, and are held accountable by the organization for clinical, operational, and financial performance.

Introduced in 2006, *ACOs* are one of three innovative healthcare delivery models featured in the PPACA. There are now more than 500 Medicare and commercial ACOs in the United States, with significantly mixed results. All models, whether by fee for service or capitation, are based on placing providers at risk for compliance with 33 quality metrics approved by the Centers for Medicare & Medicaid Services (CMS) and reducing costs over a defined period, resulting in either shared savings or losses based upon quality compliance and financial performance. ACOs must cover at least 5,000 beneficiaries, be provider led, and meet requirements published by CMS on March 30, 2011, in their updated rules. According to these rules, ACO governance must include at least 75 percent providers who are "dedicated physician leaders with a proven ability to motivate physicians to participate in the development and implementation of quality improvement" (CMS 2011).

In addition, there must be one Medicare beneficiary (for Medicare ACOs) to serve as a patient advocate and represent patient interests along with professional management on the board to better oversee and manage operational and financial performance. Similar to JOCs/MOCs, most ACO governing bodies are subsidiary, operating, or operational bodies that are accountable to a corporate structure often through a chief or system operating officer. ACO operating boards tend to have a mixture of primary care and referral specialties represented in addition to managers to reflect the demographics of the entity and the need to merge clinical and operational oversight and expertise. These governing entities also have fewer community members, and every board member is expected to bring essential expertise to ensure organizational success. Interestingly, some states such as Colorado and Texas encourage the inclusion of a convening or corporate sponsor on the board to ensure that the community's strategic business interests (e.g., cost-effective healthcare services for employers) are met. Some commercial ACOs also have strategic business partnerships with important vendors (e.g., IT and supply chain) due to the importance of creating an integrated healthcare network supported by a sophisticated IT infrastructure, seamless supply chain and revenue cycle processes, and greater standardization of high-cost supply chain items. Both CMS and the Office of Inspector General have given all PPACA-related demonstration projects consent to develop more effective collaborative partnerships in an attempt to improve quality and reduce costs.

The second innovative model, *PCMH*, focuses more on primary care, community health, and primary and secondary prevention, and it often serves as the foundational base of an ACO. The operating boards for these entities typically reflect these competencies because of their emphasis on continuity of care through the use of patient registries, to track health data across the continuum of care via health information exchanges, and nurse navigators, who personally assist patients and their families in efficiently utilizing the system. Hence, there are few if any specialists represented, and convening or corporate sponsors tend to reflect potential products and services helpful to community-based populations.

For instance, the Texas Medical Home Initiative of Dallas, Texas, partners with Pfizer Pharmaceuticals to support research and development of pharmaceutical products that benefit preventive healthcare strategies and care plans. This enables the PCMH to serve as a beta site for ongoing research and gives it financial credibility to obtain capital investment. Some organizations such as Rush University Medical Center in Chicago, Illinois, create a patient family advisory group to expand on the patient advocacy concept made up of 7 to 15 individuals to validate clinical and operational initiatives from a patient experience perspective. Many of these groups significantly affect planning, development, and operations due to their important insights regarding access, privacy, way finding, coordination of services, noise, cleanliness, food options, ease of utilization, and cost. Thus, physicians work closely with management, nursing, patient advocates, and corporate partners to develop and oversee improved models for population health and primary care.

The final PPACA innovative model is the *CMS acute care episode (ACE) bundled payment initiative,* which focuses on high-volume/high-cost services (e.g., cardiology, orthopedics, urology) to optimize quality and reduce costs through more collaborative oversight and management between physicians and executive leaders. Prospective bundled payments combine Medicare parts A and B so that both physicians and the healthcare organization are held accountable for their operating costs and margins.

An example of a successful ACE program is Baptist Health System in San Antonio, Texas, which uses an operating council of physicians and managers and significantly reduced almost $10 million in supply chain costs over a three-year period. To further incentivize savings, CMS authorized permission to utilize a gainsharing agreement (increased from 25 percent of savings to 50 percent of savings) to incentivize both physicians and the organization to continually reduce costs while optimizing quality. Incidentally, gainsharing agreements cannot inure to the personal benefit of physicians but must constitute reinvestment in the clinical unit as a whole, and so one of the key functions of the operating council is to allocate and direct gainsharing savings funds back into clinical areas that it feels will have significant impact and result in better outcomes at lower costs. Case management is essential to achievement of these results, and a case manager is often asked to serve as a member of the operating board or council to ensure efficient flow and continuity of care and services. Since management of a gainsharing program is complex, one of the functions of the operating council is to develop a gainsharing plan (in conjunction with a compensation plan) to properly administer program savings consistent with federal and legal requirements.

Todd Sagin, MD, JD, president and national medical director of Sagin Healthcare Consulting LLC, discusses some of the best ways to utilize contracting as an alignment tool.

Contracting for Hospital–Physician Alignment

The evolving twenty-first century business model of healthcare necessitates strong alignment between hospitals and physicians. The coming decades will see doctors and hospitals tied at the hip more than ever as the imperative grows for more integrated care and as the fee-for-service payment world is replaced by a value-based reimbursement environment. Leaders of healthcare organizations must find ways to structure symbiotic relationships with physicians, whether they are employed by the organization or independent, as they attempt the transition from volume-based success to value-driven delivery.

Hospital–physician alignment can take various forms, and there is no single best approach that will work in every community to ensure success. Unfortunately, most arrangements trigger a host of legal concerns. The laws implicated are numerous and can include the following:

◆ Federal laws meant to prevent fraud and abuse, such as the anti-kickback statutes, Stark laws, or the False Claims Act
◆ Federal antitrust laws aimed at preventing anticompetitive behavior
◆ Federal tax laws that aim to prevent not-for-profit hospitals from enriching physicians through illegal private inurement
◆ Laws that block gainsharing practices, such as civil monetary penalty rules
◆ State antitrust laws
◆ State antifraud laws

Some observers have noted that it is almost always illegal for a hospital (particularly a not-for-profit hospital) to pay money to a doctor without running afoul of the law unless a clear Stark exception or an anti-kickback safe harbor to the applicable law applies. Fortunately, many exceptions written into the statutes and regulations are available.

Each arrangement between a hospital and doctor raises unique legal concerns. However, some generalities should be noted. Hospitals should always seek to pay doctors in a manner consistent with fair market value for their services. Payments that exceed fair market value can put both parties at risk. Payment that motivates directed referrals or obligates admissions

(continued)

and quota-based utilization will raise legal liabilities under most alignment arrangements. Contracts that include restrictive covenants will generally raise concerns about anticompetitive impact.

There is no single correct strategy for any particular institution or medical community. Whatever the alignment strategy deployed, it is often challenged by the consequences of past battles and the entrenched ways of interacting developed by hospitals and independent physicians over many decades. Layer on the legal barriers to collaboration created by various statutes and regulations and it is not surprising that many alignment strategies stumble or fail. Nevertheless, the imperatives of the twenty-first century marketplace will continue to demand alignment, and the growing employment of physicians by health systems will likely predominate as the foundation for hospital–physician collaboration in the foreseeable future.

SUMMARY

Physician integration and alignment may be the most important strategic initiative to pursue in healthcare transformation. Organizations must lay the initial foundation for such a strategy by building trusting and compatible relations with individual physicians (cultural alignment) and be open to many kinds of contractual relationships (economic alignment) that will best meet the needs of individual physicians and their healthcare organizations. Finally, collaborative structures and processes must be in place to negotiate, establish, and monitor clinical metrics and targets to support a coordinated effort between the medical staff, management, and board to achieve world-class quality at a fraction of the cost (clinical alignment). The challenge will be for organizations to embark upon this strategy in a timely way so that they are not excluded from the narrow networks necessary to compete in an increasingly global healthcare market. To do so, both physicians and management will need to sacrifice some personal and professional autonomy to build a new coalition based on interdependence and mutual respect. This is the key to create a medical staff that can work with management in solidarity to place the interests of the organization's mission and the needs of the community above all else and to secure an alignment that can last over time.

REFERENCES

Accenture. 2014. "Clinical Transformation: Dramatic Changes as Physician Employment Grows." Published March 28. www.accenture.com/Site CollectionDocuments/PDF/Accenture_Clinical_Transformation.pdf.

Beaulieu-Volk, D. 2012. "Physician Employment Could Hit 75%, Eclipsing Private Practice." Published July 18. www.fiercehealthcare.com/story /study-hospitals-employ-75-physicians-2014/2012-07-18.

Buerhaus, P. 2005. "The State of the RN Workforce in the United States." *Nursing Economics* 23 (2): 58–60.

Center for Medicare & Medicaid Services (CMS). 2011. "Proposed Rule to Implement Section 3022 of the PPACA." *Federal Register* 76 (67): 19536.

Leapfrog Group. 2012. *National Survey of Corporate Health Promotion Programs.* Washington, DC: Leapfrog Group.

Mack, K. 2012. "Physician Integration Strategies: Advanced Lessons from Successful Organizations." Seminar presented at American College of Healthcare Executives cluster program, Anchorage, Alaska, August.

Merritt Hawkins. 2012. "A Survey of America's Physicians—Practice Patterns and Perspectives." The Physicians Foundation. Published in September. www .physiciansfoundation.org/uploads/default/Physicians_Foundation_2012 _Biennial_Survey.pdf.

Rosenstein, A. 2011. "The Quality and Economic Impact of Disruptive Behaviors on Clinical Outcomes of Patient Care." *American Journal of Clinical Quality* 26 (5): 372–79.

Vaidya, A. 2013. "Survey: Number of Employed Hospital Physicians Up by 6%." *Becker's Hospital Review.* Published June 18. www.beckershospitalreview.com /hospital-physician-relationships/survey-number-of-hospital-employed -physicians-up-6.html.

Wofford, D., and S. Messinger. 2013. *The New Hospital–Physician Enterprise: Meeting the Challenges of Value-Based Care.* Chicago: Health Administration Press.

CHAPTER 12

Best Practice Medical Staffs—
Examples from the Field

Excellence is never an accident. It is always the result of high intention, sincere effort, and intelligent execution; it represents the wise choice of many alternatives—choice, not chance, determines your destiny.
—*Aristotle (384–322 BC)*

Excellence does not happen by chance; it is a deliberate and carefully considered choice. The decision to be a positive deviant or outlier is not easy, as the natural tendency is for organizations to trend toward the mean and conform to societal norms and expectations. Every decision has a cost, and the pursuit of excellence and top performance may require the following difficult actions:

- Excluding marginal or below-average performers from the organization at every level
- Setting public, professional, and legal expectations at higher-than-benchmarked norms, thus inviting potential risk and liability
- Addressing performance issues at the earliest possible opportunity and acting in a committed, definitive, and timely way to correct for improvement
- Committing to a culture of continuous performance improvement and innovation with no tolerance for remnants of the status quo or vested interests
- Forgoing a significant degree of autonomy to achieve a higher order of performance
- Humbling oneself as a leader and practitioner to always seek guidance and support from world-class experts as needed to innovate and continually improve

Most organizations are unwilling to execute these measures. However, those that are willing to commit to innovation; excellence; continuous improvement; and a culture of world-class quality, safety, service, and cost-effectiveness will realize incalculable and unparalleled opportunities to serve and expand one's service area.

This chapter celebrates organizations of all sizes that have been willing to sever their ties with the past in order to embrace a future of opportunity and achievement. Many made significant sacrifices to pursue their vision, and they continue to do so as they realize that the mandate for innovation and change will only accelerate as the competition for world-class, cost-effective healthcare services intensifies.

DEFINING SUCCESS

Defining success is not a trivial exercise. Healthcare stakeholders characterize success in a multitude of ways, including the following:

- *Reimbursement levels.* Receiving an adequate level of payment to continue operating in the future will require optimizing volume and at-risk incentives as the organization works to achieve the Centers for Medicare & Medicaid Services (CMS) Core Measures, Hospital Consumer Assessment of Healthcare Providers and Systems (HCAHPS) top-box scores, optimum quality outcomes, meaningful use, and so on.
- *Thomson Reuters, Truven Health Analytics,* US News and World Report, *and other commercial surveys.* These somewhat arbitrarily derived rankings, which are typically based on mortality and morbidity rates, CMS at-risk measures, average length of stay (ALOS), average cost per adjusted discharge, and operating margin, are popular and influential with the public, third-party payers, and large employers.
- *Baldrige Performance Excellence program criteria.* The Malcolm Baldrige National Quality Award is the culmination of what may be the most prestigious national performance excellence process. It assesses organizations in the categories of leadership; strategic planning; customer focus; measurement, analysis, and knowledge management; workforce; operations; and quality, safety, service, engagement, and financial criteria and results. Very few healthcare organizations are recognized with the Baldrige Award.
- *Strategic goals and objectives.* Beyond the regulatory and reimbursement criteria that define minimum expectations lie opportunities to achieve excellence. The goals and objectives that frame these opportunities can only be accomplished through a strategic vision that energizes and galvanizes an organization

to go far past normative expectations to set itself apart from its competitors or, even more ideally, create a new market with no strategic opposition at all.

The latter concept is described by Kim and Mauborgne (2005) in *Blue Ocean Strategy: How to Create Uncontested Market Space and Make the Competition Irrelevant*. Examples of this approach in healthcare delivery are adopting a downloadable software application that enables virtual physician, nurse practitioner, or physician assistant appointments 24/7 or outsourcing clinical services to world-class providers overseas that permit a price point far below the cost structure of traditional fee-for-service enterprise models in this country.

◆ *Customer criteria.* Customer needs and wants may be the most important, yet most disregarded, set of success criteria of all, as they focus on unmet or pent-up market demand that few, if any, organizations are meeting. Interestingly, customer criteria are little recognized as a success factor because so few organizations ask their customers what they want and need. Were they to query, healthcare providers might find demand for lower-cost after-hours services, same-day access to outpatient venues and services seven days a week, same-day interpretation of diagnostic tests (particularly those with life-threatening implications), and access to specialty services that currently require customers to marshal substantial resources to access. Significantly, addressing these criteria may drive customer loyalty and market share even though they may have little to do with more recognized criteria, such as publicly reported performance measures.

Once an organization defines success, its strategic vision can be created collaboratively, disseminated, and integrated into strategic tactics, operating plans, the project management structure, and operating and capital budgets to ensure effective execution. Everyone in the organization needs to be engaged and aligned with this new vision, contracts modified to include appropriate financial incentives, and operations redesigned to designate resources efficiently to support it. The role of leadership is to continually articulate and reinforce the new vision so that everyone understands his essential role in its achievement.

SELECTING ORGANIZATIONS AS EXAMPLES FOR INCLUSION

Numerous organizations strive for and achieve excellence, and it is not possible to include them all in this chapter. Therefore, a sample of organizations was selected from the Truven Health Analytics (2013) 100 Top Hospitals list that offers, in the author's opinion, a cross-sectional representation of differentiating characteristics that enable a medical staff to support its organization's pursuit of high performance.

First, we discuss the characteristics identified by the physician and executive leaders at these organizations as necessary to make the 100 Top Hospitals list. The presentation of the organizations that follows moves from small to large in terms of operating revenue and demonstrates the performance excellence factors that drive an organization from ordinary to extraordinary performance.

CHARACTERISTICS OF SUCCESSFUL ORGANIZATIONS AND MEDICAL STAFFS TODAY

The following paragraphs discuss the characteristics that all of the organizations and medical staffs surveyed share and that seem to be universal for achieving a high level of performance in today's healthcare climate.

Willingness to sacrifice normative behavior. Organizations, regardless of size, that commit to excellence understand that this pursuit may require the painful separation of normative behavior and standards from its culture to achieve breakthrough performance.

Culture of collaboration and interdependency. The era of command-and-control, top-down management has rapidly evolved into a more complex and integrated matrix management system with flattened hierarchies, shared decision making and authority, and collaborative leadership and governance. Successful organizations recognize that outstanding outcomes are greater than the sum of their parts. They create collaborative and interdependent structures and processes to enable higher levels of performance.

Culture of continuous improvement and innovation. High-performing organizations embrace a culture of continual improvement and innovation and recognize that it is not the result of a technique (e.g., Six Sigma, Lean) or an approach, but rather a part of its everyday culture.

Optimization of performance through evidence-based practices. One of the greatest sources of lackluster performance and waste is the tolerance of non-value-added variation. Organizations that have good cost accounting systems and that accurately measure direct variable costs per practitioner note up to 1,000 percent, or tenfold, variation in cost, with superior quality outcomes clustered around lower-cost cases (IOM 2012). In addition, many organizations have higher-than-average labor or supply chain costs due to their insistence on using homegrown operational methodologies, which simply do not work effectively. High-performing organizations standardize their operational, financial, and clinical practices according to national research to hardwire effective processes into their systems.

Continuous focus on customer loyalty. Customer loyalty is the single greatest driver of quality outcomes, financial performance, and market share. Frontline practitioners and staff are responsible for securing customer loyalty; it is management's job to help them understand what their roles are; learn tactics and techniques that work; and embrace the deeper personal values of service, making attention to customer loyalty a part of their everyday culture.

Collaboration to reduce inefficiencies and costs. With the global competition heating up for high-quality, low-cost healthcare services, US hospitals and health systems will need to lower their cost structure by 50 percent or more. This dramatic reduction sounds impossible, and it is, if improvement efforts are made incrementally. What is required is a complete redesign and transformation of the way we deliver healthcare services, and high-performing organizations are doing just that by

- reducing labor costs through quality staffing, redeployment, and elimination of non-value-added work (e.g., administrative duties) for clinical personnel;
- reducing supply chain costs through consolidation of supplies and vendors, just-in-time inventory management, and elimination of non-value-added steps;
- supporting improved revenue cycle management and documentation through nonclinical certified coders, who enable physicians and nurses to improve their clinical efficiency and focus;
- adopting Lean and Six Sigma methodologies to achieve fewer errors, greater efficiency, and improved quality and service;
- leveraging the skills of physicians as clinicians, clinical supervisors, and managers to oversee a defined population through the use of mid-level practitioners and nurse navigators;
- adopting low-cost, cloud-based delivery models to provide 24/7 access to healthy individuals who require transactional healthcare services; and
- outsourcing operational and clinical services that can be performed far more cost-effectively overseas.

Commitment to leadership succession planning at all levels. Succession planning requires the identification, ongoing training and coaching, and retention of the most gifted and committed physician leaders so that they may rise to executive positions while continuing to lead and mentor their colleagues. Ten of the 17 *U.S. News & World Report* top-rated healthcare organizations in 2013 were led by physician

CEOs. That trend is rising as organizations realize the necessity of leaders who are adept at managing clinical, operational, and financial issues in a pay-for-value era.

Continuous health information management innovation. One of the most important and challenging aspects of healthcare transformation is the complete transition to a digitized system that features big data and comprehensive clinical, business, and operational analytics. Organizations that can produce actionable information out of seemingly overwhelming data in real time that are both generic and specific to immediate clinical and operational challenges far outperform those that cannot. Effective clinical and business analytics are a necessary cost of doing business and are no longer optional.

Expanded focus on disease management and population health. Forward-thinking organizations are moving from the care of acute disease to its prevention through the implementation of disease management and population health. Successful organizations will need to embrace health, prevention, and disease management as their primary strategies for healthcare transformation as this is where the greatest potential for clinical improvement and cost reductions lies.

Complete physician integration and alignment. Top-performing organizations have either completely integrated their physicians with the organization or are in the process of doing so, for they realize that world-class quality and low costs cannot be accomplished by management alone or by unaligned physicians performing in autonomous clinical and economic silos.

ELEVEN SUCCESSFUL ORGANIZATIONS AND THEIR MEDICAL STAFFS

Each of the following case examples represents a unique environment in which leaders are willing to confront challenges in meaningful and lasting ways that lead to a high level of performance from both a clinical and a financial perspective.

Hill Country Memorial Hospital, Fredericksburg, Texas

Approximate operating revenue: $132 million

Approximate number of active physicians: 65

Differentiating strengths: Hill Country Memorial had a significant cultural challenge with a great deal of factional conflict between physicians, management, and staff that undermined its performance and morale. All parties realized that something had to be done and embarked on a journey from "traditional" values to "remarkable" values. The concept is based on the work that Ann Rhoades (2011) has done with Jet Blue, Southwest Airlines, and other innovative companies. Hill Country Memorial held a series of retreats to define the organization's desired values and their impact on recruitment and retention of physicians, management, and staff at all levels.

The following remarkable values (RVs) were created as a result of these discussions:

RVs #1: Others First
- Anticipate and exceed expectations to serve others (internal and external)
- Listen empathetically at all times
- Teamwork
- Embrace and honor diversity
- Recognize the contribution of others
- Respect one another at all times

RVs #2: Compassion
- Consistently treat others with courtesy, respect, kindness, and patience
- Show genuine interest in what is important to others
- Display a helpful and friendly attitude
- Support and encourage always

RVs #3: Innovation
- Embrace evidence-based practices
- Learn from experience, and share with others
- Create unique ways to provide remarkable care
- Incorporate technology to improve patient and team member experience/ outcomes
- Always think "beyond the box"

RVs #4: Accountability
- Provide safe care
- Lead by example at all times
- Be open and honest about successes and failures
- Take initiative for personal growth and development
- Make appropriate decisions in difficult situations

RVs #5: Stewardship
- Demonstrate ownership of continuous improvement
- Actively participate in financial success by optimizing resources
- Make a positive contribution to our community

Note: Everyone in the organization is required to sign off on these values annually.

As management expected, implementing these values was traumatic, as many individuals who had been with the organization for a long time were unable to live them and were asked to leave. This consequence was both painful and promising, as the vacancies provided an opportunity to recruit individuals who were better prepared and suited to embrace the values and support the organization's new mission and vision.

Other initiatives included the following:

- Embedding Core Measures, Surgical Care Improvement Project (SCIP) measures, and other key quality measures into the computerized provider order entry system
- Establishing electronic health record–embedded order sets
- Adopting the Thomson Reuters quality platform to track ongoing performance and provide feedback to physicians and other healthcare practitioners
- Implementing software to identify relevant comorbidities, track present-on-admission and discharge conditions, and create a disease management registry
- Adopting the Chasing Zero patient safety program

Performance highlights: As a result of these steps, the organization became a Press Ganey Mentoring Hospital with 99th percentile ratings; achieved top 10th percentile ratings in Core Measures and safety measures; increased its Medicare case mix index (CMI) from 1.3 to 1.7, with a significant impact on net margin (moving from a negative percentage to +3 percent); and was awarded the Texas Quality Award. Most importantly, because of its new and improved culture, Hill Country Memorial is now able to attract top physician talent nationally from such organizations as Mayo Clinic and Cleveland Clinic because of its unique environment in a relatively rural area. The organization is currently on the Baldrige performance excellence journey, achieving honorable mention in 2013 and winning the award in 2014, and continues to seek ever-higher performance for itself and long-term improvements to the health of its community.

Sutter Davis (California) Hospital

Approximate operating revenue: $254 million

Approximate number of active physicians: 80

Differentiating strengths: Many organizations pursue high-margin services in the areas of cardiology, neuroscience, orthopedics, and other specialties in a fee-for-service (FFS) environment that rewards ancillary and procedural revenue. Management at Sutter Davis realized that, with the continued drop in FFS reimbursement and the movement to a more capitated environment, it was essential to address the high-risk pool of indigent workers in their community who accounted for significant costs to the hospital and preventable readmissions. The organization created indigent care and population health programs to manage chronic diseases among low-income families and improve quality outcomes, reduce cost per case, and drive prevention and overall community health. The community is afforded the means to conduct self-evaluations and adopt accountable behaviors informed by meaningful data. This effort resulted in the creation of Sutter Davis's culture of caring in which it hires for attitude, an approach reminiscent of Herb Kelleher's leadership style as cofounding CEO of Southwest Airlines.

Eighty-five percent of Sutter Davis physicians were contracted through the Sutter Medical Foundation, which requires a strong commitment to and alignment with organizational goals and objectives. As was the case with several organizations described in this chapter, Sutter Davis developed a physician-centric business model that leveraged the skills of visionary physicians around specific centers of excellence and invested heavily in their shared success.

The organization built a solid horizontal and vertical integrative model linking inpatient and outpatient services to enhance continuity of care across the continuum. Its quality program was created as the result of a close examination of culture, processes, and outcomes, part of Sutter Davis's Baldrige journey of the past five years.

Finally, the organization boasts a strong midwifery service that links low cost with high-quality outcomes and highlights a strong culture of service.

Performance highlights: Bestowed the Governor's Award for Performance Excellence from the California Council for Excellence and the Studer Group's Healthcare Organization Fire Starter Award in 2012, not surprisingly, Sutter Davis's Core Measures, safety measures, and HCAHPS measures are all in the top decile, while its readmission rate is in the lowest decile. Its ALOS is 2.9 days (almost 40 percent below the national average of 4.8 days), a result of its focus on population health, and its net margin is 7.3 percent.

St. Elizabeth Community Hospital, Red Bluff, California

Approximate operating revenue: $265 million

Approximate number of active physicians: 60

Differentiating strengths: In response to the State of California Medical Practice Act, Business and Professions Code section 2052 (the Corporate Practice of Medicine Act), physicians and management at St. Elizabeth created the Catholic Health West (CHW) Foundation, a legal structure that enabled physician leadership and employment models for physicians consistent with state law. Their ability to serve in leadership roles brought physicians into strong alignment with the organization because it demonstrated its commitment to quality, safety, service, accountability, and active physician participation in leadership at all levels. Contrary to national trends, at St. Elizabeth, physicians led the way in utilization management by adopting software to gain control of length of stay, CMI, and cost per case.

Other initiatives include the use of quality software for ongoing and focused professional practice evaluation activities and customized software for retrospective reviews and remote access.

Performance highlights: As a result of these activities, ALOS was reduced to 2.557 days; net margin increased to 3.9 percent; and the organization achieved high-level quality scores at the 98.8th percentile in national value-based measures, top 10th percentile in HCAHPS scores, and a CHW composite quality score in the 98th percentile.

Mercy Medical Center, Baltimore, Maryland

Approximate operating revenue: $396 million

Approximate number of active physicians: 250

Differentiating strengths: First, a rigorous quality program was established whereby a multidisciplinary quality committee oversaw the performance management of all departments and divisions. Indicators with targets were established for all significant performance objectives, and ongoing feedback and improvement plans were created to ensure that physicians were completely aligned with the organization's quality plan and its relationship to the overall strategic plan.

Similar to Sutter Davis (discussed earlier) and Mercy Medical Center North Iowa (see later), Mercy Baltimore developed a strongly physician-centric business plan. With Mercy's location in Baltimore sandwiched between two corporate healthcare giants—Johns Hopkins Hospital ($1.8 billion in operating revenues) and University of Maryland Medical Center ($2.4 billion in operating revenues)—the physician-centered approach became a core strategy. Mercy was able to recruit rising stars from both of those organizations who were interested in building a center of excellence or service line. The argument was compelling: These outstanding physicians could be part of building a service line or center of excellence now at Mercy Baltimore, rather than wait 20 years to build it at one of the large academic centers. In general, the service lines were led through a triad model of a physician or nursing leader who oversaw quality, operations, and financial performance in collaboration with a member of the executive team. Each service line developed a rigorous quality and cost management oversight process with careful attention to market differentiation and share.

Performance highlights: As a result of this strategy, Mercy became the most profitable healthcare organization in Baltimore, achieving an enviable +7.5 percent net margin in 2012, or $31,389,000 net income out of total gross revenues of $418,031,747. In addition, it enjoyed top 10th percentile quality, safety, and service metrics and was able to compete successfully with two juggernauts for business, reputation, and share. Many organizations in Mercy Baltimore's position would have taken a defeatist attitude, citing lack of access to capital or scale as prohibitive. But this organization chose a more agile and adaptive approach by recognizing that many large organizations have entrenched bureaucracies that do not permit rapid advancement of high-performing individuals seeking to make a difference and to leave a legacy. Thus, Mercy Baltimore leveraged a weakness of its competitors into an advantage with results that speak for themselves.

Advocate Good Samaritan Hospital, Downers Grove, Illinois

Approximate operating revenue: $410 million

Approximate number of active physicians: 450

Differentiating strengths: Advocate Good Samaritan's approach to performance improvement is a classic example of a deliberative commitment to excellence. In 2004, the CEO and governing body invested in achieving top 1 percentile quality and safety performance, regardless of what was required to do so. They understood that changes in the management team and hospital and medical staff would be needed—actions that would be traumatic for some and deeply satisfying for others. Like many top-performing organizations, Advocate Good Samaritan realized that excellence is a long-term journey. It invested in Lean, Six Sigma, and Plan-Do-Check-Act rapid-cycle improvement initiatives, demonstrating a continuous obsession with measurable improvement opportunities. Management realized that it had to lead this initiative, and it developed the Good Samaritan Leadership System to hardwire evidence-based management practices throughout the hospital. The other necessary ingredient was a strong, collaborative culture among management, associates, physicians, and staff. At the same time, Advocate Good Samaritan's joint venture organization with its physicians, Advocate Physician Partners, initiated a pay-for-performance clinical integration (CI) program in 2004 and the nation's largest commercial accountable care organization (ACO) in 2011. The ACO has an operating board made up of physicians and managers working together toward shared savings by optimizing quality and reducing costs for a defined population; it represents the best of Advocate Good Samaritan's new culture of partnership with physicians.

Performance highlights: The relentless commitment to quality and safety paid rare dividends. Over a seven-year period, the organization reduced its risk-adjusted mortality index (actual mortality ÷ expected mortality) from 0.73 (27 percent lower than expected) to 0.61 (39 percent lower than expected), which represents top-decile performance. It achieved top 10th percentile performance in all quality, safety, and service (Press Ganey) metrics and decreased its postoperative renal failure index from a high of 3.00 (300 percent greater than expected) to 0.86 (14 percent lower than expected) over a two-year period through the performance of failure mode and effects analysis. Equally important was the increase of physician and associate satisfaction to the 97th percentile, which represented the high value that physicians assigned to working in a high-performing environment.

As secondary benefits, Advocate Good Samaritan's liability costs declined by 83 percent over a five-year period, gross days in accounts receivable declined by 25 percent with an increase in net operating margin of 9 percent, and market share rose 17 percent with almost no additional incremental investment. The hospital won the Baldrige Award in 2010 and is an example of an organization that set high aspirational goals for itself ten years ago and worked relentlessly toward their achievement by recruiting the commitment and participation of everyone, every step of the way.

Baptist Medical Center East, Montgomery, Alabama

Approximate operating gross revenue: $450 million

Approximate number of active physicians: 150

Differentiating strengths: The root of BMCE's success is its strong physician relations management program. The program is founded on the CEO's philosophy that you can ask committed individuals to do almost anything and they will deliver. He made it a point to meet with every significant physician on a monthly or bimonthly basis and develop a professional and personal relationship with them to better understand their needs, challenges, and personal goals by linking the physicians to the organization whenever possible. The CEO developed quarterly leadership development retreats (LDRs) that focused on a specific leadership skill (e.g., communicating effectively, building trust, inspiring followers). The format of the LDRs was a formal physician leadership curriculum, and the program encouraged a strong culture of innovation. BMCE became the primary avenue for the physicians' personal and professional success, and the distinctions between the organization's and clinicians' accomplishments became blurred and aligned.

Through his dedication and care, the CEO developed an unusually strong relationship between individual and aggregate physicians and his management team that resulted in responsive and timely collaboration, a willingness to adopt new approaches to clinical and functional challenges, and a desire to support the organization's success.

Performance highlights: Performance metrics in all areas reflect this strong alignment. ALOS is 3.2 days, and CMI is 1.8, demonstrating the strong physician involvement in utilization and revenue cycle management. BMCE was recognized as a Truven Top 100 hospital three times in 2010–2014 because of its achievements in Core Measures, safety measures, and HCAHPS measures and financial performance. The most important benefit was the growth in physicians interested in partnering with BMCE in a competitive two-system community where revenues depend strongly on physician loyalty and performance.

Mercy Medical Center North Iowa, Mason City

Approximate operating revenue: $647 million

Approximate number of active physicians: 75

Differentiating strengths: Mercy North Iowa took a multipronged approach to achieving its outstanding results. First, it developed a strong Lean culture with an open environment to address medical errors and potential sentinel events. This was a painful process initially, as it uncovered a large number of serious safety events that had previously been suspected by physicians and management but not validated. Paradoxically, but not surprisingly, top-performing organizations tend to report a significantly higher incidence of safety events, and lower-performing organizations tend to either deny or ignore the near misses that eventually lead to sentinel and safety events.

Second, Mercy North Iowa addressed issues surrounding conduct after years of debate and discussion. The organization found that, as is often the case, some of its most generative and highly productive physicians were the source of some culture-based problems. A rigorous code of conduct, complete with accountability and follow-through policies, was put in place, resulting in a level of turnover that was both painful and necessary for the organization to improve its professional culture. Finally, similar to Sutter Davis and Mercy Baltimore, Mercy North Iowa developed a physician-centric business model that attracted top-level practitioners from Mayo Clinic, the University of Minnesota, and the Chicagoland area, who drove the development of new service lines and centers of excellence.

Performance highlights: Mercy North Iowa has achieved top 10th percentile performance in quality, safety, service, and HCAHPS scores, with a healthy net operating margin of 4 percent. It continues to thrive in its new culture of excellence, professionalism, and high reliability as a result of its commitment to a higher level of aspiration and performance.

Sarasota (Florida) Memorial Hospital

Approximate operating revenue: $1.6 billion

Approximate number of active physicians: 500

Differentiating strengths: Sarasota Memorial's physician alignment approach focused on the development of a strong service line strategy whereby 35 medical directors reported to both the medical executive committee and executive management. Each physician director was paired with a nurse manager (dyad model), and together they were held accountable for the clinical, operational, and financial performance of the service line. To develop this level of physician leadership, the organization invested in a physician leadership academy, yielding more than 15 highly qualified physician leaders at any one time who would be equally effective and collaborative in the chief of staff role. Some of the medical directors performed so well that they were being groomed for potential executive positions within the organization. Physicians actively participated in leadership roles at every level of the organization (e.g., service line, medical staff, executive team, governing board) and led most of the major strategic initiatives involving physician input and participation.

Physicians partnered with management to develop a physician-friendly electronic health record ten years before the meaningful use criteria were created. They had understood that only through rapid-cycle improvements could imperfect IT programs be refined to the point that they saved time and costs and supported clinical decision making at all levels. Acting on this understanding, Sarasota Memorial implemented customized software to focus on both clinical decision making and operational efficiency.

Performance highlights: The organization's regulatory quality performance shot up to the top 10th percentile, and both its severity- and risk-adjusted mortality and morbidity indices dropped to 0.75 (25 percent lower than expected). Several of its service lines were certified by external accreditors as centers of excellence and have won numerous awards for high quality and service. Sarasota Memorial's net operating margin is a healthy 4.5 percent, and its physician leadership bench grew and deepened to the point that appointment to physician leadership positions has become both desirable and competitive. Physician leaders are influential and provide input at the highest levels.

St. Joseph Mercy Hospital, Ann Arbor, Michigan

Approximate operating revenue: $1.6 billion

Approximate number of active physicians: 550

Differentiating strengths: St. Joseph Mercy took a two-pronged approach to physician alignment by focusing on its service line strategy and its large, multispecialty practice subsidiary. A dyad model was implemented in every unit, department, and service line to ensure strong physician, nursing, and management collaboration. In addition, all physician and nursing leaders received formal training in quality and safety techniques and in conducting crucial conversations with members of their unit, department, or service line to ensure optimum performance. Physician leadership and employment or co-management contracts were shifted from a guaranteed salary base model to an at-risk model, in which approximately 15 to 20 percent of total compensation was tied to the achievement of joint physician–management strategic organizational goals and objectives.

Performance highlights: Improvements were noted in all areas. Quality measures, CMS Core Measures, SCIP reporting, and safety measures launched St. Joseph Mercy to the top 10th percentile; 97 percent of patient safety events were reported within five days; CMI increased more than 20 percent to 1.5387; and net margin increased to 5 percent, with a rapidly growing physician group and market share as a result of the more aligned and collaborative culture. The hospital's 2013 Culture of Safety survey indicated an 11.2 percent increase in physicians' and employees' perception of St. Joseph Mercy's commitment to safe care, up from 61.2 percent in 2012.

Memorial Hermann Health System, Houston, Texas

Approximate operating revenue: $2.9 billion

Approximate number of active physicians: 3,900

Differentiating strengths: Of the 3,900 physicians in the entire system, 2,000 enrolled in a physician-led CI program that required a high level of commitment and dedication to evidence-based practices, safety, service, and operational best practices. The program was operationalized through the creation of clinical program committees (CPCs) that standardized 400 order sets and clinical or functional pathways in real time. For instance, when evidence emerged that the prostate-specific antigen screening test for prostate cancer may not be cost-effective, the relevant CPC met to decide how to integrate this new information into its existing pathways for the screening, diagnosis, and treatment of prostate cancer. The pathways were modified accordingly in real time, demonstrating that standardization can lead to greater agility and innovative change.

Memorial Hermann also created a National Committee for Quality Assurance–designated patient-centered medical home that implemented the rigorous My Health Advocate Disease Management and Community Outreach for Personal Empowerment program for the prevention, identification, and management of the most commonly encountered chronic diseases. This program was predicated on the assumption that disease management cannot be successfully implemented without the full and equal partnership of patients and their families. In addition, an ACO was created to partner physicians and management under at-risk contracts to care for a defined population. Part of this cost-reduction strategy resulted in the development of a palliative life program to enhance the quality of life for those with terminal diseases.

Memorial Hermann adopted software enhancements that helped the organization create patient portals, a continuum-of-care patient registry to track patient interactions and treatments in all clinical settings and at home, and a health information exchange to share patient-relevant information among caregivers inside and outside of the organization.

Performance highlights: The results from the physician-led CI program for 2012 were striking compared to the other organizations that had partnered with the patient data software vendor, as shown in the following table.

Measurement	Memorial Hermann CI physicians	Other vendor partners	Difference
Length of stay	4.52	4.74	(5%)
Hospital-acquired infections	0.68%	7.56%	(91%)
General complications	1.24%	2.82%	(66%)
30-day readmissions	5.92%	10.38%	(43%)
Mortality rate	1.95%	2.52%	(23%)

Source: Data from Memorial Hermann Health System. Used with permission.

The resulting benefits to the organization were equally astounding. For example, when Aetna (one of the three major third-party payers in the Houston market) saw these data, its representatives approached leadership at Memorial Hermann and asked to create a new contract for the integrated group with an immediate increase of 8 percent in FFS reimbursement and a guaranteed 3 percent increase the year after. In addition, for every 10 percent of market share moved to the integrated group, Aetna committed a physician bonus of $7.5 million and an organizational bonus of $8.0 million. It also invested in marketing resources to better compete with UnitedHealth and Blue Cross and Blue Shield (BCBS) to build new market share collaboratively. (Interestingly, UnitedHealth duplicated Aetna's offer, and when BCBS declined to match it, Memorial Hermann threatened to sever their agreement, which caused BCBS to capitulate.)

Improved reimbursement and market share were not the only advantages. Because the integrated physician group was willing to standardize approaches to supply chain management by eliminating non-value-added suppliers and vendors, the supply chain ratio (total supply chain costs to net operating revenue) dropped from 18.7 percent (near national average) to 13.7 percent, resulting in a net cash flow increase of $150 million in one year with an additional $150 million savings achieved in 2013.

Finally, this success led to an interesting shift in culture, as those few physicians in the CI program who were unwilling or unable to standardize their practices were asked to leave by the other physicians, who did not want a few resistors to undermine their clinical, operational, and financial performance or their chances for securing financial bonuses from third-party payers.

Baylor Scott & White, Dallas, Texas

Approximate operating revenue: $7.8 billion

Approximate number of active physicians: 4,000

Differentiating strengths: Baylor has a longstanding history of innovation, integration, and alignment with physicians, payers, and large employers in the Dallas–Fort Worth metroplex. Because of this history, the Baylor brand is powerful, and physicians tend to want to be a part of it. As at Memorial Hermann, this desire has helped Baylor develop a physician culture with little tolerance for those colleagues who do not share deep professional values regarding the provision of world-class quality, safety, service, and conduct.

Physicians who seek leadership roles are required to participate in a leadership boot camp every February; those participants who demonstrate both aptitude and commitment may enroll in a two-year executive MBA program that Baylor offers, which now boasts more than 150 graduates, many of whom have gone on to executive leadership positions. Baylor also created the Physician Leadership Council to unite all 30 medical staffs in the Baylor system with identical bylaws, rules and regulations, and policies and procedures so that physicians credentialed and privileged at one organization could be a part of and monitored by the other 29.

A high degree of alignment around quality and safety is pervasive throughout the system. Approximately 35 percent of every physician compensation agreement is placed at risk through mutually agreed on quality and safety metrics and targets. For self-employed physicians, a management services organization was created so that these physicians could gain access to opportunities for higher reimbursement and lower costs in their individual practices in exchange for working with Baylor to achieve high quality and low costs within the system.

The Baylor Quality Alliance was launched as a physician-led ACO with more than 1,850 physicians and a physician-led operating board to focus on population health. It features a rigorous disease management program and a shared savings reimbursement mechanism.

Every Baylor organization supports system-level training and rounding for quality, safety, and service outcomes in a partnership that includes executive leaders, physicians, and nurses.

Performance highlights: Baylor achieved top scores in almost every dimension of performance. These include Core Measures and safety measures in the 97th percentile, 74.5 percent HCAHPS top-box scores, cost per adjusted discharge of $4,900, readmission rates in the lowest 10th percentile (top 10th percentile performance), a systemwide mortality index of 0.7 (30 percent lower than expected), and total assets of $5.3 billion with a net operating margin of 7.4 percent.

Like many of the organizations featured in this chapter, these results did not occur overnight, but rather over decades with succeeding generations of physicians and leaders who saw the value in working together to achieve something that could not have been accomplished alone.

Note: Contributor articles by Paul Convery, MD, and Carl Couch, MD, describing additional efforts at Baylor are available upon request from the author.

SUMMARY

Being a top performer is a choice that must be made through careful deliberation. It requires the complete integration and alignment of the medical staff, physicians, management, hospital staff, and governance to accomplish the Institute of Healthcare Improvement Triple Aim of improving the experience of care, improving the health of populations, and reducing the per capita cost of healthcare. It requires individuals who are willing to sacrifice self-interest to pursue a higher mission of world-class quality, safety, service, and cost-effectiveness. It requires agility, speed, and the willingness to continually improve all aspects of operating performance in response to a rapidly changing external and internal environment. It requires people who are willing to work together in new and interdependent ways and to leave a respected past behind. And it requires a culture of continuous innovation, service, and respect and the humility to be the architect of a system that has never been designed before and will have to be completed in a frustratingly short period.

Organizations that choose not to embark on this journey will become fungible commodities that continually lose revenue and market share. Organizations willing to make the sacrifices necessary to pursue excellence will not only be rewarded with high levels of performance but also experience the internal satisfaction of service and of leaving something personal and important behind to sow the seeds of excellence in the ever-accelerating transformation that is healthcare today.

REFERENCES

Institute of Medicine (IOM). 2012. *Best Care at Lower Cost: The Path to Continuously Learning Healthcare in America*. Washington, DC: National Academies Press.

Kim, W. C., and R. Mauborgne. 2005. *Blue Ocean Strategy: How to Create Uncontested Market Space and Make the Competition Irrelevant*. Cambridge, MA: Harvard Business School Press.

Rhoades, A. 2011. *Built on Values: Creating an Enviable Culture That Outperforms the Competition*. San Francisco: Jossey-Bass.

Truven Health Analytics. 2013. "Truven Health Analytics Announces 100 Top Hospitals Award Winners." Press release. Published February 25. http://100tophospitals.com/portals/2/assets/100_Top_Hospitals_2013_Press_Release.pdf.

U.S. News & World Report. 2013. "U.S. News & World Report Releases 2013-14 Best Hospitals Rankings." Published July 16. www.usnews.com/info/blogs/press-room/2013/07/16/us-news--world-report-releases-2013-14-best-hospitals-rankings.

Index

Collaboration
  organizational culture of, 258
  on performance issues, 202–8
  physician engagement in, 197–202
  physician–manager partnerships, 102–5
  physicians' attitudes toward, 39, 40–41
  to reduce inefficiency and costs, 259
  in service line–oriented organizations, 17
Collective culture, 102
Co-management agreements, 237–38
Committees. *See also specific types of*
  physicians as members of, 22
Communication
  crucial conversations, 4, 176–78
  effect on clinical outcomes, 192–93
  failure in, 85, 86
Compensation
  in co-management practices, 237, 238
  for employed physicians, 235
  for physician leaders, 11–12
  work relative value units–based, 111
Competition
  achievement-based, 199
  disruptive, 208
Confidentiality
  of meetings, 69
  of negligent credentialing cases, 69
  of peer review, 69, 168–70, 197
Conflict, 18
  collaborative, 201
  contract-related, 40
  disruptive, 208
  focused professional practice evaluation–
    related, 149–50
  new technology–related, 82
  peer review–related, 156
Conflict of interest, 18
  focused professional practice evaluation–
    related, 149–50
  new technology–related, 82
  peer review–related, 156
  policies for, 42, 46
  referrals-related, 193
Consumer satisfaction, importance of, 10
Continuous quality improvement (CQI), 5,
    258
Contracts. *See also* Agreement types; Contractual
    relationships
  aligned risk, 235–36
  behavioral, 207
  exclusive, 43
  noncompete/nonsolicitation terms of, 40
  performance expectations component of, 212

for physician integration and alignment, 17,
    251–52
  role in physician performance management,
    120
  as strategic partnerships, 37–38
Contractual relationships
  physician performance management systems
    in, 108
  as strategic medical staff development plan-
    ning consideration, 36–38
  types of, 36–37
Core Measures, of Centers for Medicare &
    Medicaid Services, 10, 53, 108, 256
Corporate compliance, 194–95
Corporate negligence, 64–69
Corrective action, against disruptive or impaired
    physicians, 48–49, 82–84, 194–97, 211–27
  absence of, 212
  due process in, 214–23
    appellate review, 214, 215, 220
    cost of, 223
    fair or judicial hearings, 218–20,
      221–23
    investigations, 215–18, 221–23
    for nonphysicians/nondentists, 215
  mandated reporting to state licensing boards,
    217, 223
  need for, 211–14
  performance management basis for, 195–97
Cost per adjusted discharge, 10
Costs, strategies for reduction of, 259
Credentialing
  of advanced practice professionals, 93
  case studies of, 54–63, 69–70
  criteria for, 57–59, 87–88
  definition of, 52, 53
  economic, 42–49, 61
    definition of, 42, 43
    reappointment decisions based on,
      45–46
    successful, 47–49
  failures in, 212
  negligent credentialing claims, 63–69
  peer recommendations for, 56–57
  software for, 95–98
  without privileges, 53–54, 78
Credentialing Resource Center, 58, 59
Credentials committees, 15
Criminal activity
  as basis for denial of medical staff member-
    ship, 61–63
  fraud and abuse, 52, 204, 205, 208, 214,
    251

About the Author

Jonathan H. Burroughs, MD, FACHE, FAAPL, is president and CEO of the Burroughs Healthcare Consulting Network Inc. He works with some of the nation's top healthcare consulting organizations to provide best practice solutions and training to healthcare organizations in the areas of governance, physician–hospital alignment strategies, credentialing, privileging, peer review and performance improvement/patient safety, medical staff development planning, strategic planning, and physician performance and behavior management. He helps hospitals across the country develop new ways for physicians and managers to work together to solve quality, safety, operational, and financial challenges through innovative business solutions and contracting.

Dr. Burroughs serves on the national faculty of the American College of Healthcare Executives and the American Association for Physician Leadership, consistently rated as a top speaker and educator. He is the author or coauthor of the following books: *The Complete Guide to FPPE* (2012), *Medical Staff Leadership Essentials* (2011), *Engage and Align the Medical Staff and Hospital Management: Expert Strategies and Field Tested Tools* (2010), *A Practical Guide to Managing Disruptive and Impaired Physicians* (2010), *The Top 40 Medical Staff Policies and Procedures,* 4th edition (2010), *Emergency Department On-Call Strategies: Solutions for Physician-Hospital Alignment* (2009), and *Peer Review Best Practices: Case Studies and Lessons Learned* (2008).

A former senior consultant and director of education services for the Greeley Company, Dr. Burroughs was rated as one of the company's top healthcare consultants and educators. He is also a past medical staff president, a past president of the New Hampshire chapter of the American College of Emergency Physicians, and an emergency department medical director. As a member of the governing board of Memorial Hospital in New Hampshire, he chaired the ethics, succession planning, and bylaws committees and sat on the joint conference, strategic planning, and medical executive committees. He previously served as a member of the clinical faculty of Dartmouth Medical School, where his research interests included introducing EMT (emergency medical technician) defibrillation and automatic defibrillation into the field.

Dr. Burroughs' passion for the outdoors has led him to serve as a physician on mountaineering expeditions throughout the United States, Mexico, South America,

Europe, Africa, and Russia, and he is the coeditor of the 26th edition of the *White Mountain Guide* and the first edition of the *Southern New Hampshire Trail Guide*. He has reached the summits of Mts. McKinley (Alaska), Grand Teton (Wyoming), Blanc (France/Italy), Elbrus (Russia), Kilimanjaro (Tanzania), Orizaba (Mexico), Rosa (Switzerland), and Rainier (Washington state), to name a few.

Dr. Burroughs received his bachelor's degree at Johns Hopkins University, his MD from Case Western Reserve University, and a healthcare MBA with honors from the Isenberg School of Management. He is a certified healthcare and physician executive and is a fellow of the American College of Healthcare Executives and the American Association for Physician Leadership.